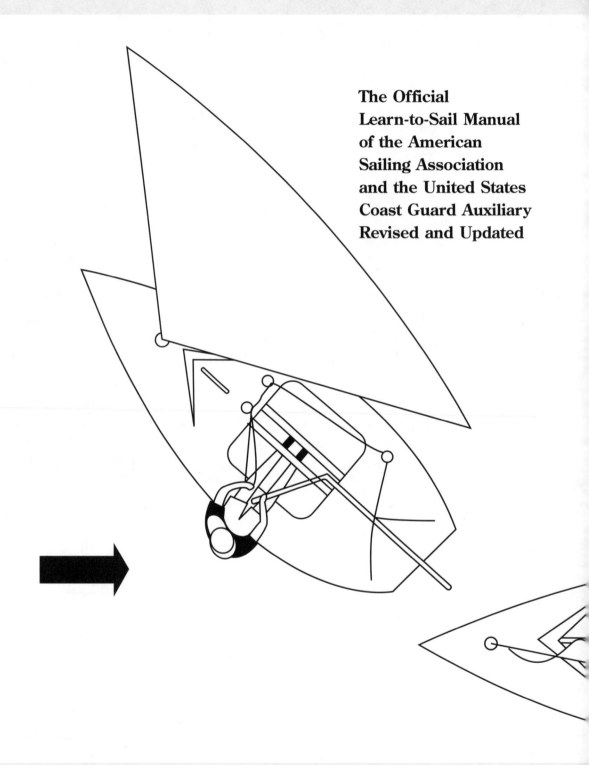

**The Official
Learn-to-Sail Manual
of the American
Sailing Association
and the United States
Coast Guard Auxiliary
Revised and Updated**

ILLUSTRATIONS BY MARTI BETZ

SAILING

FUNDAMENTALS

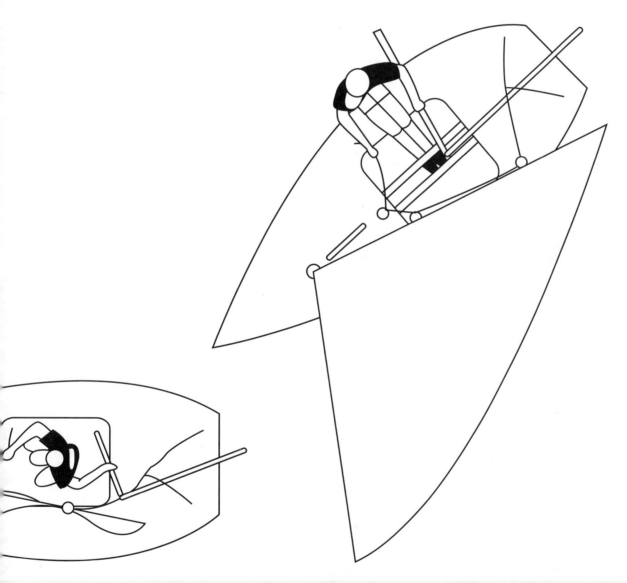

BY GARY JOBSON

A FIRESIDE BOOK
PUBLISHED BY SIMON & SCHUSTER

FIRESIDE
Rockefeller Center
1230 Avenue of the Americas
New York, NY 10020

Designed by Barbara Marks

Manufactured in the United States of America

10 9 8

Library of Congress Cataloging-in-Publication Data
Jobson, Gary
Sailing fundamentals.
Includes index.
1. Sailing. 2. American Sailing Association.
1. American Sailing Association. II. Title.
GV811.J62   1986   797.1'24   86-20338
ISBN 0-684-84994-1

CONTENTS

THE AMERICAN SAILING ASSOCIATION

by Harry Munns, Executive Vice President, ASA

The American Sailing Association is a nationwide network of sailors, sailing instructors, sailing schools, and charter fleets. Since 1982, the ASA has created and maintained professional standards within the sailing community. We promote boating safety through education. Our mission is to ensure that every sailor learns to sail properly and that he or she is rewarded with valuable credentials.

A comprehensive set of sailing standards lies at the heart of the ASA system. Detailed outlines of the standards are printed in the ASA Sailing Log Book. These performance objectives provide sailors with a credible evaluation of their sailing knowledge and seamanship skills.

ASA certification provides individual sailors with the most accepted means of proving their abilities to rental and charter fleets throughout the world. With the ASA Log Book–which also includes space for certification seals and a record of sailing experience–the ASA sailor has a passport to present to charter and rental agents in any of the thousands of sailing areas to which he or she may travel. Charter/rental agents use the ASA *Sailing Log Book* as an efficient way to gauge a prospective client's qualifications. Without it, they may have to decipher pages of resumes that often contain vague accounts of training and experience. With the ASA system, agents simply examine the internationally recognized logbook, which documents both knowledge and experience in a clear, concise format.

Sailing Fundamentals contains the knowledge and skills necessary to achieve Basic Keelboat Sailing and Basic Coastal

> **Progression of Training**
> * **BASIC KEELBOAT SAILING**
> * **BASIC COASTAL CRUISING**
> * **BAREBOAT CHARTERING**
> * **COASTAL NAVIGATION**
>   **(within sight of land)**
> * **ADVANCED COASTAL CRUISING**
>   **(by day and night)**
> * **CELESTIAL NAVIGATION**
> * **OFFSHORE PASSAGE MAKING**
>
> **CONTINUING EDUCATION**

Cruising certification. The material is divided into parts one through seven. Satisfactory completion of the first four parts qualifies students for certification to ASA Basic Keelboat Sailing. By completing parts five and six, sailors qualify for the Basic Coastal Cruising rating. Anyone planning to take the ASA or United States Coast Guard Auxiliary written exam for Basic Keelboat Sailing should read the entire book. Students who pass Basic Keelboat Sailing also achieve certification for having passed a National Association of State Boating Law Administrators (NASBLA) – recognized safe boating class. (An ASA membership application form is included in the back of this book.)

To qualify for ASA Basic Keelboat Sailing, you must be able to sail a boat about 20 feet long in light to moderate winds and sea conditions in familiar waters without supervision. This is a preparatory standard with no auxiliary (engine) or navigation skills required. For the Basic Coastal Cruising standard, you must be able to cruise safely in familiar waters as both skipper and crew of an auxiliary powered sailing vessel 20 to 30 feet long, in moderate winds and sea conditions.

UNITED STATES COAST GUARD AUXILIARY

Sailing Fundamentals is also the official sailing textbook of the United States Coast Guard Auxiliary (USCGAUX). The USCGAUX is the volunteer civilian component of the United States Coast Guard (USCG). It consists of approximately 35,000 members who wish to further their boating education and who provide administrative, operational, and other support to the USCG.

Safe boating education is one of the major missions of the USCGAUX. USCGAUX courses include both classroom and distance-learning (home-study) classes. The USCGAUX does not offer on-the-water courses to the general public, although such training is made available to members who wish to engage in search and rescue (SAR), aids to navigation (ATON), and other operational activities that require boat-crew qualification.

The USCGAUX public education program includes special courses for children and the Boating Safely Course (BSC), an eight-hour course for powerboaters, operators of personal watercraft (PWC), hunters and fishermen, and others interested in boating safety. The Skipper's Safe Boating course is a distance-learning course for those whose schedules do not permit classroom attendance. The core program includes the Boating Skills and Seamanship (BS&S) course for powerboaters and the Sailing Fundamentals course for sailors. Boaters with an interest in coastal navigation may take the USCGAUX Basic Coastal Navigation (BCN) and Advanced Coastal Navigation (ACN) courses. Members of the USCGAUX are eligible to take advanced training in a variety of topics, including communications, seamanship, SAR, and navigation, and courses on related topics offered through the USCG Institute.

The Skipper's Safe Boating Course, BSC, BS&S, and Sailing Fundamentals courses are approved by the National Association of State Boating Law Administrators (NASBLA) and graduates may satisfy state requirements for certification in those states that have mandatory education requirements. (Check with your state Boating Law Administrator [BLA] to see if this course is approved in your state.) Additionally, students who graduate from the S&S course also pass the classroom portion of the ASA Basic Keelboat Sailing Standard.

HOW TO USE THIS BOOK

Each of the first six parts of this book is divided into two sections, Sailing Knowledge and Sailing Skills.

Sailing Knowledge covers terminology, sailing theory, safety, and government regulations–all the things you need to know before going out on the water. To reinforce what you have learned, you will find review questions at the end of each Sailing Knowledge section. Answers are provided in Appendix A.

The Sailing Knowledge sections are covered in detail in the USCGAUX Sailing Fundamentals course. Questions in the written final Sailing Fundamentals examination cover material from the Sailing Knowledge section of each chapter. USCGAUX students are not tested on topics covered only in the Sailing Skills sections (see below), but are encouraged to read this material as a course supplement and in preparation for later on-the-water training offered by ASA schools.

Although this is principally a text about sailing, some of the topics covered in the Sailing Knowledge sections of this book apply to powerboats. This material is included to give the reader additional background and to satisfy the boating–safety education standards set by NASBLA and the USCG. If your vessel has an engine (as many sailboats do) and the engine is in operation–regardless of whether or not the sails are raised–you are considered to be operating a powerboat under the navigation rules and must comply with all regulations applicable to these craft. Moreover, engine equipped vessels must satisfy other federal and state regulations, such as carriage of additional required safety equipment.

The Sailing Skills sections describe exercises and maneuvers designed to teach boat handling. Although the basic principles of sailing are the same for all craft from sailboards to 12-meter yachts, the exercises in this book are designed for a boat of about 14 to 30 feet with at least two people aboard. In practicing each maneuver, switch roles with your fellow crew members so that everyone learns every skill.

Each exercise teaches a particular task. Many of the skills will build upon lessons learned in previous exercises. Each Sailing Skills section is designed to take two to three hours to complete on the water. The ideal way to learn is with the hands-on knowledge imparted by a qualified instructor or experienced sailor. The sequence of exercises in this book allows for a knowledgeable sailor on board with you, although the book itself can be your instructor.

Certain fundamental maneuvers–such as leaving the dock under sail–have purposely been left to later parts. By that point, your skills will have been developed sufficiently for you to attempt these more complicated maneuvers. We deal only with sailboats in Parts One through Four; we will cover handling a vessel under power in Part Five.

Important terms are explained in the text as well as defined in the Glossary beginning on p. 205. Illustrations or photographs give a more detailed explanation of terms when necessary. Each subject area is explored in increasing depth in subsequent parts as you gain knowledge and develop basic skills.

Good luck and smooth sailing.

Introduction to Sailing

OVERVIEW: THE SAILBOAT AND THE WIND

To illustrate the way the wind interacts with the sails, let me tell you a story.

In my early days of sailing I was once sailing a little ten-foot boat on Toms River, a body of water off Barnegat Bay along the coast of New Jersey. It was a particularly difficult day to be out on the water. Not only was the wind strong, but it was frequently shifting direction. Every time I got settled down on a desirable course, with the sails set at a correct angle to the wind and the boat moving fast, the wind would shift. I often had to make an unscheduled, drastic change in course to keep the sails filled with wind. Sometimes I did not move fast enough, and my boat was left lying stopped in the river with her sails flapping helplessly.

An older friend, named Tom Chapman, was watching from the nearby shore. At the time, Tom was one of the top sailors on Barnegat Bay, but he understood my frustration. Instead of watching in amusement as some people might do, he coached me back to shore, hopped into the boat with me, and gave me some good advice.

"First, he said, "you must understand where the wind is coming from. Your problem is that you aren't aware of any changes in direction. Here's what I do," he continued. "Before I head out, I stand on the shore and simply look at wind indicators. I look at flags on shore and on boats. I study the direction that water ripples blow in, and I watch other boats that are out sailing. This helps me understand how the wind is shifting in direction and strength so I'm not surprised once I push out.

"The next thing I do is plan in advance where I want to sail. Say I want to sail from here to that island." He pointed into the wind. "Obviously, I can't sail straight to it because that would mean sailing directly into the wind, and this boat can't sail closer to the wind than about 45 degrees. So I'll sail a series of short legs on a course of 45 degrees to the wind, first with the wind on one side and then with the wind on the other, and so on back and forth until I get to my destination. To get started, I push off, pick the first course, get sailing at 45 degrees to the wind, and adjust the sail so it catches the wind just right, without flapping. When a boat is sailing that close to the wind, the sail should be pulled in quite far, until it is right over the boat.

"Now, suppose that I'd decided to sail to that marina down there." He pointed directly downwind. "Then I'd be sailing with the wind behind me. That means that the sail should be adjusted so it is way out over the water at about a right angle to the boat. As you can see, the way I adjust the sail depends entirely on the course I choose."

Tom and I pushed off and sailed out into the river. I decided to sail toward the island upwind, so I headed about 45 degrees to the wind and pulled the sail in close. Tom resumed coaching. "I watch what the wind is doing to my sail," he said, "and adjust the course so I stay at that 45-degree angle. If the sail begins to flap, I'm probably sailing too close to the wind. I should change my course to get back to that 45-degree angle. On the other hand, if I let the sail out a little and it does not flap, that means I'm sailing too wide and should alter my course until I'm sailing closer to the wind."

"But don't look only at the sail. I spend about half my time watching the water beyond the bow of my boat so I can try to understand what the wind will do. I try to remember what I observed while I was on shore, but I also learn through experience. For example, if the wind shifts 20 degrees to the left side, it will ripple the water at a new angle. Whenever I see that kind of ripple on the water," he said, pointing and adjusting our course, "I anticipate another wind shift to the left".

"When you're sailing in a shifty wind, at first you'll be making big swoops between sailing either too close to the wind or too wide off it," Tom warned. "But with experience and practice you will be able to steer a straighter course, and you won't find your boat sailing quite as high or quite as low."

On the way back to shore, Tom had one last bit of advice. "In shifty winds, it's important to be able to make rapid adjustments to the sail. So keep the sheet (the rope leading to the sail) in your hand so you can adjust it whenever the wind changes direction."

That afternoon, in less than an hour, Tom's lessons set me on the right course. I was learning how to sail.

In this first lesson, the parts of the boat and the two most frequently used knots are introduced. Knots are an essential part of a sailor's knowledge and should be attempted before the first lesson. Upon completion of this part you will be able to raise the sails, come about, jibe, and leave the boat in ship-shape fashion after a sail.

SAILING KNOWLEDGE

ALL ABOUT BOATS

PROPULSION TYPES

Recreational boats are designed to use one or more of three propulsion types. Self-propelled vessels, including kayaks, rowboats, rafts, and canoes, are designed to be propelled by people using paddles, oars, or poles. Power-driven vessels (powerboats) typically use gasoline or diesel motors for propulsion. Sailing vessels (sailboats) are wind powered, using sails to capture the wind's power (see below).

POWERBOAT–a recreational boat typically powered by a gasoline or diesel engine. Powerboats may be subdivided into several types, including utility boats (prams, skiffs, dinghies, inflatables, and utility outboards), runabouts (bowriders, open fishermen, center consoles), cruisers (trawlers, houseboats, larger sportfishing vessels), pontoon boats, and personal watercraft (PWC). Each type has certain uses, characteristics, and limitations. Utility boats, for example, are used as tenders for larger craft and as platforms for fishing and hunting in protected waters. Because utility boats are generally small with limited stability, boaters should enter them carefully to avoid overloading. Caution should also be exercised when moving within these boats to avoid tipping them over. Runabouts are generally fast, maneuverable craft, used for fishing, hunting, cruising, and waterskiing. Cruisers are generally larger, more seaworthy (except for houseboats) craft, equipped with berths (sleeping areas), a head (marine toilet), galley (marine kitchen), and other facilities necessary for living aboard. Powerboats are subject to particular navigation rules and have specific responsibilities under those rules.

PERSONAL WATERCRAFT–also called "water scooters" as well as a variety of trade names. They are highly maneuverable, fast, fun-to-operate, low-cost, power-driven (jet drive) craft capable of operation in very shallow water. Many PWC are designed for one person, but larger models are available for use by two or three people. PWC are not toys and are governed by navigation rules applicable to power-driven vessels. In addition, most states and many localities have established specific laws that regulate PWC activities, such as prohibition of night operations, speed limitations, prohibitions of specific activities (e.g., wake jumping), limitations on operator age, and education requirements. These popular craft have unique operating capabilities (e.g., high speed, shallow draft), but are also subject to limitations. For example, PWC are steered by altering (via handlebars) the direction of the jet drive, and if power is not applied, steering is lost (the so-called off-throttle steering problem). Operators who are unfamiliar with this design feature may have difficulty controlling the vessel. PWC are designed for operation in relatively calm waters, have limited fuel capacity, and are not highly stable or maneuverable at slow speeds.

PWC operators often focus their attention on nearby waves or wakes, which can impair their ability to maintain a proper lookout. Operators of other vessels should exercise caution when operating in the vicinity of PWC to minimize the likelihood of collision.

Persons using PWC can expect to be thrown into the water and should wear personal flotation devices (PFDs) suitable for PWC use. The ability to swim and knowing how to reboard a PWC from the water are also essential. Many PWC are equipped with engine kill switches rigged to shut the engine off if the riders are thrown from the craft. Fuel management is very important for PWC. Not all PWC are equipped with fuel gauges. Instead, they have reserve tanks and riders need to know how to switch to the reserve tanks and must know the PWC's endurance when using the reserve tanks. Weight and balance are important for PWC operators. Thorough familiarity with owners' manuals and strict adherence to the published limitations are essential. Finally, it is important that operators of PWC (as well as other craft) display environmental sensitivity. Operations in shallow water areas may disturb a fragile ecosystem and its inhabitants.

PWC operators must observe restrictions on loud noise in populated areas. This can be both a matter of courtesy and regulation.

SAILING VESSEL–as noted above, this is a wind-powered vessel that uses only sails for power. Many sailboats are also equipped with gas or diesel motors for use (either as primary or supplemental power) when winds are light or from the wrong direction, for docking or other precise maneuvering, and for operation in waters (e.g., certain canals) where use of sails is prohibited. A sailboat is a power-driven vessel, as defined in the navigation rules, when the motor is in operation, and must observe regulations applicable to this type of vessel. When powered solely by sail, a sailboat is termed a sailing vessel and is subject to other specific regulations and (because of its limited maneuverability) enjoys certain privileges under the navigation rules. Various types of sailboat are discussed later in this text.

Most large powerboats like this one do not have the ability to plane.

SAILBOARD–a modified surfboard with a mast attached that holds a sail and is capable of swiveling. They are one-person craft, so the "skipper" operates the sail, steers, and acts as lookout. Visibility on these high-speed craft may be limited when the operator is positioned behind the sail. Skippers of other craft should understand this limitation and exercise caution when operating in the vicinity of sailboards.

HULL

The hull is the basic boat minus the rigging. The hull comprises the bottom, topsides, buoyancy tanks, and deck. One way to classify boats is based on hull design. Displacement-hull boats move through the water and push it aside or displace it. Planing-hull vessels move faster and, after gaining speed, ride more nearly on top of the water. All boats at rest or moving slowly are displacement boats. Each displaces a volume of water equal in weight to its own weight when operating in displacement mode.

A displacement-hull vessel always displaces a volume of water equal to its own weight, regardless of its speed. At slow speeds, it is easy for a displacement-hull boat to push the water aside, forming a bow wave. As speed increases, the bow wave becomes higher and the boat tries to climb it. But the boat is not designed to do this so there is a practical limit to its speed. Displacement vessels with longer waterlines have the capability of attaining higher speeds as long as they have adequate power. Most sailboats (except sailboards and certain other light-weight boats such as racing dinghies), tugs, freighters, and true trawlers are displacement-hull vessels. The theoretical upper limit (the hull speed) of a displacement hull can be calculated with relative precision. Hull speed in knots (nautical miles per hour) is approximately 1.34 times the square root of the waterline length in feet. Thus, a displacement-hull vessel with a waterline length of 36 feet has a maximum speed of approximately 8 knots (9.2 statute miles per hour). Despite their slow speed, displacement–hull vessels have many advantages and special uses. They are steady and comfortable and can handle rougher water than their planing hull cousins (see below). Engine-powered displacement-hull vessels are typically highly fuel efficient.

Above hull-speed a planing-hull vessel rides on its bow wave or "on-plane." When planing, it uses most of its power to move forward instead of pushing the water aside and displaces a volume of water less than its own weight. Generally, flatter hull bottoms allow boats to plane more easily. Runabouts, speedboats, sportfishing boats, and PWC are examples of planing-hull vessels. Power-driven planing-hull vessels are generally less fuel efficient than displacement-hull vessels of comparable size and weight.

As the name implies, a semidisplacement hull has both displacement and planing characteristics. Up to a certain power and speed, a semidisplacement hull behaves as a displacement hull. Beyond that point, the hull can rise to a partial plane. Increasing the power of a semidisplacement hull vessel increases its speed. It never gets fully "on top," however, and is not as fast as a vessel with a true planing hull. Most trawlers and many cruisers fit into this category.

Multihull vessels include sailing catamarans (two hulls) and trimarans (three hulls). Although technically a displacement-hull vessel, a multihull is able to escape the restriction of hull speed because the narrow hulls create very little wave resistance and because this type of vessel typically carries a great deal of sail. These boats may be difficult to maneuver at docking speeds because they lack the momentum that heavier, ballasted boats use to maintain forward motion.

There is no single, all-purpose, perfect hull design. Boat builders strive to find a happy compromise among conflicting design objectives.

THE BASIC BOAT

Learning to sail is rather like going to a foreign country. Everyone seems to speak a different language. But don't let this trouble you, for the language will soon become familiar. Once you cast off from shore, your boat becomes a self-contained world. To function within that world you need to learn the parts of your boat and their uses. Go over them often so there is no question in your mind.

KEEL–a weighted fin that, when attached to the bottom of a sailboat, keeps the boat from capsizing or slipping sideways in the water, which allows it to sail upwind.

CENTERBOARD–A sailboat without a keel may have a centerboard. A centerboard is a wooden or metal fin housed in a centerboard trunk. It can be lowered to overcome the boat's lateral motion.

BEAM–the maximum width of the hull.

DECK–the horizontal upper surface of the boat.

STERN–the back of the boat.

BOW–the front of the boat.

AFT, AFTER–toward the stern.

FORWARD–toward the bow.

WINDWARD–toward the wind.

LEEWARD–away from the wind.

ALOFT–overhead.

RUDDER–the fin at the stern of the boat used for steering.

TILLER–the wooden or metal steering arm attached to the rudder. It is used as a lever to turn the rudder.

TILLER EXTENSION–a wooden or metal pivoting extension attached to the tiller. It is usually found in dinghies and enables the skipper to steer accurately while hiking out.

WHEEL–on larger boats the wheel replaces the tiller and is used to turn the rudder.

MAST–the vertical pole or spar that supports the sails and boom. The top of the mast is called the masthead.

BOOM–the horizontal spar which is attached to the mast to support the bottom part of the mainsail.

HIKING OUT–leaning the weight of the crew over the windward side to help keep the boat on an "even keel."

PORT–the left side of the boat as you face forward.

STARBOARD–the right side of the boat as you face forward.

MAINSHEET–the line used to make major adjustments to the trim of the mainsail.

BOOM VANG–an adjustable tackle or rod that prevents the boom from lifting. A rod type boom vang also keeps the boom from dropping on deck.

LIFELINES–plastic-coated wires enclosing the deck to keep the crew from failing overboard. Lifelines are suspended from metal supports, called pulpits and stanchions.

TRAVELER–a slide, running across the boat, to which the mainsheet is led. The crew can change the trim of the mainsail by adjusting the slide position.

TOPSIDES–the sides of the hull above the waterline.

The **STANDING RIGGING** is a collection of

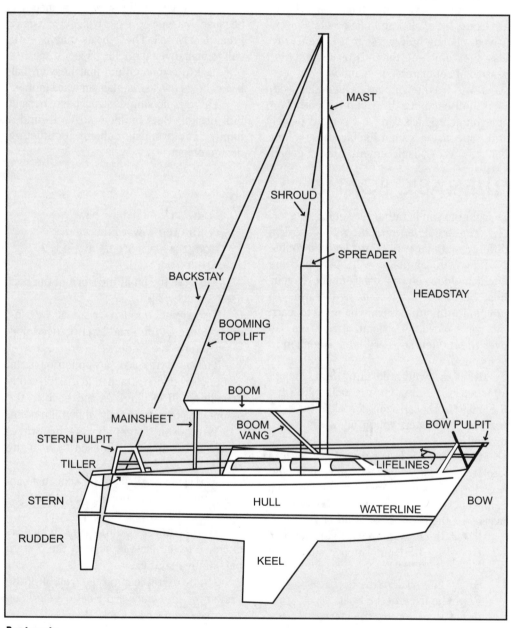

Boat parts

wires that supports the mast. On more sophisticated boats, the standing rigging is more complex and can be adjusted to optimize a sail's performance. The basic standing rigging consists of:

HEADSTAY–a wire that runs from the top of the mast (or near the masthead) to the bow and onto which the jib is attached. It supports the mast, preventing it from falling backwards.

BACKSTAY–a wire that runs from the top of the mast to the stern and supports the mast.

SHROUDS (SIDESTAYS)–wires that run from the masthead (or near the masthead) to the sides of the boat to support the mast and prevent it from swaying.

SAILS–are the power supply of the sailboat. They are most frequently made of Dacron, a synthetic fiber, used because of

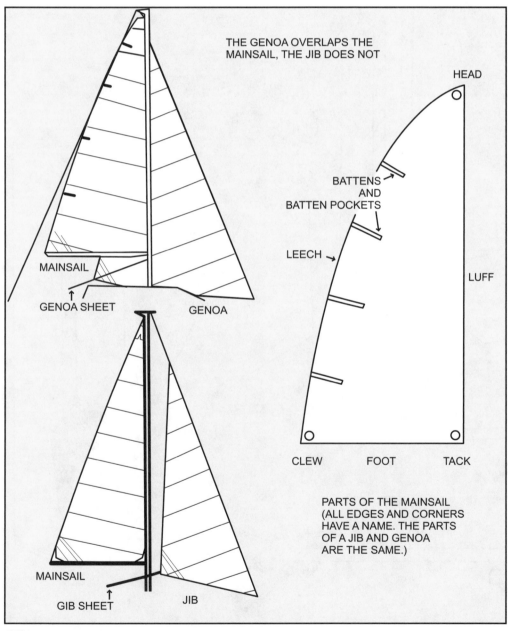

THE GENOA OVERLAPS THE MAINSAIL, THE JIB DOES NOT

MAINSAIL

GENOA SHEET

GENOA

MAINSAIL

GIB SHEET

JIB

HEAD

BATTENS AND BATTEN POCKETS

LEECH

LUFF

CLEW   FOOT   TACK

PARTS OF THE MAINSAIL (ALL EDGES AND CORNERS HAVE A NAME. THE PARTS OF A JIB AND GENOA ARE THE SAME.)

Sail parts

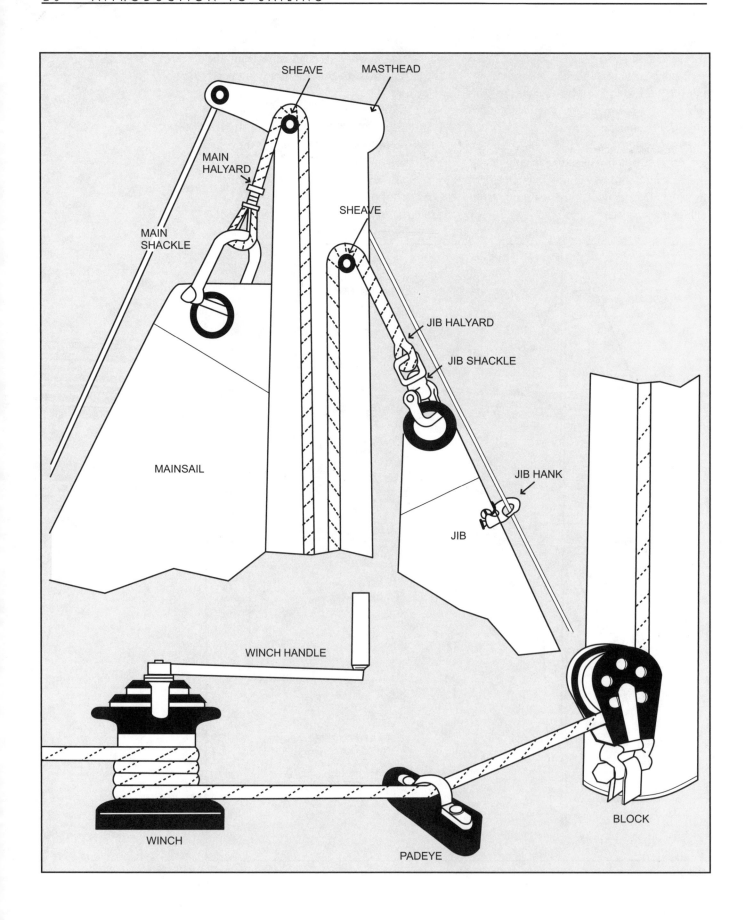

SHEAVE
MASTHEAD
MAIN HALYARD
MAIN SHACKLE
SHEAVE
JIB HALYARD
JIB SHACKLE
MAINSAIL
JIB HANK
JIB
WINCH HANDLE
BLOCK
WINCH
PADEYE

its resistance to stretching. Other materials such as nylon, Mylar, and Kevlar are also used in sailmaking. Types of sails are:

MAINSAIL–the primary and most easily controlled source of sail power, attached along the aft edge to the mast and along the top edge to the boom.

SPINNAKER (CHUTE)–a balloonlike sail, often colored, used when running (sailing downwind).

JIB (HEADSAIL)–the sail set forward of the mainsail and attached to the forestay using jib hanks or a headfoil track for a bolt rope.

GENOA (HEADSAIL)–a large jib with an overlap aft of the mast.

Each part of a sail has a name:
HEAD–the top comer of the sail.
TACK–the forward lower comer of a sail.
CLEW–the back lower comer of a sail.
LUFF–the leading edge (front) of a sail. The luff of the mainsail attaches to the mast, and the luff of the jib attaches to the forestay.

FOOT–the bottom edge of a sail. The foot of the mainsail attaches to the boom. The foot of the jib is unattached and consequently more difficult to control.

LEECH–the trailing (back) edge of a sail.

BATTENS–support sticks held in pockets to keep the leech from flapping and to add support to the sail.

DRAFT–the fullness or roundness of a sail.

The **RUNNING RIGGING** consists of ropes (called lines) that pull the sails up and adjust the sails' shape. Unlike the standing rigging, the running rigging is not stationary. When sailors speak of "trimming" sails to find the most efficient shape, they mean that the sheets are being let out (eased) or pulled in (trimmed).

The running rigging includes:

HALYARDS–lines used to raise (hoist) sails and hold them up.

MAINSHEET–a line used to trim the mainsail; it is led through a series of blocks to form a block and tackle.

JIB SHEETS TWO lines, one on each side of the boat, to trim the jib.

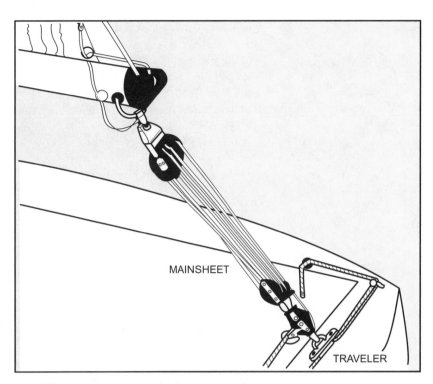

MAINSHEET

TRAVELER

The **TOPPING LIFT**, which prevents the boom from dropping on deck, is part of the running rigging. The **DOWNHAUL, OUTHAUL,** and **CUNNINGHAM** are also running rigging. We will discuss them later.

HALYARDS attach to the top or head of a sail. Halyards run through the top of the mast by means of a **SHEAVE** or **BLOCK** (pulley) and then down to the bottom of the mast. A halyard can be **INTERNAL**, inside the mast, or **EXTERNAL**, outside the mast. The **MAIN HALYARD** raises the mainsail and the **JIB HALYARD** raises the jib.

Halyards sometimes terminate at the base of the mast, requiring the crew to be at the mast when hoisting and lowering the sails. A better system is to have the halyard lead back to the cockpit through **TURNING BLOCKS** and **PADEYES** (blocks and eyes through which a line is threaded to give it a clear, safe run). The sail can then be hoisted by the crew without leaving the safety of the cockpit.

Most boats have **WINCHES** on the mast or on the deck to aid in the hoisting of sails. Winches pull on lines mechanically and safely. They consist of a drum that rotates only in a clockwise direction around which

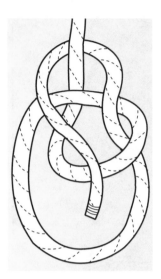

Bowline knot

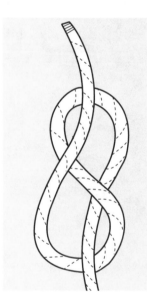

Figure eight knot or "stopper knot"

The windward or "lazy" jib sheet becomes the new working sheet when the boat tacks.

the line is wrapped. A crank handle rotates the drum. Winches are discussed in the Sailing Skills section of this part.

SHEETS control the shape of the sail and **SAIL TRIM** or position of the sail. The mainsheet and jib sheets are quite different from one another. The mainsheet is a multiple-part block and tackle used to increase an individual's pulling power. By giving a sheet a 2:1, 4:1, or 8:1 advantage, the device lets you trim your sails more easily. This is particularly helpful in strong winds.

The jib sheet consists of two lines connected to the clew of the jib that lead along each side of the boat to the cockpit. Although the actual leading of the jib sheets varies from boat to boat, the system illustrated in this book is among the most common.

The jib sheets are attached to the clew of the jib with a knot called a **BOWLINE** This knot provides a temporary loop that allows the jib sheet to be securely attached to the sail. The key feature of the bowline, like any property tied knot, is that it unties remarkably easily, even after being under prolonged, heavy strain.

The other end of the jib sheet leads through a **BLOCK** (a pulley), or series of blocks, around a winch, to a cam cleat or deck **CLEAT** (a wooden, plastic, or metal fitting used to secure lines). The crew controls the sail trim by pulling in or letting out

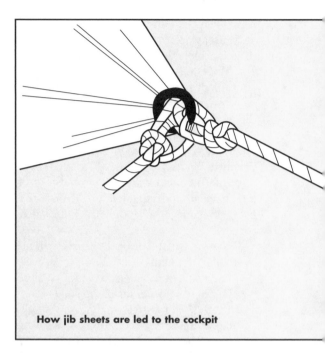

How jib sheets are led to the cockpit

the sheet.

Since the jib sheets are led along both the **WINDWARD** (toward the wind) and the **LEEWARD** (away from the wind) sides of the boat, they are referred to as the **LEEWARD** and **WINDWARD SHEETS**. The leeward sheet is led along the leeward side of the boat. It is the working sheet and will be taut when the jib is in use; the windward sheet is the nonworking or "lazy" sheet and will be slack. Of course, as the side of the boat

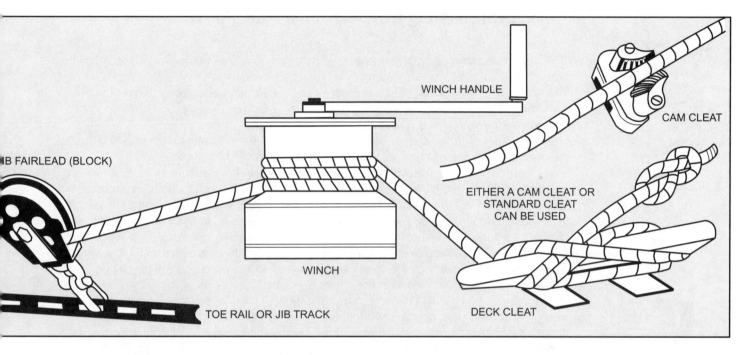

JIB FAIRLEAD (BLOCK)

WINCH HANDLE

CAM CLEAT

EITHER A CAM CLEAT OR
STANDARD CLEAT
CAN BE USED

WINCH

TOE RAIL OR JIB TRACK

DECK CLEAT

the wind is blowing from changes, reference to the windward or leeward jib sheets also changes.

At the tail end of the jib sheet will be a **FIGURE EIGHT** or **STOPPER** knot. The knot will keep the line from pulling through the turning block or fairlead.

The topping lift, or boom lift, holds the boom off the deck when the sail is not being used. If the mainsail is lowered without the topping lift attached, the boom will fall to the deck.

A topping lift should be adjustable, either from the cabin top or from the boom itself One of the simplest types of topping lift attaches to the backstay and consists of a few feet of wire with a clip or shackle on the end. Although this type of topping lift serves the basic purpose of support for the boom, it is difficult to use and almost impossible to adjust or disconnect once the sail has been raised.

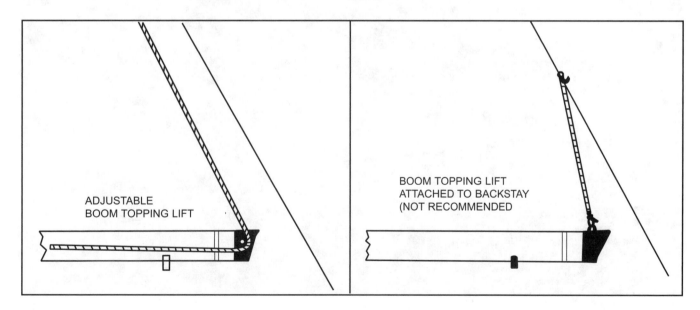

ADJUSTABLE
BOOM TOPPING LIFT

BOOM TOPPING LIFT
ATTACHED TO BACKSTAY
(NOT RECOMMENDED

RESPONSIBILITIES OF THE SKIPPER AND CREW

The terms **HELMSMAN** and **SKIPPER** are often used interchangeably; however, they are not the same. The skipper (whether on deck, at the wheel, or taking a nap below) is the person responsible for the safe operation of the vessel. The helmsman is the person steering the boat, a role which may be performed by any member of the crew, including the skipper. The crew (including the helmsman) is responsible for assisting the skipper in the safe operation of the boat.

Traditionally, the captain of a vessel is responsible for the safety of the vessel and all persons aboard. This is particularly true on commercial vessels. However, on a recreational boat the operator (skipper) assumes many of the responsibilities of the captain. If the boat is boarded by federal, state, or local law-enforcement personnel, the skipper must answer for the condition and conduct of the boat. For example, the skipper is responsible for ensuring that:

Organize the crew by giving each person a specific task

- The boat carries all required safety equipment.
- Proper lights are displayed at night.
- Correct sound signals are used when required.
- No-wake zones and restricted areas are correctly observed.
- The boat isn't operated in a manner that will endanger life, limb, or property of any person. Negligent or grossly negligent operations could include: operating in a hazardous manner, operating in a designated swimming area, excessive speed in the vicinity of other boats, hazardous waterskiing practices, overloading, overpowering, boating in hazardous weather, bowriding (or riding on a gunwale or transom), and operating under the influence of alcohol or drugs.
- The boat complies with the rules for preventing collisions.
- Proper registration numbers are displayed and the certificate of number is carried on board.

• An accident report is prepared if the boat or persons aboard are involved in an accident that involves a fatality or disappearance (Report within 48 hours), injuries requiring more than first aid, more than $2000 damage to vessels or property, or the complete loss of a vessel (within 10 days).

• Assistance is rendered to persons overboard and to other boats needing help. (The operator or any person in charge of a vessel is obligated by law to provide assistance that can be safely provided to any individual in danger at sea. The Good Samaritan rule in the Federal Boat Safety Act of 1971 will protect you from liability if you act reasonably and prudently. The operator is subject to a line and/or imprisonment for failure to do so.)

• Trash, oil, and other pollutants are properly disposed of, and that permanently installed marine toilets comply with United States Coast Guard (USCG) regulations.

• The owner is responsible along with the operator if an injury occurs or if the boat causes damage.

The above list is illustrative, not exhaustive. It identifies some of the specific required actions and responsibilities of the skipper. Being a good skipper, however, entails more than satisfying the specific requirements listed above. It is also a matter of attitude. To a degree unmatched by many other forms of transportation, passengers and other boaters are dependent upon the skipper's skills and responsible approach to boating. In boating, responsibility and fun go hand in hand.

To ensure the safety of the crew, the skipper must organize the operation of the boat so that tasks will be performed efficiently. This means delegating jobs according to the abilities of different crew members.

As a skipper, be tactful when giving an order; as a crew member, be willing and able to obey all reasonable commands. The great General "Stonewall" Jackson once said, "Obedience to orders, instant and unhesitating, is not only the life blood of armies and navies, but the security of states." This statement applies perfectly on sailboats.

Give orders in a friendly but firm tone of voice. Never shout: it only makes the crew nervous and leads to mistakes. Explain commands to inexperienced crew members in advance so they feel more relaxed. Give commands in exact terms. For example, ask for sails to be trimmed in four inches instead of "a little." By putting commands in precise terms, you leave no doubt as to what you want. The best skippers are those who ask the advice of the rest of the crew. However, in times of quick action, the crew must obey commands immediately and ask questions later.

One of the greatest yachtsmen of all time, Ted Turner, establishes the role of each crew member when that person steps on board the yacht. He clearly defines the job of every person on the boat. In case there is an emergency or an important maneuver, each person is assigned a specific task. Turner has earned great loyalty from his crews over the years because they have faith in his ability to make clear decisions in the heat of battle. His secret? Taking good advice when asked for, assigning specific duties, and motivating the crew by giving everyone on board a reason to excel.

This book will introduce and develop the skills you must have to be a good skipper and crew member. Whether you are tending docking lines, trimming the mainsail, or maneuvering through a crowded marina, each task undertaken and learned in this course will make you a better and safer sailor. More on the duties and responsibilities of a skipper will be discussed in

ALCOHOL AND DRUG ABUSE

The National Transportation Safety Board (NTSB) estimates that between 37 and 76 percent of all boating fatalities can be traced to operators with measurable levels of alcohol in their blood. Moreover, studies show that, compared with sober operators, legally drunk boaters are ten times more likely to be fatally injured.

Alcohol consumption while boating is problematic for several reasons:

• Boating exposes the operator to natural stressors (e.g., noise, shock, extreme temperatures, vibration, sun, glare, and wind) that increase fatigue, decrease dexterity, and interfere with judgment. Alcohol exacerbates these effects.

• Complex reaction time (that associated with more difficult tasks or divided attention) is increased with moderate alcohol use. In tasks requiring vigilance (i.e., prolonged periods of task concentration or attention to task) accuracy decreases and the time required for correct response increases with blood alcohol content.

• Alcohol impairs the psychomotor performance of tasks that are vital to safe boat operation, such as steering and signal anticipation. Visual acuity is reduced in low contrast situations such as twilight and night conditions.

• Fatigue increases with alcohol consumption.

• Intellectual functions are sensitive to the effects of alcohol. Verbal performance, problem solving, and short-term memory are adversely affected by alcohol.

• Balance is adversely affected by alcohol, increasing the likelihood of falling from the boat.

• Judgment is adversely affected by alcohol. Persons under the influence appear to be willing to take greater risks and to underestimate their degree of impairment.

These are all excellent reasons to refrain from consumption of alcohol while boating. Nonetheless, the American Red Cross National Boating Survey reveals that 29 percent of all boaters reported using alcohol during typical outings, and the percentages for operators of cabin cruisers and cabin sailboats were higher, 44.6 percent and 41.6 percent respectively.

Here are some ideas to reduce alcohol related risks:

• Refrain from alcohol consumption until safely tied up at the end of the day. This is the best strategy.

• Limit consumption to one drink or less per hour.

• Eat before and while drinking.

• Alternate between drinking alcoholic and nonalcoholic beverages. Use nonalcoholic beverages to quench thirst before drinking alcoholic beverages.

• Don't invite people who characteristically drink to excess.

• Don't bring large amounts of alcohol.

• Don't stop at waterside drinking establishments.

Operating a vessel while intoxicated became a specific federal offense effective January 13, 1988. The final rule set standards for determining when an individual is intoxicated. If the blood alcohol content (BAC) is 0.10 percent or greater for operators of recreational vessels being used solely for pleasure, violators are subject to a civil penalty not to exceed $1,000 or a criminal penalty not to exceed $5,000, one-year imprisonment, or both. State laws may have other penalties, such as forfeiture of vessel (or motor vehicle) operating privileges. Most states have an implied consent law and refusal to take a blood alcohol test can be used against the boater.

A 160-pound person who consumes five drinks (twelve ounces of beer equals five ounces of wine equals one ounce of eighty-proof liquor equals one drink) in a two-hour period will raise his or her BAC to 0.1 percent.

Intoxicating drugs may not show up in a sobriety test designed for alcohol. However, many jurisdictions give law-enforcement officers great latitude in determining the probability of drug use by operators. If behavior and/or other outward signs indicate that drugs may be present, the officer may charge the operator with boating under the influence (BUI).

FEDERAL REQUIREMENTS FOR RECREATIONAL BOATS

As noted above, the prudent skipper ensures that the recreational vessel carries all required safety equipment (e.g., personal flotation devices, fire extinguishers, appropriate lights, sound-producing devices) and operates the vessel in full conformity with the navigation rules (both topics are covered in parts two and five). Additionally, the operator must comply with other federal and state requirements, such as registration or documentation, numbering, display of capacity information, ventilation systems, use of approved backfire-flame arresters, appropriate pollution placards, and marine sanitation devices (MSDs).

REGISTRATION AND DOCUMENTATION

A vessel of five or more net tons may be documented through the USCG. Documentation is a form of national registration available to citizens or corporations of the United States. In the documentation process, USCG issues papers similar to those issued for large ships. Bills of sale, mortgages, and other papers of title may be recorded with federal authorities, giving legal notice that such documents exist. Documentation may provide additional security and aids in financing and transfer of title. Many states also require that you register documented vessels (see below). If a documented vessel is registered, a decal issued by the state is displayed in lieu of the usual registration number. The decal must be in a clearly visible location. The name and hailing port of a documented vessel must be displayed on an exterior surface that is clearly visible (typically a transom). The original documentation papers (not copies) must be carried aboard.

If your vessel is not documented, registration in the state of its principal use is probably required. Check with state authorities to determine if your vessel must be registered. If you use it mainly on an ocean, gulf, or other similar water, register it in the state where you moor it. Registration fees vary with state, vessel length, and type of propulsion. The period of registration also varies with the state and may be one year or more.

All states, except Alaska, register boats. (The USCG issues the registration numbers in Alaska.) You must have the original registration certificate (certificate of number) aboard (not a copy) when the boat is in use. Some states will issue duplicate originals for a small additional fee for operators concerned over the certificate's security or susceptibility to water damage.

***In most cases, a boat which is legally registered in one state can travel to another state without a specific application to do so. The operator bears responsibility for determining whether any additional legal obligations prevail when operating in another state. ***

An alpha-numeric sequence (the registration number) is provided on the certificate of registration. It usually consists of three groups: two letters (indicating the state), up to four numerals, followed by one or two additional letters. Registered vessels must have their registration number painted or permanently attached on both sides of the forward half of the hull. This registration number must be clearly visible in block characters (of contrasting color to the background) at least three inches high, which can be read from left to right. The three character groups must be separated by a space or hyphen. Most states issue a decal, along with the registration, which identifies the expiration date of the registration. This decal must be affixed in close proximity to the registration number.

Unlike state registration numbers that appear near the boat's bow, the Hull Identification Number is quite small and is attached to the transom.

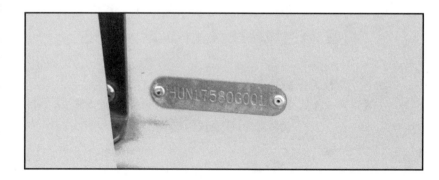

HULL IDENTIFICATION NUMBER

A boat manufactured for use in the United States after 1972 must have a hull identification number (HIN) permanently attached to the transom on the starboard side, above the waterline. The number must also be located in an unexposed location. The vessel's HIN should be recorded by the owner. It may be helpful in identifying a lost or stolen boat. Moreover, the HIN is required on many state registration forms.

CAPACITY INFORMATION

Manufacturers must put capacity plates on most monohull recreational motorboats less than 20 feet long. Sailboats, canoes, kayaks, and inflatable boats are exempt. Outboard boats must display the maximum permitted horsepower of their engines. The plates must also show the allowable maximum weight of the people on board. And they must show the allowable maximum combined weights of people, motors, and gear. Inboards and stern drive boats need not show the weight of their engines on their capacity plate.

The capacity plate must appear where it is clearly visible to the operator when getting underway. This information reminds the operator of the vessel's maximum capacity under normal circumstances. On windy days or in rough water, don't load your boat as heavily as on calm days in smooth water. Overloaded boats can swamp, capsize, and sink. Law-enforcement officers may consider operation of an overloaded boat to be an act of reckless endangerment or negligent operation. For home-built or other boats not required to have a capacity plate the following formula can be used to estimate the maximum number of persons who can safely ride in the boat on a calm day. Multiply the length (in feet) by the width (in feet) and divide this by 15. Round the result down to the nearest whole number. For example, a boat with a length of 20 feet and a beam of 6 feet could safely carry $(20 \times 6) / 15 = 8$ persons on a calm day. This formula assumes that the average weight of a person is 150 pounds-adjustments should be made if this assumption is incorrect. Note that the length of the boat is measured along a straight line from its bow to its stern. The length does not include bowsprits nor does it include rudders, brackets, outboard motors, diving platforms, or other attachments.

Remember that the number of seats in a boat is not a reliable indicator of how many people the boat can safely carry!

VENTILATION

The largest cause of fire and explosions aboard recreational boats is gasoline vapor collecting in the lower compartments of the boat. Gasoline vapor is heavier than air and sinks to the lower compartments. If a flow of air is not present to ventilate gas vapors, a spark from a source such as a cigarette ash, an electric switch, or static electricity could cause trapped gasoline vapors to explode.

Technology has not as yet provided us with a completely foolproof ventilation system. However, natural or powered ventilation systems are required by law because they significantly reduce the chance of explosion. Both powered and natural ventilation are required for boats with permanently installed gasoline engines that have cranking motors. An engine compartment is exempt if its engine is open to the atmosphere. Diesel-powered boats are also exempt.

Fresh air is directed into engine and fueltank compartments using wind scoops (cowls), often assisted by electric blowers. A tube leads to the exhaust cowl

---

U.S. Coast Guard

Maximum Capacities

XX PERSONS OR XXX LBS.
XXX LBS. PERSONS, MOTORS, GEAR
XXX HP MOTOR

where the collected vapor is vented overboard. The tubes connecting the lower areas with the intake and exhaust cowls should be at least two inches in diameter. A powered blower should have a marine-type, spark-proof switch.

Ventilation systems are particularly important for inboard, engine-powered sailboats. The engine location in the lower portion of a deep hull can make routing the ventilation ducts very difficult. It is important that ventilation in this type of boat not be neglected. Because sailboats spend a great deal of time operating with the engine shut down, engine "breathing" doesn't help ventilate the engine compartment. When the wind dies and it's time to start the engine, the engine compartment must be free of vapors.

A ventilation system will not remove spilled fuel or oil from the bilge or bottom of a boat! Wipe up any spilled fuel or oil (and dispose of it properly)! Remember the following points:

• Always ventilate the engine compartment before turning on any switches or starting the engine.

• Operate the bilge blower for at least five minutes before starting an inboard engine. If the blower fails to operate, fix or replace it before attempting to start the engine.

• Even if your boat is equipped with fuel vapor detectors, sniff your bilges. Your nose is the best fuel and vapor detector.

A BRIEF DIGRESSION:
SAFE FUELING PROCEDURES

While on the subject of ventilation, it is useful to provide a few pointers on safe fueling procedures. Most boat fires occur just after fueling and most are preventable. Fuel can leak from punctured hoses, lines, and tanks. Fittings, loosened through normal operation, can also fail. Periodically inspect the entire fuel system and tighten fittings when necessary. Gasoline that requires an oil mixture (for two-stroke motors) should have the oil added on shore in a separate container. (This procedure minimizes the impact of an oil spill

and reduces the hazard.) The gas-oil mixture should then be poured into the boat's tank. Leave air space for expansion at the top. If it is necessary to keep additional gasoline onboard, keep it in a safety-approved tank with adequate air supply. All combustibles should be kept away from the boat's engine(s) and batteries.

Here are key safety tips to follow when fueling. You may wish to summarize these in a checklist for onboard review:

• Ensure that you are familiar with the locations of all fire extinguishers.

• Label your deck-mounted fuel fill to prevent mistaking it for the water or sewage tank.

• Portable tanks must not be fueled on the boat.

• Refuel during daylight hours to minimize the likelihood of spills.

• Turn off motor or any other source of sparks or heat. Electrical equipment and compressed cooking-gas tanks should all be off.

• Close all hatches and ports and seal off all cabin areas. Ventilating cabins during fueling can allow fumes to be trapped below.

• Ask your crew to stand on the dock away from the fueling operation.

• No smoking!

• Verify that the correct fuel pump (gas or diesel) is being used. Hold the spout or nozzle firmly against the tank or filler pipe. This keeps the two grounded and prevents sparks from static electricity. Remember that the automatic shut-off on the fuel nozzle may not work on your boat. Never leave a fuel hose unattended while refueling!

• Do not overfill the tank (see below). To minimize the likelihood of a spill, estimate the amount of fuel that you will need and have one of your crew call out the amount delivered if you cannot see the dial on the fuel pump.

• Wipe up all spills. Your clean-up rags should be allowed to dry in the open air, not in the boat. If rags must be stored, store them in an air-tight container. Better yet, use disposable rags.

• When fueling is completed, open all hatches and ports. Enclosed areas should be allowed to air-out for at least five minutes. Use the blower for at least five minutes before starting the engine.

• Check all fuel lines and connections again for leaks. Check enclosed areas for fumes. Start the engine and invite your crew back aboard.

BACKFIRE-FLAME ARRESTERS

Gasoline engines, other than outboards, must have acceptable means of backfire control. Backfires occur when flames from an engine exit through the carburetor instead of the exhaust system. A backfire control keeps the flames from entering the engine compartment. The usual method of controlling backfires is by a backfire-flame arrester mounted atop the engine's carburetor. A flame arrester works by rapidly dissipating the heat of the flame. Thus, the flame is kept out of the engine compartment. An acceptable backfire-flame arrester bears a Coast Guard approval number, or it shows that it complies with Underwriters Laboratories Standard UL 1111. The label may also state that it complies with the Society of Automotive Engineers Standard SAE J-1928.

To be effective, flame arresters must be free of oil, grease, and dirt. Grease dissolving detergents are available for this purpose. Other than periodic cleaning, backfire-flame arresters do not need servicing or replacement.

MARINE SANITATION DEVICES

There is no requirement to equip your boat with a marine toilet. However, installed toilets must have Type I, II, or III marine sanitation devices (MSDs), certified by the Coast Guard. Most pleasure boats have Type III MSDs, which use holding tanks to contain waste until it can be properly disposed of onshore. Vessels over 65 feet long must use Type I or Type 11 MSDs. Pumpout stations-shoreside facilities designed to empty the holding tank-can be found at many marinas.

Additives are often used to sanitize and deodorize waste while it is stored onboard. These additives may contain chlorine, quaternary ammonia, or formaldehyde. Marine life and septic systems can both suffer when these substances are introduced. Boaters should make an effort to use products that do not contain environmentally damaging substances.

Some systems use Y valves to direct

Typical dumping placard.

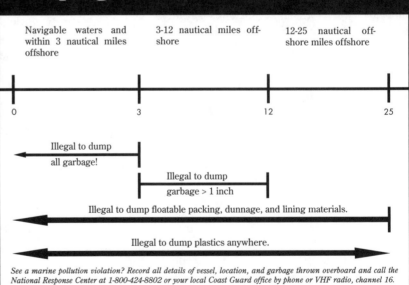

Garbage Dumping Restrictions

Under Federal law, it is illegal to discharge plastic or garbage mixed with plastic into any waters. Regional, state, or local regulations may also apply. All discharge of garbage is prohibited in the Great Lakes and their connecting or tributary waters.

Violators are subject to substantial civil penalties and/or criminal sanctions, including fines and imprisonment.

Navigable waters and within 3 nautical miles offshore

3-12 nautical miles offshore

12-25 nautical offshore miles offshore

0   3   12   25

Illegal to dump all garbage!

Illegal to dump garbage > 1 inch

Illegal to dump floatable packing, dunnage, and lining materials.

Illegal to dump plastics anywhere.

See a marine pollution violation? Record all details of vessel, location, and garbage thrown overboard and call the National Response Center at 1-800-424-8802 or your local Coast Guard office by phone or VHF radio, channel 16.

waste into the holding tank or directly overboard. Boats with a Y valve that can direct waste overboard must use special caution on inland waters, in a "No-discharge Area," or within the three-mile coastal limit. Consult state and local rules regarding the operation of this system.

POLLUTION

For too many years, it was thought that the sheer volume of rivers, bays, and oceans was so great that there was little man could do to cause significant environmental damage. Today, we recognize the fallacy of that assumption and understand that we all share a responsibility to help keep our waters clean and to avoid damage to fragile wetlands and other sensitive areas. There is much that all boaters (both power and sail) can do to reduce environmental impacts. Here are a few suggestions:

• Observe dumping restrictions (see below). These are easily complied with and can significantly reduce environmental impact. Stow all loose items, plastic bags, drink cups, and other articles properly so that they do not fall into the water. Use onshore toilet facilities instead of MSDs whenever possible.

• Develop a waste-management plan that specifies the measures you will take to comply with applicable laws and the procedures you will use to collect, process, and move waste for proper disposal. Identify the person responsible (usually the skipper) for ipllementing this plan. Vessels more than 40 feet in length with a galley and berths are required to have such a plan. A simple written statement to the effect that the skipper is in charge of trash and trash disposal in accordance with the Act to Prevent Pollution from Ships (MARPOL Annex V) is all that is required.

• Check the bilge frequently for signs of oily wastes and use approved absorbent pads to collect this waste. (This is a good safely measure as well as an environmentally sound practice.) If you spill fuel or oil into the water, do not disperse it with detergent or soap. This only sends the problem down to the seafloor where it becomes more toxic and more difficult to clean up.

• Keep engines properly tuned to reduce hydrocarbon emissions. This will improve your fuel efficiency and lower fuel bills as well. Clean your boat's bottom regularly to reduce drag and improve performance.

• Exercise care when fueling. To minimize the likelihood of a spill through the vent tube, do not fill fuel tanks to the top.

• Use only environmentally friendly antifouling bottom paints.

• Use environmentally friendly cleaning products (look for the words phosphate-free and biodegradable on the label) when washing your boat. Rinsing your boat with clean water after each use will reduce your need for cleaners and heavy-duty products.

• Do not anchor in rubble, coral reefs, or sea grass. This practice is unsafe and will damage the underwater environment.

• Stay in marked channels whenever possible to lower the likelihood of running aground and damaging bottom vegetation.

• Take steps to prevent the introduction of zebra mussels into uninfested waters. These steps include: use of antifouling paints, cleaning your vessel with hot water, removal of all bait and emptying bait wells and bait buckets and flushing them with water containing chlorine bleach.

• Operate at slow speeds in manatee areas to lower the likelihood of harming this vulnerable mammal. In general, do not disturb wildlife.

DISCHARGE OF OIL

All vessels under 100 gross tons must have a fixed or portable means of discharging oily bilge stops into a container-a bucket or bailer is acceptable. Any discharge that causes a sheen on the water is a violation of the Federal Water Pollution Control Act. If your vessel is 26 feet or more in length you must post a placard stating the federal requirements. The placard must be at least 5 by 8 inches and made of a durable material. Post it in the machinery space or at the bilge and ballast pump control station. The placard must state:

DISCHARGE OF OIL PROHIBITED

The Federal Water Pollution Control Act prohibits the discharge of oil or oily waste into or upon the navigable waters of the United States or the waters of the contiguous zone if such discharge causes a film or sheen upon, or discoloration of the surface of the water or causes a sludge or emulsion beneath the surface of the water. Violators are subject to a penalty of $5,000.

These placards are commonly available at marine supply stores. You are encouraged (required, if you are the source) to report any pollution discharge to the nearest USCG office. Report its location, source, size, color, substance (if known), and the time you saw it. If you are uncertain what substance has been discharged, keep flames away from it and avoid physical contact and inhalation of vapors. The USCG oil spill and pollution telephone number is 1-800-424-8802.

PLASTICS

It is illegal to dump plastics anywhere on the water. Plastics are lightweight, strong,

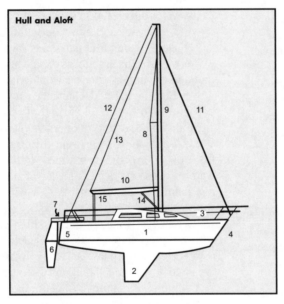

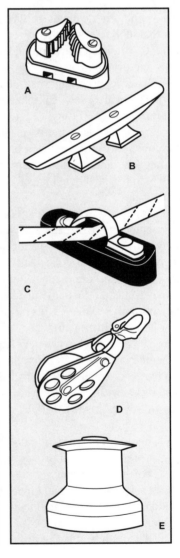

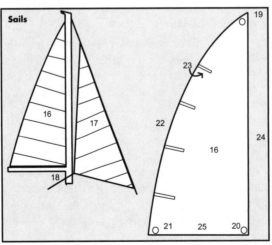

SAILING KNOWLEDGE • 33

and durable. On land, these may be very desirable qualities; but on the water these same characteristics are responsible for environmental damage. Because plastics are lightweight, they tend to float or remain in the water column. Birds, marine mammals, and fish can either ingest or become entangled in plastics. Both are major problems. Because plastics are strong, it may be difficult or impossible for marine animals to break free once they have become entangled. And, because plastics are durable, the threat to marine animals is persistent.

GARBAGE

It is illegal to dump garbage in any U.S. lakes, rivers, bays, harbors, and so on. Limited dumping offshore of trash and garbage is permitted beyond the 3-mile limit. If you have a vessel 26 feet or more in length, you are required to have a placard summarizing dumping restrictions. This placard (shown in the illustration on page 30) notifies guests and crew of applicable discharge restrictions. It is available in most marine stores.

Regional, state, or local regulations may impose additional restrictions.

REVIEW QUESTIONS

1. Match the following parts of the boat with the numbers on the illustrations.

A. Aloft
headstay _____
backstay _____
shroud _____
mast _____
boom _____
boom vang _____
topping lift _____
mainsheet _____

B. On Deck and Below
tiller _____
lifelines _____
rudder _____
stern _____
hull _____
bow _____
keel _____

C. Sails
jib _____
jib sheet _____
mainsail _____
head _____
clew _____
tack _____
luff _____
foot _____
leech _____
batten _____

2. In what direction can a boat not sail?
a) with the wind blowing across the boat (abeam)
b) into the wind
c) with (in the same direction as) the wind

3. From the illustrations, identify:
deck cleat _____
winch _____
block _____
padeye _____
cam cleat _____

4. Two major types of boat hulls are _____ hulls and _____ hulls.

5. A sailboat with an operating engine is considered a _____ under the navigation rules even if the sail is raised.

6. True or false: A backfire-flame arrester is required on a diesel engine.

7. True or false: Any discharge that causes a sheen on the water is a violation of the Federal Water Pollution Control Act.

8. A boat with a length of 16 feet and a width of 5 feet can carry a maximum of _____ 150 pound passengers on a calm day.

Answers in Appendix A, p. 201.

SAILING SKILLS

BOARDING

Boarding a sailboat for the first time is an exciting experience for everyone, but it can be traumatic. This is normal. Be careful when boarding a boat; even experienced sailors have fallen in the water. Always wear nonskid deck shoes for better footing, and also to protect the deck. Wearing socks with your shoes will increase traction.

Board the boat quickly. To steady yourself, hold onto a shroud or rail while stepping on board, or hold the steadying hand of a person already on the boat. Don't step from dock to deck with an armful of gear. Pass your gear across to the boat first. Step into the boat as close to the middle (between bow and stern) as you can. On smaller boats it is imperative to step into the middle of the boat while keeping your weight low. It often helps to put the centerboard down to give the boat added stability while you're loading. Keep the deck clear by stowing your gear as it is passed on board. Most importantly, relax when board-

Sit with the hiking stick at about a 90-degree angle to the tiller.

ing, but don't take unnecessary chances. Falling into the water between the boat and dock can be dangerous because a wave might push the boat back against the dock, causing you injury.

Each crew member should have a specific place to sit when the boat is leaving the dock and when it's underway. Make sure the helmsman has room to move the tiller, and always keep your head low to avoid being hit by the boom. Normally, most of the crew weight is kept at the beamiest (widest) part of the boat.

The helmsman has to sit near the tiller. He or she should try to sit so the hiking stick is at a 90 degree angle to the tiller. On a boat with a wheel, standing may give the helmsman a better view of the sails and the boat's heading.

Run through all the motions of boarding on land first, then practice from a dock to get the feeling of the boat in the water.

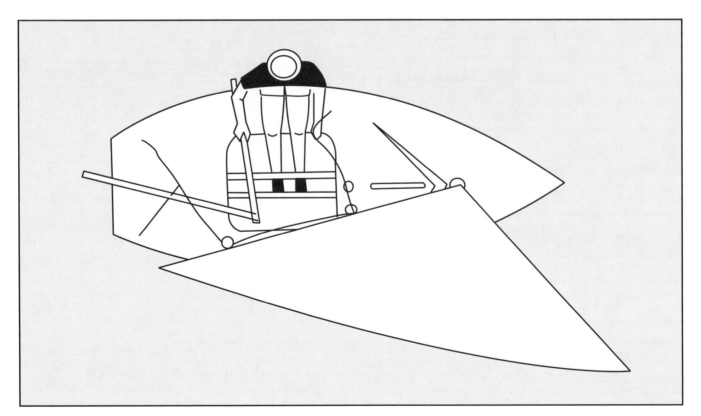

SAILING CHECKLIST

It is now time for your first sail. Use the following checklist to ensure that all required equipment is on board and that the boat is properly prepared to sail.

1. Check the weather report (see Part Six, Weather, p. 166).

2. Open hatches and ventilate the boat. Check below. If gasoline, stove fuel, or a holding tank for the **head** (toilet) are on board, the crew must check to make sure there are no fumes present before any flames are lit or the engine is started.

3. Check bilges and pump. The floor boards in the bottom of the boat should be lifted. They cover the **bilge** (the lowest part of the interior of the boat), and water will collect there from the natural "sweating" of a closed boat or from rain. Water will also seep in around loose keel bolts (the bolts that attach the keel to the boat). Use the bilge pump or a bucket and sponge to empty the bilge so the water won't slosh around while you're sailing.

4. Make sure there is one **PFD** (personal flotation device or life jacket) for each person aboard, plus one Type IV. (See Essential Safety Equipment, p. 144 for more details.)

5. Stow all gear in a safe, accessible place. Equipment must be close at hand in case of an emergency. Loose gear may roll around and injure someone during the sail. Be sure gear is stowed securely so it doesn't fall into the cabin when the boat heels over.

6. Make sure that the horn or whistle is operational.

7. Plan the day's sail and course.

8. Check the rigging and sails. Are the halyards clear and the sails ready to go up? Are the battens in their pockets? It is important that all lines be uncoiled and ready so they do not foul up in a block while you are attempting to leave the dock.

9. Assign specific jobs to each member of the crew and spell out the goal for the day.

ATTACHING THE SAILS

THE MAINSAIL

The mainsail may be furled (folded or rolled) on the boom, secured with sail ties, and protected with a sail cover, or it may be stored off the boom, folded and kept in a sail bag below. Newer Mylar and Kevlar sails are best rolled when lowered. This keeps the material from cracking. In either case, there are several steps necessary to prepare the mainsail for hoisting.

If the sail is off the boom, it will be taken out of the bag and laid along the deck. The crew will feed the clew into the groove in the boom. The sail will then be slid onto the boom until the tack is at the **gooseneck** (the fitting that attaches the boom to the mast). The **tack pin** (the pin that holds the tack of the sail to the boom) will be attached, as well as the **outhaul** (the line that attaches to the clew and is used to tension the foot of the sail).

If the mainsail is stored on the boom, the crew simply has to remove the sail cover, feed the luff or the attached plastic slugs into the groove of the mast, and attach the **main halyard shackle** to the head of the sail. Ensure that the battens are in the batten pockets, flexible end first. The crew should take up any slack from the halyard.

THE JIB

The jib is always stored in a sail bag when not in use. To set the jib, remove it from the sail bag and spread it on the foredeck. Locate the head, tack, and clew of the sail, the head being the narrowest angle of the three corners. Many sailmakers will mark the corners of the sail with *head, tack,* and *clew.* If this has not been done, it is easy to do with an indelible marker providing an easy reference.

The luff of the jib will usually be **hanked**

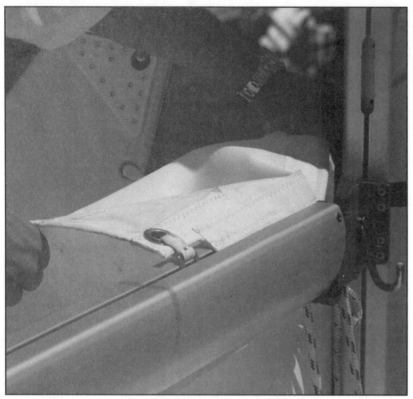

Attaching the mainsail's clew and tack

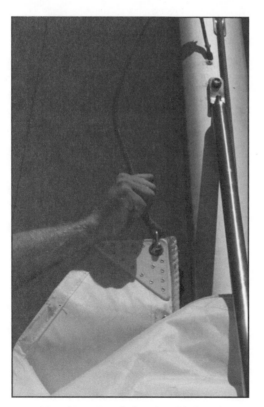

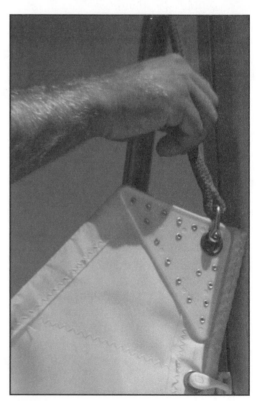

Attaching the mainsail's head and halyard

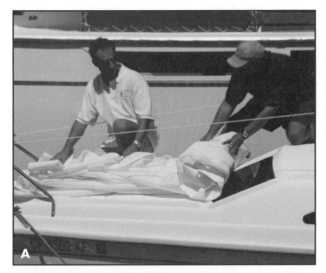

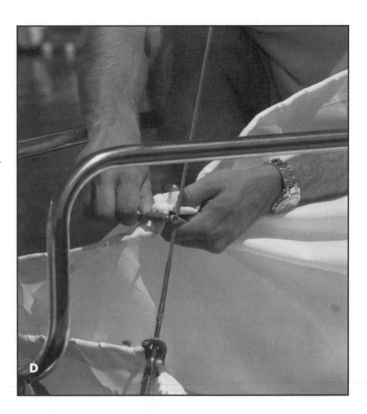

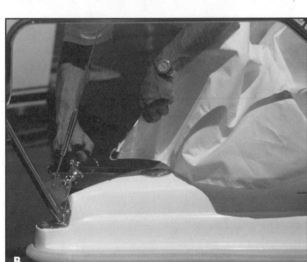

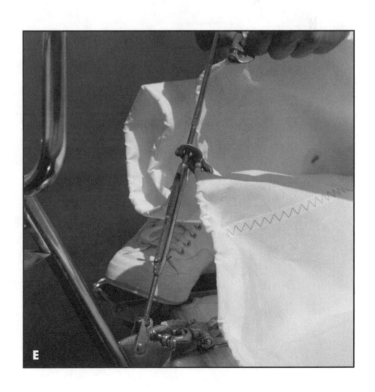

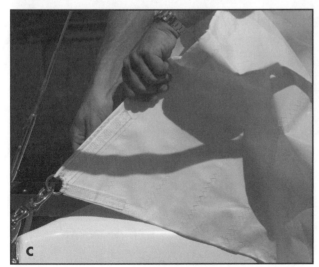

Attaching the jib

(with small brass or plastic snip fittings on the jib) onto the headstay and the jib sheets will be attached to the clew of the jib with bowline knots. If the headstay has a groove, then the jib will have a **bolt rope** (rope sewn into the luff of the sail) instead of hanks. In that case, insert the bolt rope into the **prefeeder** (a device which makes raising sails easier) and then into the groove.

The next step is to lash the jib to the side of the boat farthest from the dock. This will keep the sail out of the way while you leave the dock. To keep the jib from creeping up the forestay before it is time to hoist the sail, either tie a line around the sail and halyard or undo the top hank of the sail and attach it to the lifeline.

RIGGING CHECKLIST

The mainsail:
1. Remove sailcover.
2. Attach outhaul to the clew.
3. Attach tack pin to tack.
4. Attach main halyard to head of sail.
5. Uncoil and uncleat mainsheet.
6. Loosen boom vang.

The jib:
1. Attach jib to headstay.

2. Attach jib halyard to head.
3. Attach jib sheets to clew of jib with bowlines.
4. Lead jib sheets according to your particular boat's design, either inboard or outboard of shrouds.
5. Lead jib sheets to winches.
6. Tie the jib to lifelines to keep deck clear and secure head of jib to lifelines or bow pulpit.

Winches make many jobs on a sailboat easier and safer.

USING WINCHES

An important piece of gear on boats larger than about 20 feet is the winch, a drum turned by a handle that gives a mechanical advantage when hoisting sails and trimming sheets. All winches work the same way:

1. Before there is a strain on the line, make one or two clockwise loops around the drum.

2. Pull on the line hand-over-hand until the strain is heavy.

3. Make one or two more clockwise loops depending on load.

4. Insert the winch handle. With one hand, rotate the handle. With the other hand, pull on the line. (In some boats, the winch handle is permanently installed. When sailing on larger boats with very heavy strains, it may be necessary to have one crew member turn the handle with two hands while another crew member "tails," or pulls on the line.) Keep winching the line in until the halyard is hoisted or the sheet is trimmed properly. Be careful not to let fingers, hair, clothing, watch straps, etc., catch in the turns.

5. Once the line is cleated, remove the winch handle from the winch. If it's left in, it may trip somebody or fall out and be lost overboard.

RAISING THE MAINSAIL

The mainsail is always hoisted first because it is the primary source of power and because a sailboat handles better under mainsail alone than under jib alone. Since the mainsail is attached to the mast and boom, it is also easier to control than the jib.

Whether you raise the mainsail at the dock or while motoring out of the harbor, the bow of the boat should point into the wind. Check all shackles to be sure they are secure. Many are of the twist-locking type with a little groove for the pin. Make sure the pin is in the proper place. Keep enough slack in the mainsheet so that the sail can be fully hoisted. It is best to keep passengers and extra crew out of the way of the boom, which will swing radically during the hoisting procedure. Keep the mainsheet clear of winches, cleats, and the stern of the boat. Be sure to stay low so you don't get hit in the head as the boom swings while the main is raised.

PREPARATION

1. Position one person at the mast at the point where the sail enters the luff groove.

2. A second crew member should be at the end of the halyard, prepared to raise the sail.

3. A third crew member (if there is one) should keep the end of the boom from jumping around by controlling the mainsheet as the sail is being raised.

4. Crew members in the cockpit should slacken the topping lift, the mainsheet, and the boom vang. Some boats use the main halyard for the boom lift, so someone will have to hold the boom while the sail is being raised.

5. Don't begin hoisting until the bow is aimed directly into the wind.

PROCEDURE

When the skipper orders, "Hoist the mainsail":

1. Wrap the main halyard once around the winch.

2. Release sail ties.

3. Pull the halyard to start raising the sail.

4. Feed the luff of the sail into the slot to keep it from jamming. If it jams, lower the sail a few inches and hoist again.

5. The crew member on the halyard will

keep pulling by hand until the sail reaches the top of the mast. Use the winch to raise the halyard if the sail gets too heavy to hoist.

FINISHING OFF

1. When the sail reaches the top of the mast, take an additional wrap or two around the winch.

2. Place the winch handle in the winch and turn slowly until one vertical wrinkle appears in the luff of the sail, indicating proper tension. This wrinkle will smooth out when the boat begins sailing.

3. Coil and stow the halyard.

The jib may be hoisted now, or hoisting may be delayed until the boat is in open water if you leave the dock under power.

Raising the mainsail

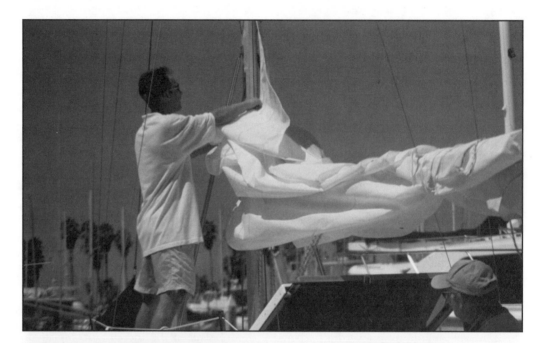

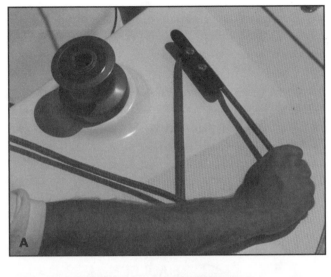

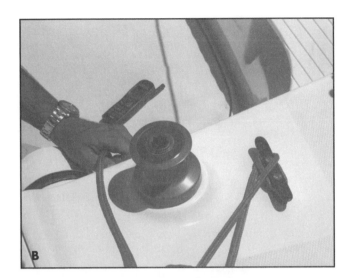

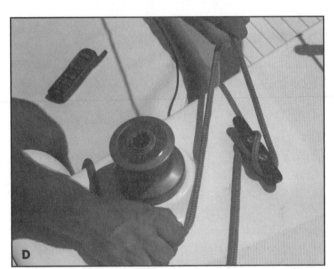

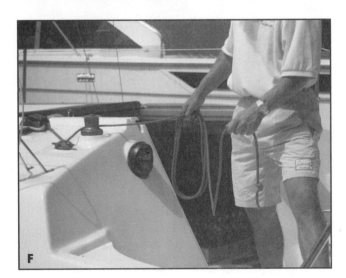

Cleating and coiling a line

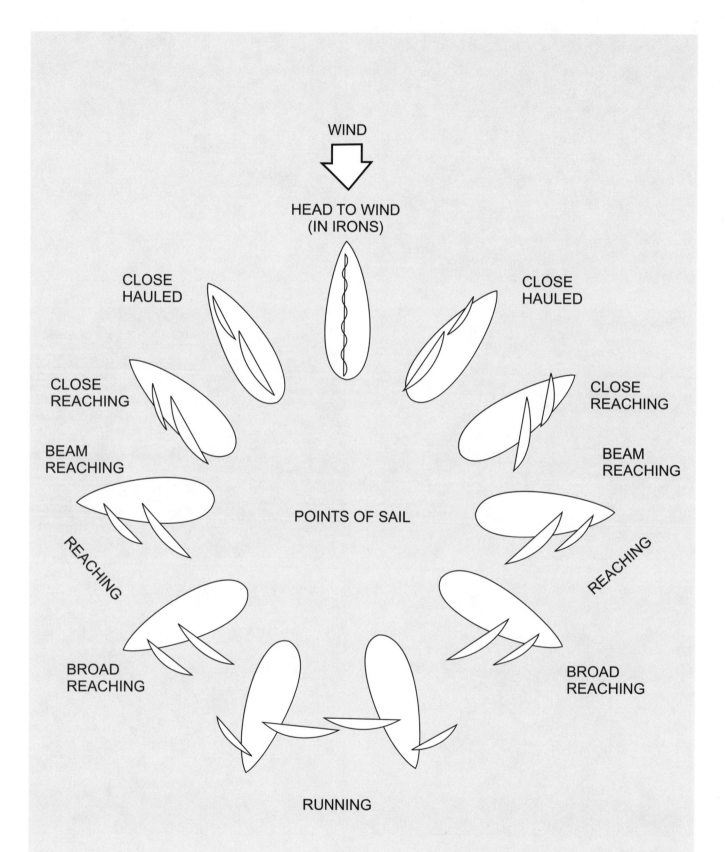

WIND

HEAD TO WIND
(IN IRONS)

CLOSE
HAULED

CLOSE
HAULED

CLOSE
REACHING

CLOSE
REACHING

BEAM
REACHING

BEAM
REACHING

POINTS OF SAIL

REACHING

REACHING

BROAD
REACHING

BROAD
REACHING

RUNNING

GETTING THE BOAT MOVING

The best wind for learning lies between 4 and 12 knots. Lighter winds make it difficult to maneuver, while heavier winds require greater skill. Light to moderate breezes and small waves allow the boat to sail easily. In addition, the crew feels more secure. Here, we'll look at basic skills while sailing under mainsail alone.

When steering, sit on the windward side where you can see the sail working while watching the approaching wind and waves. The windward side gives you the clearest view of where you are heading and what is happening on your boat.

When picking a course to sail, keep in mind that sailboats cannot sail directly into the wind. A sailboat's directional heading with respect to the wind is called her point of sail. There are three basic courses: beating (wind is from ahead), reaching (wind is from the side), and running (wind is from astern). The three different winds of reaching and more will be explained in Part II, Basic Sailing.

Sailing around with just the mainsail is an excellent way to learn the principles and mechanics of changing direction, but it is not as much fun as sailing with both the jib and mainsail. Sailing with the jib requires more coordination between the helmsman and crew and provides better boat performance and more pleasurable sailing.

Understanding how the wind acts on sails will enable you to sail to any destination you choose. The set of the sail in relation to the boat and the wind is called sail trim. To trim a sail is to adjust its position by pulling in or letting out its sheet.

Without going too deeply into the physics of what makes a sailboat sail, let's look at the airflow over a well-trimmed sail. A sail acts much like the wing of an airplane. As air flows over the two surfaces of the sail, lift develops, just like the lift on an airplane's wing. This lift pulls the sail forward and with it the boat.

As long as the sail's angle relative to the wind is correct (properly trimmed), smooth airflow over the sail will be main-

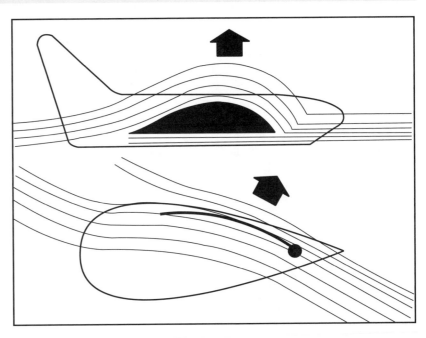

tained and a strong lift will result. If for some reason the sail is pointing too close to the wind or too far away from it, the flow of air on the sail will be turbulent, destroying the lift effect. Imagine an airplane with its wings installed improperly. How well do you think it will fly? The same thing happens to the sailboat if the sails are not properly trimmed. The sailboat will not perform any better than an airplane would with vertically mounted wings.

Good airflow is most critical when you're beating and reaching. Although airflow does affect the other points of sail, it does so to a lesser degree.

Trimming sails is a fascinating game all sailors can play. The techniques are logical and simple if you follow a few basic principles. Our first sailing exercise requires trimming just the mainsail. The main objective will be to gain a feel for how the boat sails, to learn to steer, and to learn to control the trim of the mainsail while sailing in a straight line.

Most sailors enjoy steering. You become attuned to the boat and feel close to the wind and waves.

The wind powers a sailboat just as it helps an airplane lift off.

EXERCISE: **GETTING THE BOAT MOVING**

1. The helmsman should position the boat so it is about 90 degrees to the wind. This is a reaching course and the easiest point of sail.

2. The crew should ease (let out) the mainsheet until the sail starts to luff (flap), then pull in slowly until the sail just stops luffing. This will indicate the best trim. In other words: Let the sail out as far as it can go without luffing.

3. To double-check whether this is exactly the right trim, the crew will again ease the sheet out slowly until the sail starts to luff and then pull it back, just until the luffing stops. This is a fine tuning in which the crew will move the mainsheet only a few inches.

Note: As the boat starts to move, the sail will begin to luff again. Don't question it now, just sheet in (pull in the sheet) until the luffing stops.

4. The helmsman will steer a straight course to the mark. The crew will continue to test the trim of the sail by easing it out until it luffs and then pulling it back in until it stops. Your goal is to steer a straight line. Make a game out of sailing. As the boat begins to sail, pick an object on shore or on the water to head for. Having a target to point

the boat toward makes it easy to watch where you go. If the target is an object in the water, such as a buoy, channel marker, or an anchored boat, watch the motion of your reference in relation to the shoreline in the background. It's easy to see if you are altering course inadvertently. Another technique is to watch the wake, or the trail of waves, coming from the stern of your boat. If you have a straight trail, you have been sailing a straight line. Don't write your name in the water. When you reach the object you have been heading for, pick another and start again.

WIND

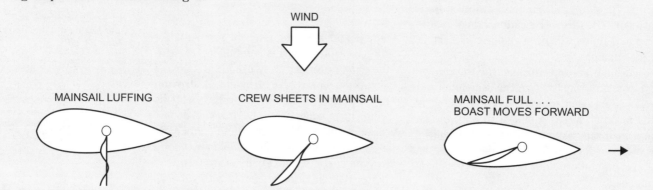

MAINSAIL LUFFING   CREW SHEETS IN MAINSAIL   MAINSAIL FULL . . . BOAST MOVES FORWARD

GETTING OUT OF IRONS

Many beginning sailors find themselves **in irons.** The term means that the boat is stopped, pointing directly into the wind, having lost all headway. It will not sail off on either tack. Not to worry, being caught in irons is an everyday occurrence. It happens to everyone at one time or another. Just be patient. Relax.

The term *irons* comes from the great days of sail, when a battleship stuck in irons could not maneuver away from its foe and therefore was unable to escape attack. The

term refers to handcuffs or leg irons, since the boat cannot move. A boat in irons was certain to be sunk as the enemy circled it. Captains were very careful to keep their boat from getting stuck in irons, but of course this was difficult, since one error in sail trim could be fatal to the vessel. These great ships were slow to maneuver, taking as long as thirty minutes to tack (change direction). A boat in irons might be stuck for several hours.

Even 12-meters can find themselves in

A boat is in irons when stopped and aimed directly into the wind. To get out of irons, back the jib to one side and the bow will move away from the wind in the opposite direction. Then release the jib and trim it on the leeward side to begin sailing.

irons. And, when sailing under a mainsail alone, I've found that it is almost impossible to get a 12-meter out of irons. I remember we were taking a lunch break while sailing on Defender during a testing session off Newport, Rhode Island, when we inadvertently got the 12-meter in irons. Our stablemate, Courageous, recognized our predicament and made continual passes by the boat lobbing spare bits of food in our direction and causing a great mess on deck. Since Defender was in irons, she was powerless to do anything about it, but the incident made for a great water fight back on shore after the day's sail testing. Defender's escape was finally made by hoisting the jib and getting the 12-meter underway.

To get out of irons, push the boom out until the sail fills with wind and the boat begins to sail backwards. This is called backing the mainsail. Now you've got to steer in reverse until the wind is coming over the side and the boat once again moves forward. To steer backwards, push

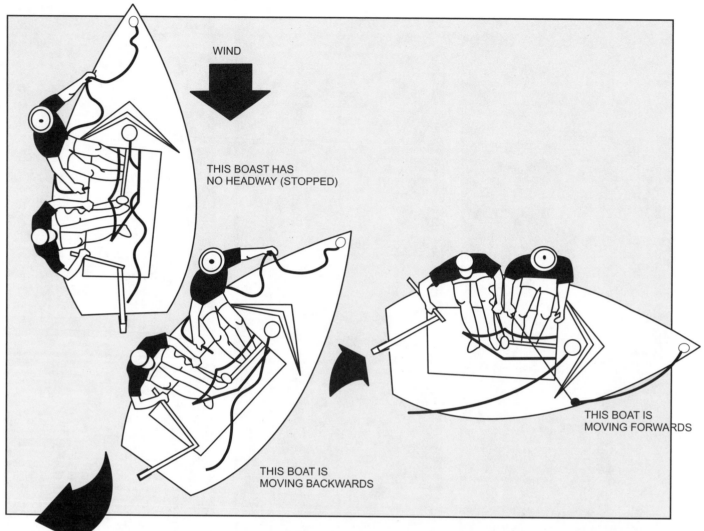

WIND

THIS BOAST HAS
NO HEADWAY (STOPPED)

THIS BOAT IS
MOVING BACKWARDS

THIS BOAT IS
MOVING FORWARDS

**Getting out of irons
(backing a jib)**

the tiller in the opposite direction that you want the stern to go, but turn the top of the steering wheel in the same direction that you want the stern to go. When the wind is coming over the side, let go of the boom, trim the mainsheet a bit, and get moving slowly. If you pull the mainsheet in too much, the boat will simply head right back into the wind again.

It's a lot easier to get out of irons when the jib is up. Although we haven't said much about sailing with the jib, let's assume that one is flying. If you're caught in irons, simply back the jib by holding the clew out to one side. You'll sail backwards slowly and the jib will push the bow off to the opposite side. For example, if you back the jib to starboard (the right-hand side), the bow will swing to port. When the wind is coming

over the starboard side, let go of the jib and trim its sheet normally, on the port side. Then trim in the mainsheet a little. The boat will quickly get sailing on a reach.

A well-balanced boat will more or less sail itself. A helmsman controls the boat and guides it along its course once the sails are set. Many sailors, particularly novices, over-correct for changes in the wind and deviate from the course steered.

Light boats are easy to maneuver because the rudder is large compared to the weight of the boat. Therefore you can rely on the rudder for all course changes. As a new sailor, you will find yourself using the rudder as a crutch. The key is to use the rudder in combination with your weight and the sails to help control and steer your boat.

COMING ABOUT OR TACKING (Mainsail Only)

Coming about or **tacking** means changing course by turning the boat into and through the wind until the sails move from one side of the boat to the other.

Coming about changes the **tack** of a sailboat. In this context the noun *tack* is not to be confused with the forward lower center of a sail, also called a tack. The tack you are sailing on is determined by the side of the boat over which the wind blows.

You can sail on either a starboard or port tack. On a **starboard tack** the wind comes over the starboard or the right-hand side of the boat. The boom is always on the port side of the boat when you sail on the starboard tack. A boat is on a **port tack** when the wind is coming over the port or left-hand side of the boat and the boom is to starboard.

I love tacking a sailboat. When I first learned to do a crisp roll tack while attending the Maritime College, I could spend hour after hour tacking back and forth. It feels so good because your body and the boat become one as you balance from tack to tack. In a **roll tack** you use your weight and sail trim and very little rudder to change the course of the boat. This is only possible in smaller boats. You can actually accelerate because you create the wind in your sails as you rock from one tack to the other.

Although roll tacking is an art form in itself that takes years of practice, it is one of the things that make sailing so special to me. The one-on-one competition found in match racing is the best. Tacking well is the essence of match-racing championships. The real goal is to turn the boat as quickly

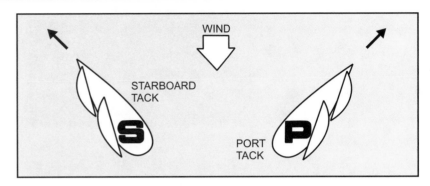

as possible without losing speed. The boat that does this best will often win a race. Even if you're not racing, you should learn to tack efficiently.

The closest angle most boats can sail from the wind is about 45 degrees, although some boats, like 12-meters, can sail 35 degrees off the wind. If you wish to reach a point directly upwind, sail as close as you can to the wind until you reach a point at which if you were to come about, you would be able to sail directly to your destination. The destination can also be reached by sailing close hauled and coming about in a series of short tacks.

SAFETY

When coming about, the helmsman and crew should always watch for other boats.

To avoid getting hit in the head, everyone must keep his head down as the boom crosses the boat during the tack. It is best to face forward when coming about so you see where your boat is heading.

The helmsman must establish a course (steer in a straight line) as soon as the mainsail fills. This will prevent the boat from going in circles and out of control.

JIBING (Mainsail Only)

There is another way to change tacks–jibing, or turning the boat away from the wind until the wind crosses the stern of the boat and the sail moves to the opposite side of the boat. To jibe, the helmsman turns the

boat in the direction away from the wind. This is called bearing away or bearing off. (In coming about, remember, the boat turns into the wind or heads up).

Jibing is one of sailing's greatest chal-

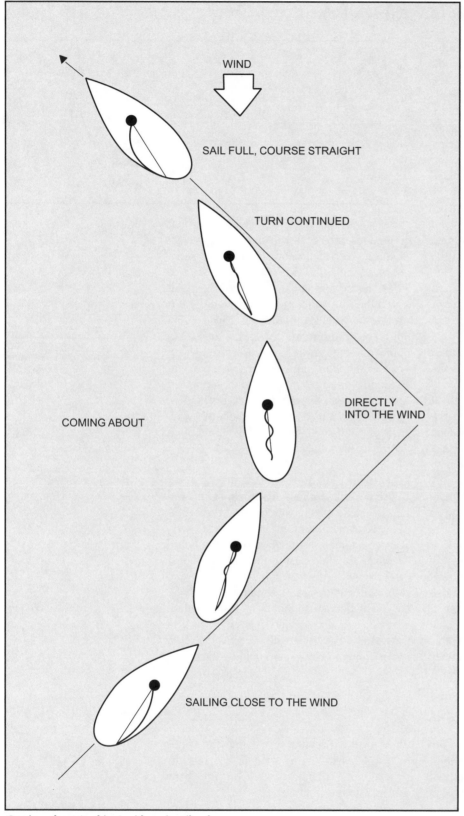

WIND

SAIL FULL, COURSE STRAIGHT

TURN CONTINUED

COMING ABOUT

DIRECTLY
INTO THE WIND

SAILING CLOSE TO THE WIND

Coming about (tacking) with mainsail only

WIND

SAIL FULL

BATTENS START
THE JIBE

SAIL JIBES
(QUICKLY EASE
THE MAIN SHEET)

JIBE COMPLETE

Jibing with mainsail only

lenges. In a dinghy, the possibility of capsizing is greater while jibing than at any other time. Since the sail shifts sides so rapidly, it is important to duck at the right moment to avoid being hit in the head by the boom. It takes many beginning sailors a couple of good bumps before they learn this important lesson.

The boat will feel unstable while running; therefore you want to jibe quickly. In jibing, the mainsail stays full of wind at all times, unlike in tacking, where the sail loses its power and luffs through the maneuver. For this reason, we must control the movement of the boom and sail during a jibe. The boom should not be allowed to fly across the cockpit in a potentially dangerous uncontrolled or accidental jibe.

In light breezes you may change course quickly and pull the boom across the boat onto the new tack. However, with a stiff breeze the boom will fly across violently. An accidental jibe can wipe out your rig.

In one regatta in San Francisco we were sailing cat-rigged (single sail) boats. All twelve competitors capsized at a jibe mark. The real race became how fast you could right your boat. I remember that the twelfth person to capsize came screaming in on a reach in a 35-knot gust going into a jibe, with the rest of us all trying to right our boats and watching the fellow. He started to jibe but lost control at the last second as his bow buried into a wave. The boat capsized, throwing the skipper head over heels into the water to the applause of all the rest of us who had reached a similar fate moments before.

There is a story about a Hudson River sloop captain who discovered an interesting jibing technique for boats with large mains. This captain was sailing his loaded vessel down the Hudson River when for navigational reasons it came time to jibe. The helmsman pushed the tiller over too far and the boat went on a flying jibe. Considering that the boom on this boat was over sixty feet long, it looked as if the sail was going to continue out on the new side and take the mast with it. But the gods, being with this sailor, allowed for the sail simply to

EXERCISE: **COMING ABOUT**

1. The helmsman should sit on the windward side of the boat, where he can measure the effect of the wind on the sail and have clear sight lines forward.

2. Before coming about, sight 90 degrees across the boat on the windward side to see the new course. Line up your new course with an object on shore or an object on the water as a reference point. Be sure before you come about that your new course is clear of other boats. A boat that is coming about should always stay clear of a boat that is on a tack.

3. The helmsman will turn the boat toward the direction of the wind by pushing the tiller to leeward slowly until the boat begins to head into the wind. This is called heading up.

4. As the boat reaches head-to-wind, the sail will luff. At that point, push the tiller over fast.

5. As the boom crosses over the center of the boat, the skipper and crew will smoothly change from one side of the boat to the other, taking as few steps as possible.

6. As the mainsail fills, the helmsman will steer the new course.

7. Repeat this maneuver, sailing an upwind, zigzag course until the helmsman can turn the boat smoothly.

The faster you turn the wheel or push the tiller over, the faster the boat will turn, but the more it will slow down. Your object when tacking is to maintain speed when turning. This takes practice.

The skipper changes from one side to the other as the boom crosses the centerline.

EXERCISE: **JIBING**

1. Bear off (or bear away) so the boat is sailing straight downwind.

2. Keep your sail overtrimmed slightly. Otherwise the force on a run may cause you to "heel" or lean to weather (windward). (Heeling to windward, the boat can capsize to windward on top of you. Heeling to leeward and overtrimmed, the boat will round itself up into the wind.) The sail will indicate when it is ready to be jibed. The leech starts to jibe first.

3. Hold onto the tiller while jibing to keep the boat from spinning out of control.

4. The crew should assist the mainsail by quickly pulling in on the mainsheet until the sail starts to cross the boat. Keep the traveler centered and securely cleated. A fast-moving traveler can cause injuries and damage.

5. The crew then releases the mainsheet as the boom passes the centerline of the boat. This allows the boom to swing fully to the new side.

6. After the jibe, resume your normal course as soon as possible. Staying dead downwind keeps the boat off balance. If the boat seems to be out of balance, sail more on a reach, heeling (leaning) the boat slightly to leeward until you are under control.

7. Repeat this exercise, sailing a downwind, zigzag course, until the boom passes from one side of the boat to the other without banging into the rigging on the other side. The helmsman and crew must be able to change sides of the boat smoothly, just as the boom crosses.

Changing hands behind during jibe

back itself as it fluttered into place. The speed of the sail as it changed sides created so much force that a wind was generated on the back side of the sail. Did the captain discover this jibing technique by accident or plan? I think he found it by accident. It might be a good technique for you to use any time you are sailing in a boat with over five thousand square feet of mainsail.

Try to keep the boat flat when jibing. Put the centerboard down halfway. Too little board will allow the bottom to spin out from under the mast; too much board will cause the board to steer the boat and tip it. In stronger winds, keep your weight aft during the jibe so the bow does not dip into the water.

Important: When steering, change hands early in a jibe so you do not get twisted up in the boat. If you are forward of the tiller, move it by passing it from one hand to the other behind you.

Getting your boat moving quickly after a jibe is difficult. The heavier the boat, the longer it will take to accelerate. A square-rigger will take minutes before it is moving at full speed. Even a 12-meter sloop will sometimes take a full minute to get up to top speed. A smaller boat, like a Sunfish, can easily reach top speed in ten seconds. To accelerate a boat, keep it on course as close to a reach as possible. Trimming your sails to the most efficient point and keeping the boat flat are essential. These combined forces will help the boat to sail at full speed.

S-JIBE AND ROLL JIBE

There are two special methods of jibing. One is the **S-jibe,** used when the wind is blowing hard and there is a chance of capsizing. In strong-wind jibing, the main boom comes over with such force that it goes too far out on the new side and the boat begins to round into the wind. At its worst, this loss of control can capsize dinghies or **broach** (spin out of control into the wind) larger keel boats. To stay upright, you must keep the boat under the mast and the boat in balance. Steering an S course when jibing can accomplish this.

As you go into an S-jibe, bear off and

keep the boat sailing slightly by the lee. This is the point of sail where the wind is coming over the corner of the stern that the boom is still on. It is a temporary point of sail only. Keep the main overtrimmed at this time. Then, as the mainsail is coming across the boat, steer back in the direction in which the main is going. This change of course reduces the power in the sail and doesn't allow the boat to round into the wind. As the main fills on the new side, keep it overtrimmed and resume course, having completed your jibe.

When there is little sea and the air is calm, use the **roll jibe** in sailing small dinghies. The advantage of this technique is that you can jibe the boat without changing course and accelerate rapidly. Basically, you sail dead downwind or slightly by the lee. With your weight, roll your boat to leeward about 10 degrees, then roll it hard to windward, giving a rapid trim on the mainsheet. Have the crew throw the boom over. When the sail is just reaching the other side, roll the boat back to the new windward side. You are, in effect, rocking the sail from one side to the other. This method will take considerable practice to master.

COMING ABOUT VERSUS JIBING

We can change tacks either by turning into the wind (coming about) or by turning away from the wind (jibing). The choice between the two depends upon which direction the boat is sailing. If you're sailing upwind, you come about; if you're sailing downwind, the obvious choice is to jibe.

There are times, however, particularly in heavy winds, when jibing can be dangerous. Since the sail does not lose any power during a jibe, it will swing with tremendous force as the boom slams across the boat and the sail crashes to a stop at the shrouds. Consequently, in strong winds coming about is the preferred maneuver even though it takes slightly longer when you're sailing downwind. Instead of jibing through, for example, a 90-degree arc, you head up and come about through 270 degrees.

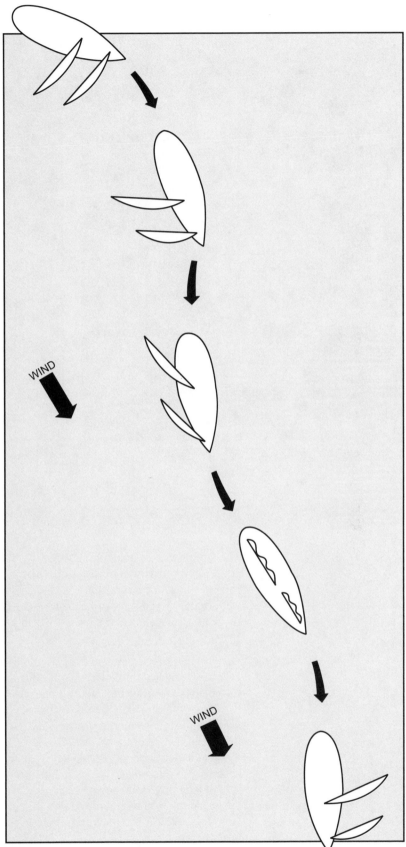

WIND

WIND

S-jibe

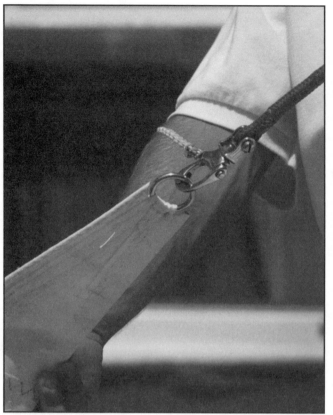

Attaching the jib halyard

Attaching the jib sheets to the clew

RAISING THE JIB

The helmsman should point the bow 30 degrees off the wind. The jib will blow away from the boat and mast as it is raised. This will protect the crew from being beaten by the flailing jib sheets and clew of the sail.

PREPARATION

1. One crew member attaches the jib tack to the tack fitting, attaches the luff to the headstay, and ties the sheets to the clew.

2. The helmsman steers a course to keep the boat 30 degrees off the wind (so the mainsail is just luffing).

3. One crew member takes a position at the headstay to feed the sail and prevent it from jamming while being raised.

4. Another crew member takes a position at the end of the halyard, prepared to raise the sail.

5. The crew unties the jib and ensures the jib sheets are clear (free of knots and tangles).

6. The helmsman makes sure the crew members are ready.

PROCEDURE

1. Foredeck crew watches to make sure the sail goes up properly (no snags).

2. The crew pulls the sail all the way up by hand with one wrap around the winch.

3. Use the winch for the final tightening of the luff.

4. The crew coils and stows the halyard.

Note: When the skipper gives commands, the crew should respond with an acknowledgment.

REACHING WITH MAINSAIL AND JIB

This exercise is a repeat of the first exercise, performed when sailing under the mainsail alone. The helmsman positions the boat so the wind is blowing over the beam (90 degrees off the bow). The crew eases both sails so they are luffing (shaking).

SAFETY

Make sure there are at least two or three wraps of the jib sheet around the winch at all times. The friction of the line around the winch will relieve some of the pressure of the sail and make it easier for the crew to hold the sheet.

Never allow fingers or clothing inside the area where the sheet comes onto the winch.

For now, the crew should not cleat the

jib sheet. If the boat has to be slowed, the jib sheet need only be released from someone's hand rather than taken off a cleat. Sheets should never be cleated in puffy winds or during a maneuver.

EXERCISE: **REACHING**

1. The crew trims the mainsail until the sail just stops luffing.

2. The helmsman keeps the boat in a straight line by using a buoy or an object on shore as a guide.

3. When the mainsail is full, the crew begins trimming the jib sheet on the leeward side of the boat (this is the side on which the sails are set).

4. As the jib starts to fill, the boat will heel and gain speed.

5. The sails will start to luff (flutter) slightly as the boat accelerates. The crew then retrims the sails until the luffing stops.

COMING ABOUT WITH MAINSAIL AND JIB

Remember how easy it was to come about under mainsail alone? It will be that easy with both sails, if the proper system is used. Remember, the helmsman should keep his weight on the windward side (the side opposite the mainsail) to balance the boat, and he should face forward. The exercise on page 49 or 56 shows how the boat is tacked.

SAILING A FIGURE EIGHT

Using two marks set in a line at right angles to the wind, sail a figure eight course, tacking only. As we'll see later, this maneuver is vital in rescuing a man overboard, so practice until you can complete every part of it smoothly. To ensure that the roles of helmsman, mainsheet trimmer, and jib sheet trimmer are learned by everyone on board, each person should rotate through each of these duties. The best-sailed boats are ones on which every crew member can perform every function.

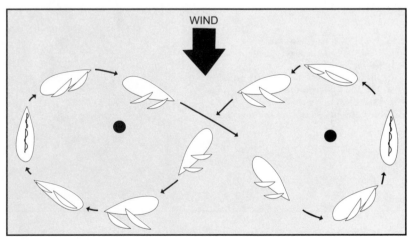

Sailing a figure eight course, tacking only, with mainsail and jib.

EXERCISE: **COMING ABOUT**

1. One crew member prepares to cast off the leeward jib sheet (the one under pressure holding the jib in).

2. Another crew member prepares to pull in on the windward sheet (the slack or "lazy" one).

3. The helmsman checks to see that no other boats are in his path and that the crew is prepared to come about.

4. The helmsman informs the crew that the boat is ready to come about by hailing, "Ready about." When prepared, the crew should respond, "Ready."

5. The helmsman pushes the tiller to the leeward side of the boat and says, "Hard alee. "

6. As the jib begins to luff, one crew member releases the leeward jib sheet.

7. As the jib is blown to the opposite side of the boat, another crew member pulls in on the jib sheet.

8. When the mainsail has filled on the new tack, the helmsman steers to the next buoy.

This exercise should be repeated until releasing **(casting off)** and trimming the jib is a smooth and coordinated effort on the part of the crew at helmsman. At this stage, the objective is to be able to keep the boat moving in a zigzag course without stopping.

A. Preparing to come about
B. Bow passes through the wind backwinding the jib
C. Jib blows clear of the mast and rigging
D. Crew begins trimming jib
E. Cruw trimming jib
F. boat begins to sail on the new tack

A

D

JIBING WITH MAINSAIL AND JIB

Here is how the boat is jibed under mainsail and jib:

EXERCISE: **JIBING**

1. A crew member prepares to cast off the leeward jib sheet with one hand and pull in the other sheet with the other hand.

2. Another crew member or helmsman takes hold of the mainsheet, checking that it is not tangled. This person should have plenty of elbow room, because he or she will have to trim the sheet quickly in the middle of the jibe.

3. The helmsman (who should be sitting to windward) makes sure that no other boats are in his path both during and after the maneuver.

4. The helmsman says, "Prepare to jibe." If they are ready, the crew say, "Ready." If not, they say, "Wait."

5. When the crew is ready, the helmsman says, "Jibe ho, " and pulls the tiller to windward with a steady motion.

6. As the boat heads off, the crew members ease their sheets.

7. When the jib is blanketed by the mainsail and hangs limply, the crew knows that the boat is running almost directly before the wind. At this point, one crew member trims the mainsheet rapidly and the other crew member lets go of the old leeward jib sheet and takes a strain on the other sheet.

8. The helmsman continues to make the turn until the boom has swung across the boat (the crew must duck their heads). The crew members trim the sails properly for the new point of sail.

As the boat either comes about or jibes, the crew and helmsman should shift from one side of the boat to the other to keep the boat balanced and to give the helmsman an unobstructed view in front and to one side of the boat.

A. Sailing on a broad reach
B. Boat turns downwind backwinding the jib
C. Jib and main jibe putting the boat on a new tack
D. Crew begins trimming jib
E. Boat sails away on the new tack

B

D

E

ENDING THE SAIL

When heading back to dock, first lower the jib, then the mainsail. How and when the sails are lowered will depend on your particular docking situation. The skipper will have to make this decision. We will assume the dock is easily accessible.

The biggest danger is approaching a dock with too much speed or on a downwind course. The key to docking is maintaining control.

LOWERING THE JIB

The jib can be lowered by one of three methods. In the first, the helmsman positions the boat into the wind, a crew member releases the halyard, and the foredeck crew pull the sail onto the foredeck.

In the second method, as the helmsman brings the boat about, with the jib sheet cleated, a crew member releases the jib halyard. As the sail drops to the deck, one of the crew pulls the luff of the sail down the forestay. The helmsman continues to turn the boat until it is sailing on the new tack.

The third way of dropping the jib is for the helmsman to head the boat directly downwind. This makes the procedure easy because the boat is upright and in a stable position. It is also easier on the foredeck crew because they will not be getting wet, since the boat is sailing with the wind.

LOWERING THE MAINSAIL

The helmsman steers the boat back to the mooring or marina under mainsail alone. The mainsail must be lowered with the boat heading into the wind so that the sail drops neatly onto the deck, but this shouldn't be done too early since the boat needs the mainsail for propulsion. If the boat is to be tied up to a mooring, the sail may be dropped after the mooring buoy is picked up. However, if she will be tied up to a float or pier, it may be best to head up into the wind, lower the mainsail several yards upwind of the float, and then drift down to it with the little bit of momentum that is left over. Sometimes, the wind and the pier may be aligned, so the mainsail can be dropped as the boat approaches the pier. Obviously, the boat should not be going so fast that she can't be easily stopped by somebody standing on the pier.

Here's how to drop the mainsail:

1. Tighten the adjustable topping lift to lift the boom parallel with the deck.

2. Close the main hatch to ensure that no one falls into the cabin.

3. Lower the halyard while a crew member pulls down the mainsail luff and gathers in the sail.

Flaking the mainsail

STOWING SAILS

Sails are stowed (put away) primarily to protect them. Two of the most damaging things to a sail are direct sunlight and chafing. The ultraviolet rays in direct sunlight break down the synthetic fibers in the sail while chafing wears the sail cloth thin.

FLAKING THE MAINSAIL

Flaking is the preferred method of stowing the mainsail. To flake the sail, a crew member should be positioned at each side of the sail (the luff and the leech).

The crew then pulls on the sail to take the wrinkles out and simultaneously layers the sail over the boom accordion-style. Keep the battens parallel when folding. Wrap the last few feet of the sail (the head) around the mainsail and boom to form a cumberbund, and then secure it with at least three sail ties.

Rubber shock cords should not be used to tie the sail down, since the end of the tie may fly around if released unexpectedly and could cause a serious eye injury.

ROLLING THE MAINSAIL

Rolling the mainsail is one of the best ways to protect it from wrinkles. Starting at the

Flaking a sail on the dock

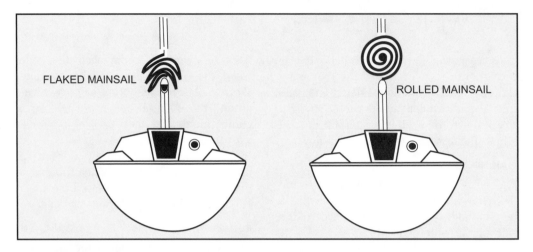

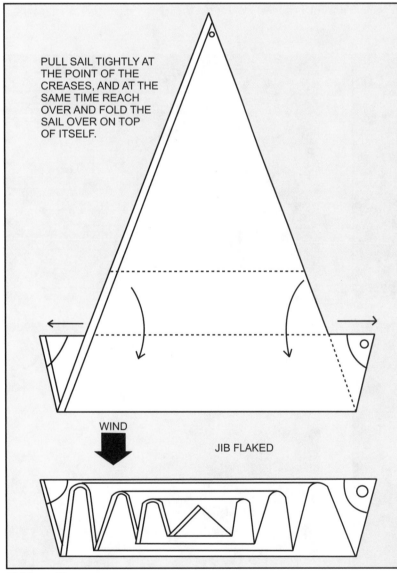

PULL SAIL TIGHTLY AT THE POINT OF THE CREASES, AND AT THE SAME TIME REACH OVER AND FOLD THE SAIL OVER ON TOP OF ITSELF.

WIND

JIB FLAKED

Flaking a jib or genoa

head of the sail, the crew rolls the sail until it sits on the boom as a neat bundle. Then it is tied to the boom with sail ties.

Taking the sail off altogether is another option if there is no sail cover; in that case the mainsail would be flaked in the same manner as the jib or genoa.

FOLDING THE JIB OR GENOA

To fold the jib or genoa, the crew spreads the sail out on a clean dry area such as a lawn or a clean dock. Wash the salt from your sails, using fresh water so they will dry properly. Salt water dries very slowly, sometimes taking days. Unless the sail is going to be used within a day or two, it should be dried completely before being folded.

The proper sail folding procedure is as follows:

1. Spread the sail flat with the foot into the wind.

2. Fold the sail accordion-style from the foot to the head, making the width of each fold slightly shorter than the length of the sail bag. Continue folding until the entire sail is folded. If the sail has a plastic window, first fold the foot of the sail over it so as not to crease the window. You'll find that the sail will fold more easily if you tension (pull) at the fold line while making the fold.

3. Fold over the ends.

4. Without pressing hard, roll or fold the sail into a rectangular shape to fit the sail bag. Slide the folded sail into the bag. Avoid stuffing; it causes creases.

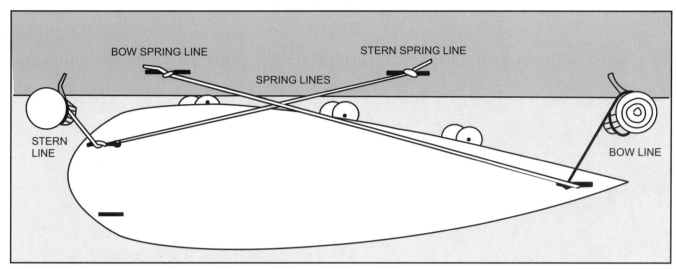

The boat is tied side-on at the dock and protected by fenders.

DOCKING

To prevent damage to the boat while it is not in use, the vessel must be secured properly. There are many types of docking and mooring systems. The most common is the side-on to the dock, as illustrated.

The crew must make sure the fenders (inflated protectors hung between the boat and a float or pier) are in place. Position at least half of the fender under the edge of the dock. If they are placed too high, the boat may scrape against the dock.

The crew secures the bow and stern lines to position the boat on the dock and then secures bow and stern spring lines to keep the boat from rotating or moving forward and backward at the dock

SUMMARY

We have covered a lot of material in this part, which should be reviewed often. The next five parts of the book will help you refine these skills and sail better and safer.

By this point, you as helmsman should be able to make the boat go in any direction by turning the tiller. Maneuvers, such as coming about and jibing, will need practice. As a crew member you should be able to trim the sails properly by easing them until they luff and pulling them back until the luffing stops. You should be able to secure the boat properly and fold the sails.

PART ONE

Basic Sailing

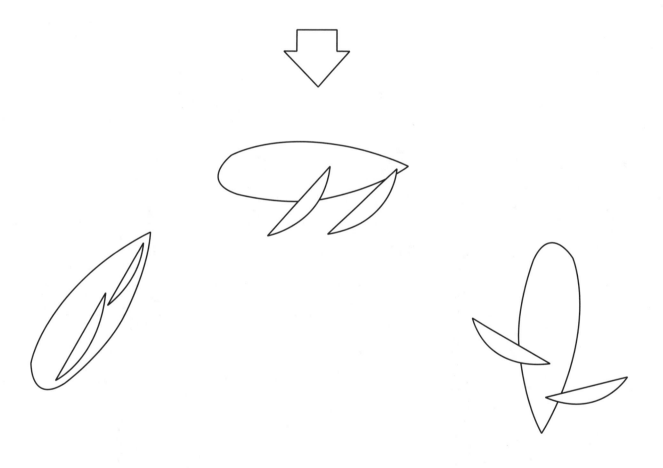

SAILING KNOWLEDGE

In Part One you were introduced to many aspects of sailing, including the parts of the boat, U.S. Coast Guard requirements for pleasure boats, the parts of the sails, how to raise and lower sails, the basic maneuvers of coming about and jibing, and putting the boat away.

Now in Part Two we will learn more about turning the tiller and sheeting the sails to achieve smooth sailing. This knowledge will be incorporated into more sophisticated maneuvers, such as stopping the boat in a predetermined location.

It is easy to understand the relationship a boat has with water: the hull "slices" through the waves as the boat moves. At the same time, the sail is "carving" its way through the wind, but this relationship is not so easy to see. The action of the wind on the sail must be seen by its results—the boat's forward motion and **heeling** (leaning).

You will learn more about how to sail a boat to an upwind destination and how to sail across the wind at the boat's greatest speed. The coordination of helmsman and crew will also be studied. By the end of this section, you will be able to describe:

• The duties of the helmsman and crew on each point of sail
• The Rules of the Road
• How to stop a boat to pick up an object or tie up to a mooring buoy or can.

SAIL TRIM

Let's begin by learning more about the importance of sail trim. While trimming your sails, watch the luff, the forward edge of the sail. Trim is correct when the wind flows evenly on both sides of the leading edge of the sail, with very little or no luffing.

If the sail is luffing, trim it in until it barely stops. When the sail is luffing you are moving slower than you should be. You'll gain speed by keeping your sails trimmed correctly at all times. As a rule of thumb, a boat will sail faster as the sails are eased just short of letting them luff. This may mean easing the sail out slowly until you see the first sign of a luff near the mast. Practice watching the luff of the sail to keep track of what the wind is doing.

TELLTALES

One of the best ways of knowing whether the flow of air over a sail is as smooth as it should be is to use telltales_pieces of yam attached to the sails and rigging. Telltales are very sensitive to changes in the flow of air over the sail's surface and therefore are good wind indicators. Any turbulence caused by even small alterations of wind direction or change of the sail's angle can be detected by the telltales long before the

sail luffs or before the boat slows down and stalls.

The best locations for telltales are at the top of the mast, on the shrouds, and on the sails themselves. They should be about six inches long and as thin as possible to flow easily. A dark color is best since it will contrast with the sails. Polyester and mohair are better than wool because they are water resistant.

When adding telltales, place them along the luff six inches from the forward edge on both sides of the jib. Space your telltales equally, with one at the top, one in the middle, and one at the bottom. Telltales are also helpful on the outer edges of the mainsail, particularly along the leech.

Reading the telltales is relatively easy. When the wind is flowing smoothly on both sides of the sail, the windward and leeward telltales flow straight aft and the sails are trimmed correctly. If the boat is pointing too close to the wind, the sail is undertrimmed and the windward telltale will flutter up and down. Change your course away from the wind or trim your sails in until both telltales flow aft evenly.

If your boat is pointing too low or the sail

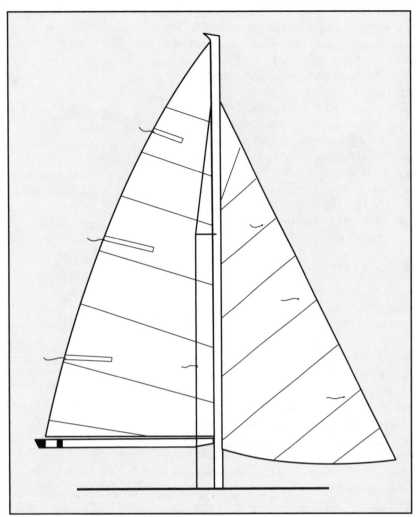

Placement of telltales

is overtrimmed (trimmed too tightly), the leeward telltale will flutter up and down. Head closer to the wind or ease your sails out until both telltales luff evenly.

READING THE WIND

Since you cannot see the wind, you must learn to read its signs. Observe how the wind affects flags on shore, trees, wind pennants, smoke from stacks, clouds, and other boats. The angle and intensity of the ripples on the water are very important wind indicators. You'll be able to predict what's about to happen if you study the effect of wind on these. Your face, neck, and ears are also very sensitive to changes in wind direction and strength.

The wind is always changing patterns during the day. Use a wind pennant at the top of your mast so you can tell what the wind is doing. This pennant is called a masthead fly. With practice, you will be able to forecast the wind. Try to predict from distant signs what the wind will do as it approaches your boat. Estimate its velocity and direction. You will get a feeling for the patterns. As studying the wind becomes a habit, you will be able to forecast wind changes accurately.

Although people smile at them, old wives' tales can be useful in forecasting the

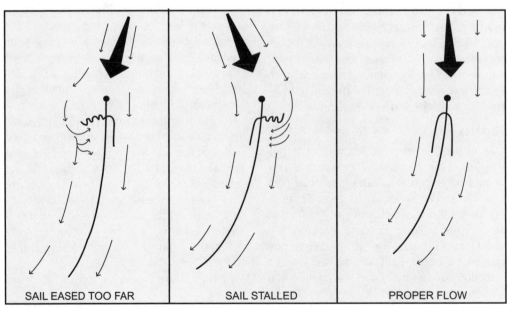

SAIL EASED TOO FAR | SAIL STALLED | PROPER FLOW

Reading jib telltales

wind. Cornelius Shields of Long Island Sound wrote a paper several years ago entitled "Corny Shields' Lore of Long Island Sound." Some of his old wives' tales are helpful. Dew in the morning means an early strong southerly wind. Cobwebs in the rigging mean a northwester in the near future. Wind from the northeast generally brings rain, at least on the eastern seaboard. Wherever you sail, you can learn from the local folk wisdom. There are other sayings that tell a story concisely: "Red sky at night, sailors delight. " "Wind before rain, set sail again. " "Rain before wind, take her in. "

Pay attention to the water. By comparing different colors in the water with the constant color of the sail, with your boat, or with an object on land, you will be able to note differences in the wind. This will help you read the direction of puffs and predict when the wind will shift and where the lulls in the wind are.

When watching the wind on the water, use both eyes and let them relax. Blink often and try not to stare. Concentrate on one section of the horizon at a time rather than making sweeping glances.

Since the wind is constantly shifting (changing direction), the sails often go out of trim without any action on the part of the helmsman or crew. Therefore, the helmsman must continuously adjust for the subtle wind changes when sailing into or away from the wind, and the crew must adjust the sails when crossing the wind.

APPARENT WIND AND TRUE WIND

There is a difference between the **apparent wind** and **true wind**. True wind is the actual direction and speed the wind is blowing over the water. Apparent wind is the wind you feel while sailing. Because a sailboat is moving, it creates its own wind. The wind you feel when sailing will be the apparent wind, a product of the true wind and your relative wind due to your motion. The apparent wind direction will be forward of the true wind.

For example, if you were on a bicycle and were stopped with the wind blowing from the side, you would feel the

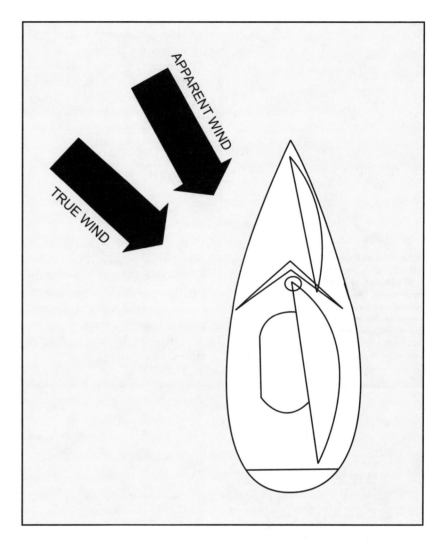

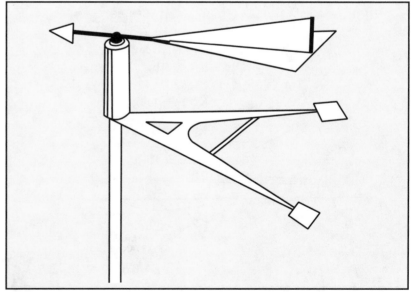

Masthead fly

wind on your side. But once you start pedaling, the faster you go, the more forward the wind will feel until it is directly ahead. Again, the combined effect of the true wind and the wind you are creating is the apparent wind. The apparent wind will be at a 30 to 35 degree angle when sailing upwind. The faster your boat is going, the farther forward the apparent wind will be. The direction of the apparent wind is indicated by any telltale or masthead fly.

WHAT MAKES A BOAT SAIL

LATERAL RESISTANCE AND HEEL

The centerboard or keel is critical to a boat's windward performance. If there were no centerboard or keel, the force of the wind would push the boat sideways. But the counteracting force of the water on the keel or centerboard allows the boat to go forward. This resistance to sideslipping is known as **lateral resistance.**

When the sail's center of effort is directly over the hull's center of lateral resistance, the boat is balanced, with neither lee nor weather helm. Heeling the boat will change this relationship and cause windward (weather) helm.

The **center of lateral resistance** is the point on the centerboard, keel, or hull under the water that acts like a pivot for the whole area of lateral resistance: one-half of the lateral resistance is to one side of the center and the other half is to the other side. In a way, the center functions like a pivot on a seesaw. There is another important center, called the **center of effort,** which acts as a pivot for the sails. When the two centers are in the same vertical plane, the boat will **balance,** which means that she will be easy to steer. (In a moment, we will have more to say about balance.)

Designers try to come up with hull shapes that work efficiently on all points of sail in all wind conditions. One major concern, besides balance, is that the boat be **stable,** which means that it not heel (tip) very far. Larger boats have keels made of lead or iron that provide stability against heeling. These boats should sail efficiently upwind at an angle of heel of 20 degrees or less. However, centerboard boats, which do not have keels, are kept upright by the weight of their crews. For best performance, they should not be allowed to heel more than 5 to 10 degrees.

Heeling has one advantage in that it lengthens the boat's waterline. Generally, a longer waterline will help the boat go faster by creating a longer wave length,. But if the boat heels too far over, it will begin to slide sideways, or make leeway. The weight of the helmsman and crew or that of the keel can keep the boat sailing "on its lines," at the optimum angle of heel; otherwise the water flow will be inefficient.

If the boat heels too much because of a

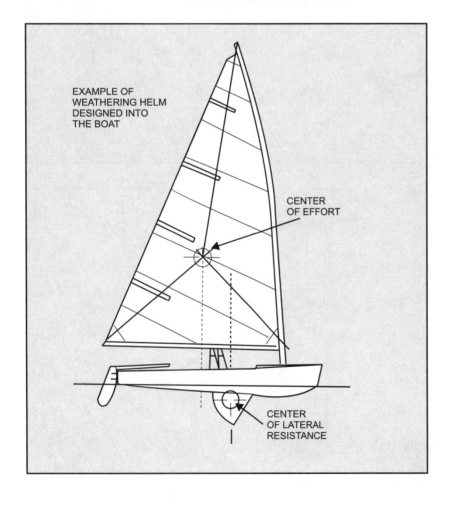

EXAMPLE OF WEATHERING HELM DESIGNED INTO THE BOAT

CENTER OF EFFORT

CENTER OF LATERAL RESISTANCE

sudden gust or too much wind, you must reduce the angle of heel by flattening your sails to reduce their power, heading into the wind, hiking out farther, or easing your sails. In puffy winds, ease your sails in a hard puff when the boat begins to heel too much. You'll discover that easing the sails and using your weight in combination with your steering will get you through the heaviest puffs while maintaining the same angle of heel. The gustier the wind, the more suddenly the boat will heel over and the more attention must be paid to sail trim.

WEATHER (WINDWARD) AND LEE (LEEWARD) HELM

Another factor to be aware of, especially while sailing close into the wind, is weather and lee helm. Weather helm is created by heeling and the wind on the sails. It is the tendency of a boat to round up into the wind when you let go of the tiller. The more the boat heels or the greater the force on the sails, the more the boat will want to round up into the wind. To reduce the windward helm force, you have several options, including hiking out until the boat is flat, heading the boat slightly into the wind to reduce heel, easing your sails, or flattening your sails.

Lee helm is the opposite of weather helm. When you let go of the tiller and the boat steers away from the wind, you have lee(ward) helm. If your sailboat has lee helm, allow it to heel to leeward somewhat until you get some weather helm. Most sailors prefer a slight amount of weather helm when sailing upwind.

Extra waterline length when heeling

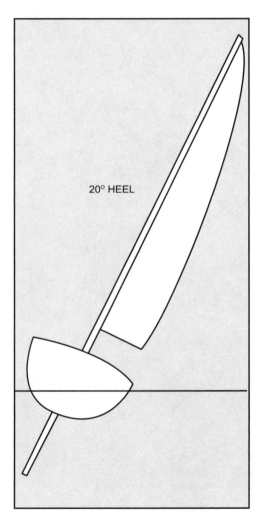

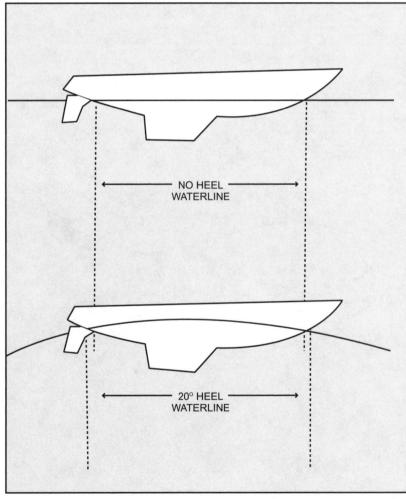

POINTS OF SAIL

Altering course from one point of sail to another can be compared to changing lanes on a highway. In going from one point of sail to another (changing lanes) you steer the boat either closer to or farther away from the direction of the wind. Steering toward the wind is called **heading up,** and steering away is referred to as **bearing away**. (To carry this analogy one step further, changing tacks by coming about or jibing can be compared to moving from one highway to another.)

As we have already learned, a boat cannot sail directly into the wind. Instead, a boat sails at various angles to the wind, the closest of which is about 45 degrees, although America's Cup 12-meter yachts can sail as close as 35 degrees. The point of sail closest to the wind is **close-hauled.** The sails are sheeted in close to the boat, and the vessel is steered as close to the wind's direction as possible without the sails luffing.

If a boat is sailing in the same direction as the wind, it is **running** with the wind coming from directly behind. A boat sailing across the wind, at an angle between close-hauled and running is on a **reach.** On each of these points of sail, sail trim varies and the duties of crew and helmsman vary as well.

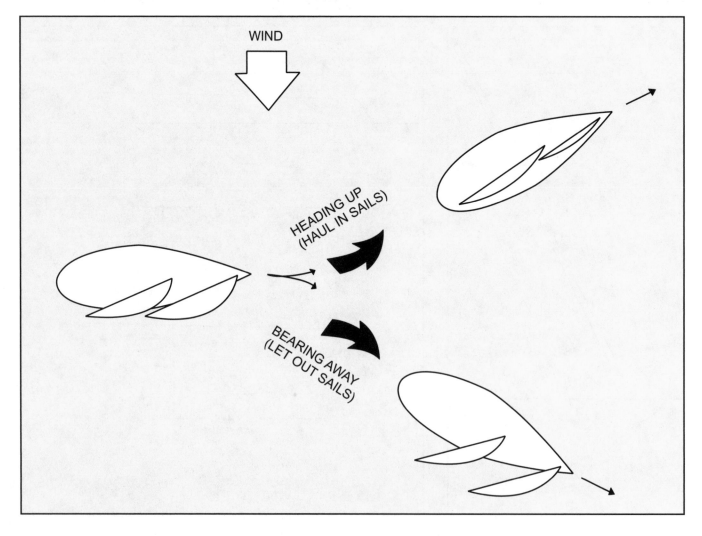

SAILING CLOSE-HAULED

Sailing close-hauled is also known as **beating to windward.**

At point A, the sail appears to be well trimmed and the boat is moving through the water. To ensure efficient wind flow, the helmsman heads up (steers the boat toward the wind) until the sail just starts to luff (point B). When the helmsman bears away again (point C, the sails fill, and the boat is once more sailing close-hauled (as close to the wind as possible).

If the helmsman bears away (point D) and the crew does not ease the sheets, the boat will continue to sail, but less effectively. The boat will slow down.

Sailing close-hauled is exciting. The wind is in your face and the boat works through the waves. Sailing to windward on a balanced boat is a thrill because you and your boat become one being as you feel every wave and puff of wind.

A boat is **balanced** when it will sail in a straight line with little action on the tiller. In fact, it is possible to balance the boat so there is no need to use the tiller at all. However, most boats perform best when there is some weather helm. This means the wind on the sails pushes the boat to turn toward the wind. It should take approximately 2 to 3 degrees of rudder to counter this force and keep your boat in balance.

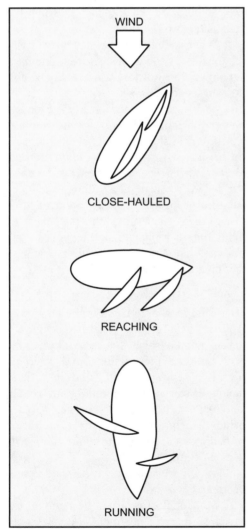

Correct sail trim

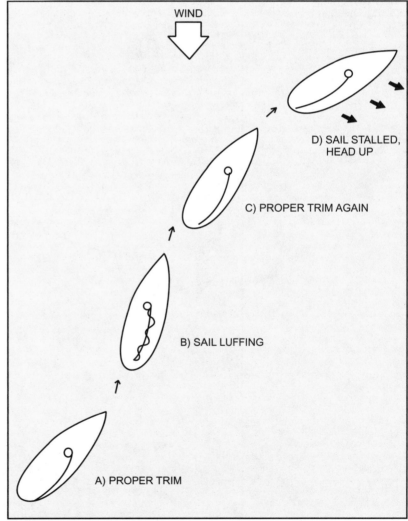

Adjusting course to correct sail trim

To get to an upwind destination as quickly as possible, sail as close to the wind as you can without allowing your sails to luff. You want to keep the boat moving at optimum speed at the closest possible course to the wind. Therefore, it is important to have a better understanding of sail trim and helm tendencies. Learning to gauge the wind by your telltales and a masthead fly will help you sail to windward efficiently.

RUNNING

A sailboat is running when the wind is blowing from behind the boat. On a run, the lifting effect of the sail is replaced by a pushing effect of the wind.

When you're sailing on a run, the wind has a pushing effect.

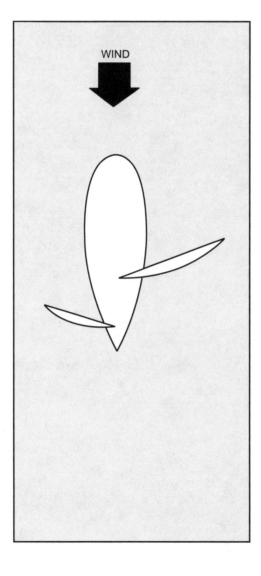

WIND

When running, the boat stands upright and moves freely along as the wind pushes the boat from astern. Running with the wind is particularly gratifying after a long beat to windward with the boat pounding into the waves, hiking for long periods of time, and tacking (coming about) back and forth. Now you can sail with the wind, running free. Like a cross-country skier coming to a slope, you simply stop pushing and let gravity take you along.

Sailing downwind is the goal of many sailors. Early skippers always made a point of sailing in the trade winds or in other reliable prevailing winds. They could be assured of sailing with the wind for long periods of time. This was particularly important in older sailing vessels, since they could not sail very close to the wind; going to a windward destination was arduous.

When sailing downwind you will also be pushed by the waves. As each one passes under your hull you will actually be able to gain speed. This is known as surfing. The boat gains extra speed as a wave passes under the hull. Although surfing requires considerable skill and practice, it will begin to happen whenever you encounter wind-driven waves or even after a powerboat passes by. You can get a sailboat surfing by steering it on a course perpendicular to a wave, then accelerating the boat by trimming the sail rapidly or shifting your weight forward. The first time you get a boat surfing on a wave is quite a thrill.

REACHING

The wind is from the side of the boat when you are sailing on a reach. Reaching-the fastest point of sail-is defined as any point of sail between close-hauled and running. Reaching can be subdivided into three points of sail: **close reach, beam reach,** and **broad reach.** A boat is on a close reach when the wind is forward of abeam. It is on a beam reach when the wind is directly abeam (hitting the boat at a 90 degree angle). On a broad reach, the wind comes from aft of abeam.

More important than the name of the reach is the sail adjustment. We have seen

that a sail has to be trimmed all the way in on a close-hauled course and eased all the way out on a run. On a reach, the sail is somewhere between these two extremes. Sails should be eased until they begin to luff, then trimmed in just a little bit to keep them from luffing.

Sometimes it's difficult to steer a straight course when reaching, because the waves as well as the wind approach from the side. In small (smooth) seas no problem exists. However, in large (choppy) seas difficulties can arise. You may need to adjust your course, sailing either higher (on a closer reach) or lower (on a broader reach), to keep from rolling too much.

Reaching, the boat will heel. Correct for this by sitting to windward. If the boat continues to heel too much, ease the sail until it luffs a little. For temporary relief, head the boat into the wind to luff the sails, or steer a new course farther away from the wind (on a broader reach) and ease your sails. This will reduce your heel angle, making the boat easier to sail.

HEAD TO WIND AND BY THE LEE

There are two final points of sail to be discussed: **head to wind** and **by the lee.**

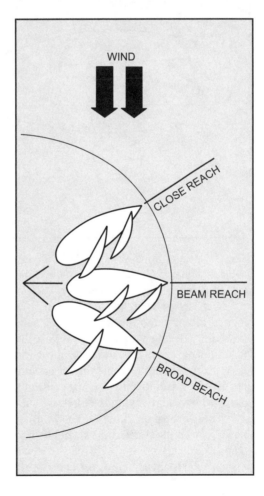

WIND

CLOSE REACH

BEAM REACH

BROAD BEACH

A sailboat can surf with the waves in windy conditions, giving the crew an exhilarating ride.

Three kinds of reaches

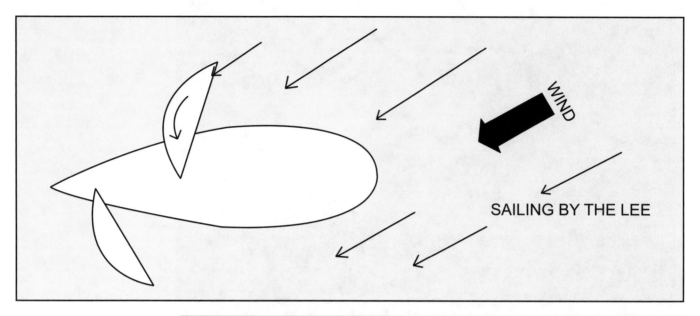

SAILING BY THE LEE

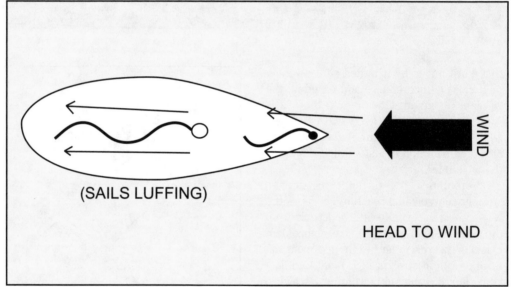

(SAILS LUFFING)

HEAD TO WIND

Neither is intentionally used while sailing because a boat can't sail on the first and the second is potentially dangerous.

A vessel is head to wind when it is pointed directly into the wind and the sails are luffing. Because the sails do not fill, the boat does not move forward. A sailboat will pass through head to wind when it is coming about. Heading into the wind is only useful when you're trying to stop the boat.

When a boat is running, the wind is blowing over its stern and the helmsman keeps the wind on the side of the stern opposite the mainsail. However, if the wind shifts or the helmsman is unable to steer a true course, the wind could begin to blow over the same side of the boat as the side on which the mainsail is set. This situation is called sailing by the lee.

Sailing by the lee carries the inherent danger of an accidental jibe. An accidental jibe is an inadvertent changing of the mainsail from one side of the boat to the other and can result in damage to the boom, rigging, and sails. Even worse, an unprepared crew member could get in the way of the flying boom and be knocked overboard and seriously injured.

RULES OF THE ROAD UNDER SAIL

There is often a chance of collision between two or more boats approaching one another. There are rules to cover these situations. These are known as the rules of the road or more properly as Navigation Rules (NAVRULES) or Collision Regulations (COLREGS). Every sailor must follow these rules for his own safety and that of others. You may think that it is impossible for two boats to collide when they have wide open spaces of water around them in which to maneuver, but it is all that open space that causes people to relax and be less vigilant.

When the helmsman and crew are sitting to windward, they are unable to see boats approaching from leeward behind the sails. One crew member should be assigned to check to leeward occasionally to be sure the course is clear. If someone other than the skipper notices a boat in their path, he should immediately report its position to the skipper. A decision is then made as to which boat (or boats) must stay out of the way and which is (or are) allowed to stay on course. The terms used to describe the boats are give-way vessel and stand-on vessel. The first is obligated to give way (or stay clear), and the second is allowed to hold its course.

There are several different sets of water traffic rules. Which set applies to you depends on where you sail. Most American sailors come under the jurisdiction of the Inland Rules of the Road, which apply to boats in bays and estuaries connected with the Atlantic or Pacific oceans or the Gulf of Mexico. Such major boating areas as Long Island Sound, Chesapeake and Biscayne bays, San Francisco Bay and Puget Sound, and the Great Lakes are covered by the Inland Rules. In the ocean or the Gulf of Mexico, you are subject to the International Rules of the Road. The boundary between these two jurisdictions is an imaginary line drawn across the mouths of rivers, harbors, and inlets along the coasts; the two sets of rules are very similar. you can purchase a copy of the "U.S. Coast Guard's "Navigation Rules, International-Inland" from most marine or ship stores, or contact your local Coast Guard office for information.

This section provides some general information and some specific rules that apply to sailing vessels (without operating engines). Additional material on the navigation rules relevant to powerboats is presented in part five.

Both Inland and International Navigation Rules require that every vessel shall maintain a proper lookout at all times-including use of all appropriate means to assess the risk of collision. Failure to maintain a proper lookout is one of the major causes of accidents. It may be advantageous to assign sec-

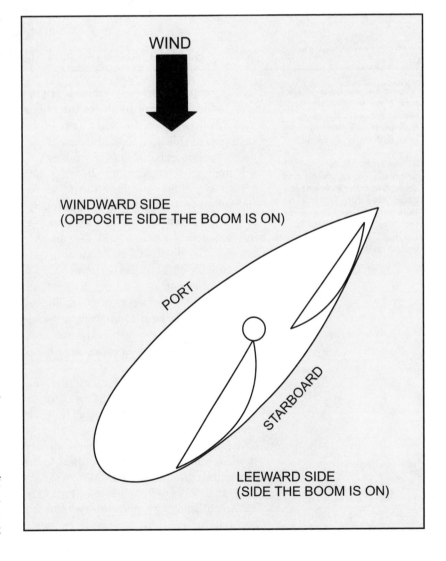

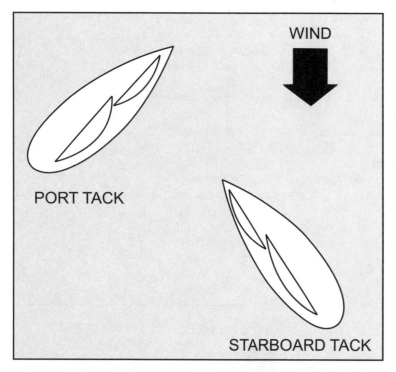

WIND

PORT TACK

STARBOARD TACK

Above: Since a boat on port tack gives way to one on starboard tack, the port tack boat will be at fault here if there is a collision.

Above right: When crews are proficient at sailing and understand the Rules of the Road, they can race in close quarters as here. The port-tack yacht on the right is staying clear of the starboard-tack boat on the left.

tors of responsibility to members of your crew, or in any event to stress the importance of advising you whenever there is possible risk of collision. Risk of collision may be deemed to exist whenever another vessel maintains a constant bearing and decreasing range. In other words, if you sight another boat at the same spot relative to your boat just off the bow for example) for any period of time and the distance between the two boats is decreasing, you are probably on a collision course.

Maintenance of a proper lookout can be a particular challenge on sailboats, where the sails restrict visibility in some sectors. Difficult or not, it is the responsibility of the skipper to keep an alert watch for other traffic.

Both Inland and International Navigation Rules require that every vessel shall proceed at a safe speed at all times, in order to insure that the vessel can take effective action to avoid collision and be stopped within a distance appropriate to the prevailing circumstances. Many sailors think that this rule applies only to powerboats, but there are instances where sailboats have been charged with negligent

operation as a result of excessive speed.

Both Inland and International Navigation Rules require that every vessel shall use all available means to determine if risk of collision exists and, if in doubt, to assume that such risk exists. "All available means" includes the proper use of radar equipment, if fitted and operational.

Both Inland and International Navigation Rules require that actions to avoid collision shall be positive and made in ample time. Alterations in course or speed shall (where possible) be large enough to be readily apparent to another vessel. If necessary to avoid collision or to allow more time to assess the situation, you should reduce your speed or take all way off (stop).

WHEN APPROACHING ANOTHER SAILBOAT

Use the following to agree with current NAVRULES:

• When each has the wind on a different side, the vessel, which has the wind on the port side shall keep out of the way of the other.

• When both have the wind on the same side, the vessel which is to windward shall keep out of the way of the vessel, which is to leeward.

• A boat that is astern or overtaking shall keep out of the way to a boat ahead.

• A boat coming about or jibing shall give way to a boat on a tack.

The give-way vessel always alters course to pass astern of the stand-on vessel. The stand-on vessel is obligated to maintain a steady course during any crossing situation. However, if a collision is imminent, the stand-on vessel should alter course to stay clear as well.

• If one boat is running and the other is close-hauled and they are on the same tack, the close-hauled boat must hold its course and speed while the running boat stays clear. This is because the running boat is to windward of the close-hauled boat.

• If a vessel with the wind on the port side sees a vessel to windward and cannot determine with certainty whether the other vessel has the wind on the port or on the starboard side, she shall keep out of the way of the other.

• If both vessels are running, but one of them is on port tack and the other is on starboard, then the boat on starboard tack is the stand-on vessel.

• For the purposes of this rule, the windward side shall be deemed to be the side opposite to that on which, the mainsail is carried or, in the case of a square-rigged vessel, the side opposite to that on which the largest fore-and-aft sail is carried.

WHEN APPROACHING A POWERED VESSEL

Use the following to agree with current NAVRULES:

In general, sailboats are stand-on vessels when approaching power-driven vessels, but there are four exceptions:

• When overtaking a power-driven vessel, a sailboat is the give-way vessel.

• A sailboat must stay clear of a vessel not under command, i.e., unable to maneuver.

• A sailboat must stay clear of a vessel engaged in fishing with nets, lines, trawls or any other fishing apparatus which restricts maneuverability, but does not include a vessel fishing with trolling lines or other fish-

The windward boat to the left must stay clear of the leeward boat (right).

In restricted channels, stay clear of passing freighters with limited visibility and steerage. This cruising boat is much too close.

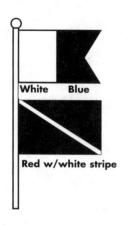

White   Blue

Red w/white stripe

Diver's flags

ing apparatus which does not restrict maneuverability.

• In a narrow channel or confined area, a sailboat must not hamper the safe passage of power-driven vessels that can navigate only inside such a channel or area. Large ships are not very maneuverable and often have poor visibility from the bridge. Therefore it is important for sailing vessels to stay away as far as possible from large steamers.

WHEN APPROACHING DIVERS

All vessels are required to keep clear of divers displaying the international code flag alpha ("A"). Although the red and white diver's flag is more readily recognized, the legal requirement is the blue and white international code flag. For safety and legal reasons, divers often fly both flags, and boaters should avoid any vessel displaying either one.

These Rules of the Road have been presented in detail because they are important. The skipper of any vessel is morally and legally responsible for avoiding collisions. Know the rules and abide by them.

A final note on sailing etiquette: When daysailing, you will undoubtedly encounter sailboat races. Although racing sailboats have no special privileges, for your own safety and enjoyment, and out of courtesy to them, try to steer clear. If that is impossible, make your way through the fleet carefully, passing to leeward of racing boats to avoid disturbing their wind.

REVIEW QUESTIONS

1. When the telltales stream straight back, they indicate
a)   turbulent air flow
b)   smooth air flow
c)   no air flow

2. The sails are trimmed in tight when the boat is
a)   close reaching
b)   close-hauled
c)   in a close call
d)   in irons

3. On a run, the sails are
a)   trimmed all the way in
b)   trimmed halfway in
c)   eased out all the way

4. One of the major safety concerns when sailing on a run is
a)   coming about
b)   reaching
c)   an accidental jibe

5. On which point of sail will a boat not sail?
a)   by the lee
b)   head to wind
c)   broad reach

6. In drawings A, B, C, and D at right, circle the boat which is stand-on vessel whenever approaching. Add arrows to indicate what course the give-way vessel should take.

7. When one sailboat is overtaking another, the _____ is the stand-on vessel.
a)   boat ahead and being overtaken
b)   boat behind and overtaking

8. Sailboats are stand-on vessels whenever approaching power-driven vessels except
a)   when overtaking
b)   when sailing on port tack
c)   when the power vessel is limited in its maneuverability by a narrow channel
d)   when the sailboat is also under power

9. A _____ tack boat shall give-way to a boat on _____ tack

10. When two sailboats are approaching on the same tack, the _____ boat shall stay out of the way of the _____ boat.

Answers in Appendix A, p. 201.

A

WIND

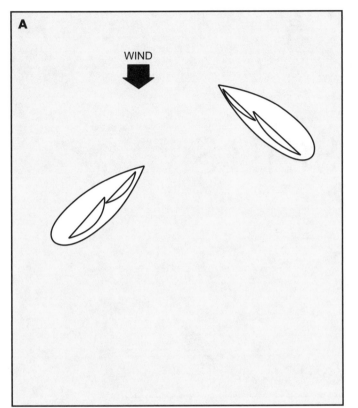

B

WIND

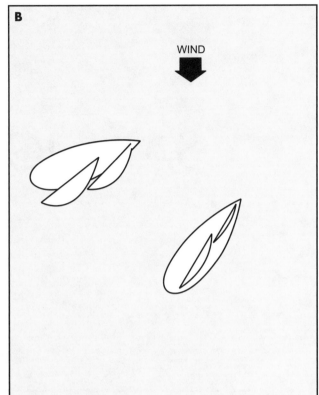

C

WIND

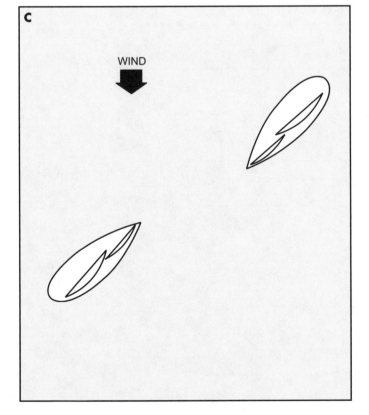

D

WIND

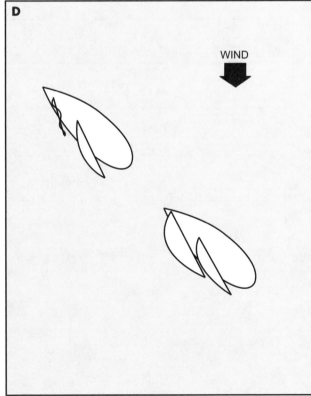

SAILING SKILLS

The following exercises have been devised to increase the competence and confidence of both helmsman and crew. They will help you evolve from the mechanical approach we took in Part One to a more intuitive or reflexive approach. Review the sail raising procedures in Part One, then let's go sailing.

Sailing close-hauled, reaching, and running each involves different techniques and skills for the person at the helm and for the crew. A good sailor will be able to perform all functions on the boat, so read the instructions once from the point of view of the helmsman, and again from the crew's point of view. Then practice each on the water. In Part One we developed the technique of sailing across the wind (reaching). By learning how to sail close-hauled, we will be able to sail closer to the wind; and, by coming about from time to time, sail to an upwind destination.

COMMUNICATIONS

When the boat is leaving the dock or maneuvering, only one voice should be heard. The helmsman should be the skipper, and he or she gives the orders. The boat will be better organized and there will be less confusion than if authority is shared. Murphy's rule of sailing confusion is, "For every additional person you add to a boat you square your problems."

To ensure that the crew understands the helmsman's intentions (and vice versa), simple, standard verbal commands have been developed. These commands should be learned and used at all times. Each time the vessel alters course and the trim of the sail is changed, the proper commands must be used to alert the others on the boat that such changes are about to take place. Although the actual wording of the commands may vary from boat to boat and from skipper to skipper, the meaning and the reason for them is the same-communication and safety. For sailing upwind and coming about these are the most frequently used commands:

HELMSMAN: "Ready about." (This means the crew will get ready to come about by putting the windward jib sheet around the winch.)

CREW: "Ready." (The crew has made sure that the jib sheets are clear and the boat is ready to come about.)

HELMSMAN: "Hard alee. " (The tiller is being pushed to the leeward side of the boat, and the boat is starting to turn.)

Another series of commands is used when heading up (steering closer to the wind):

HELMSMAN: "Prepare to head up." (The crew prepares to pull in on the sheets.)

CREW: "Ready." (The crew has made sure that all is ready.)

HELMSMAN: "Trim sheets." (The tiller is moved slightly to leeward, and the sheets are pulled in as the boat is turning.)

You probably noticed that there was a preparatory command" and then a "command of execution." It's important to have both.

SAILING CLOSE-HAULED

Sailing close-hauled is perhaps the most difficult point of sail for a helmsman because it is the least forgiving. If the helmsman steers too close to the direction of the wind or too far from it, or if the crew pulls the sails in too tight or not tight enough, the boat will not perform efficiently. The happy medium of best angle to the wind is often referred to as the "groove."

As a rule, the closer you sail to the wind, the slower the boat will go. For upwind sailing with the sails trimmed, you as helmsman should head up, easing the tiller to leeward and turning the boat until the sail

EXERCISE: **SAILING CLOSE-HAULED**

1. The helmsman starts the boat from a beam reach position.

2. The crew trims the sails for a beam reach, with the wind flowing evenly on both sides of the sail as indicated by the telltales. Watch the luff or leading edge of your mainsail along the mast and the luff of your jib. The boat should be steered so that the sails remain full, but keep testing your course by slowly heading the boat toward the wind. If the sail begins to luff, either trim it in until it stops or, if the sail is already trimmed in all the way, bear away from the wind by pulling the tiller to windward (constantly looking at the "luff " in the sails) until the sail fills.

3. When the boat has picked up speed, the helmsman gives the command "Prepare to head up." The crew responds with "Ready" when they are prepared to sheet in the sails.

4. With the command "Trim sheets," the helmsman turns the boat closer to the direction of the wind and the crew sheets the sails to prevent luffing.

5. Counteract any heeling action by moving crew weight to the windward rail as the sails are trimmed in. If you feel uncomfortable or if the boat heels excessively,

ease out your mainsail while trying to maintain your close-hauled course. A normal reaction is to bear away from the wind without letting the sails out. This will cause too much heel and weather helm. Keep the boat balanced by adjusting your mainsail trim to maintain a constant angle of heel. In strong breezes upwind, you can control the angle of heel by your mainsail trim.

6. When the sails have been sheeted in, the helmsman tests to see if the boat can be steered any higher toward the wind by heading up until the jib luffs, and then bearing away from the wind until the luffing just stops.

7. The helmsman needs to be in a position to see the telltales at all times. By indicating when the boat is a few degrees out of the groove, the telltales allow the helmsman to steer a close-hauled course. Slight tiller adjustments are required to keep both telltales streaming properly. If the windward telltales rise up in the air, your sail is probably beginning to luff and you should sail a lower course by bearing away. If your leeward telltales begin to flutter, you are sailing too low a course and you should head toward the wind or ease your sails out.

8. The helmsman sails on a close-hauled course for a minute or two and then signals coming about with the command "Ready about." When the crew replies "Ready," the helmsman turns the tiller, saying, "Hard alee."

9. The helmsman comes to a close-hauled course after each tack, and the helmsman and crew shift to the opposite side of the boat. Avoid oversteering. Since a sailboat sails about 45 degrees off the wind, coming about should be a turn of 90 degrees-45 degrees to the wind and another 45 to the opposite tack. If this 90-degree turn is anticipated and practiced, the helmsman will be able to come about from closehauled to close-hauled every time.

10. After a few minutes of testing the trim of the sails, come about again. Repeat this exercise until a predetermined upwind objective (a mark or buoy) is reached. This should require coming about at least four or five times. The helmsman will then prepare to head the boat downwind with the command: "Prepare to bear away." When the crew replies "Ready," the helmsman orders "Ease sheets" and pulls the tiller to windward.

just begins to luff. When the sails luff, bear away slightly (pull the tiller to windward to turn away from the wind) just until the sails cease luffing. Now you have found the upwind groove. Constant retesting is required to keep you in this groove.

Remember to go through maneuvers slowly and gradually both to give the crew time to react and to maintain the speed of the boat. Most maneuvering problems occur because the helm is turned too quickly.

For crew members, close-hauled is a

relatively easy point of sail. Once the sails have been sheeted in, the crew's main duty is to watch for other boats. The helmsman, on the other hand, has to continually steer the boat, making small course adjustments for the inevitable wind shifts. The most common problem for the new sailor is oversteering. Try to sail a straight course by using a compass or heading for a fixed object.

A good way to learn to sail to windward is to sail alongside another boat. You will feel more comfortable with another boat nearby, and it will give you a reference point or a benchmark. When doing this exercise, sail about two or three boat lengths apart.

In this exercise, being able to sail from the leeward to the windward mark repeatedly and efficiently is your goal. It's a major

accomplishment; don't be concerned if you do not perform well at first. Many new sailors have difficulty getting the boat on a close-hauled course the first time, but with practice you will learn to sail a close-hauled course at optimum speed.

SAILING ON A RUN

Although sailing downwind (running) may seem less demanding than upwind sailing. It takes concentration to maintain sail control and crew coordination. When running, the boat is being pushed by the wind. Running with the wind efficiently is a matter of exposing as much sail as possible. The more proficient the crew and helmsman become at sailing downwind, the more sail area they can set to catch the wind.

When sailing close-hauled, the helmsman continually tests the set of the sails by steering a few degrees into the wind until the sails luff and then back until the luff stops. Similarly, on a run, the helmsman continually tests the sails by steering away from the wind a few degrees. The idea is to sail as low a course as possible and yet maintain speed.

Sailboats can be difficult to steer dead (directly) downwind, particularly lightweight dinghies in which the weight of the crew exceeds the weight of the boat. If you reach up slightly toward the wind, the boat will gain stability and be easier to sail.

It is a good practice to position your crew so that you do not feel any pressure on the helm-that is, your boat will maintain a steady course if you let go of the tiller. Your boat will heel slightly to windward (or to leeward) to balance the helm. Don't worry, this is normal. With a balanced helm, the center of effort of the sails is directly over the center of lateral resistance of the hull under the water.

Ease your sails out as far as you can without letting them luff. Keep easing the sail out until it just begins to luff, then trim in slightly until the luffing stops.

In cat-rigged (mainsail only) boats, sailing downwind is simply a matter of bearing away from the wind and easing the mainsail out. However, in a sloop (a boat with two sails) it will help to wing your jib to wind-

EXERCISE: **SAILING ON A RUN**

1. Pick the course that you would like to sail by locating an object downwind in the water or on shore to steer toward or simply by noticing the wind direction.

2. As the boat gets onto a run, the jib is blanketed by the mainsail and loses wind. This is the first indication that the boat is on a run.

3. The crew pulls the jib to the opposite side of the boat by releasing the leeward jib sheet (the one on the same side as the mainsail). They then tighten the windward sheet. Try to keep the wind flowing slightly to one side of astern so both sails will fill. When sailing downwind in a strong breeze, the boat will have a tendency to plow into the waves ahead of you. Moving the weight of your crew aft helps to lift the bow up out of the waves. You can also head up slightly so that you are sailing at an angle to the waves.

4. The helmsman must watch the wind indicators. A masthead fly or telltale can be particularly helpful when you're sailing downwind. Watching the direction from which the wind is coming helps you to steer. Masthead flies always tell the truth. Keep the wind over your quarter. If you feel the boat become unstable or start to rock back and forth, head the boat toward the wind by pushing the tiller to leeward. Ease the sail until the boom is at a right angle to the wind. The masthead fly should create a right angle with the boom and the foot of the jib.

5. After maintaining this course and point of sail for a few minutes, the helmsman gives the command to prepare to jibe the mainsail, "Prepare to jibe. " The crew replies "Ready, " and the helmsman gives the order "Jibe ho. "

6. The jib is always jibed after the mainsail has crossed the boat, since it is less important on a run than the main.

7. In small boats, the helmsman and crew should sit on opposite sides of the boat to keep it level and to allow each crew member to watch for other boats and obstructions.

ward (set it on the opposite side from the mainsail). This helps both sails to capture the air more efficiently. If the jib is kept to leeward of the mainsail,` the main will block the wind from the jib. One crew member may hold the jib sheet on the windward side of the boat to capture the wind.

The jibe, as you learned in Part One, is the most direct approach to changing tacks downwind. This running exercise will involve a series of jibes, and with practice the helmsman should be able to jibe the mainsail without steering the boat more than a few degrees from a dead downwind course.

The commands for jibing are:
HELMSMAN: "Prepare to jibe." (The crew gets ready on the sheets.)
CREW: "Ready."
HELMSMAN: "Jibe ho." (The tiller is pulled to windward, and the boat starts to turn away from the wind.)

Sailing upwind and sailing downwind are actually two parts of the same exercise. While working through the upwind exercise for sailing close-hauled, you'll have to sail on a run to get back downwind to the leeward mark or buoy. Let us look at how to improve downwind sailing skills by doing the "Sailing on a run" exercise.

SAILING ON A REACH

Reaching differs from sailing close-hauled and running because the crew cannot just set the sails and then leave the trimming to the helmsman's course. When sailing close-hauled or on a run, the helmsman must maintain the trim of the sails by steering the boat to adjust for changes in the wind direction. On a reach, the helmsman maintains a straight course to a destination and the crew trims the sails by easing them out until they luff and pulling the sheets in until the luffing stops.

Three buoys with anchors are needed for the next exercise. Anchor them in a triangular pattern so that in order to sail the entire circuit, the helmsman must steer on a beam reach, a close reach, and a broad reach.

EXERCISE: **SAILING ON A REACH**

1. On each leg of this exercise, the helmsman steers directly for the next mark while the crew trims the sails by easing them out until they luff and then trimming them until they stop luffing.

2. Telltales are less effective on a beam reach than on an upwind course and virtually useless on a broad reach and run. On a broad reach, ease the sail until it luffs and then trim until the luffing stops. The crew continually tests to make sure the sails are properly trimmed.

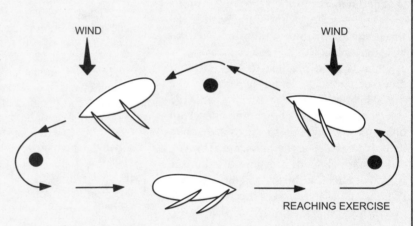

REACHING EXERCISE

STOPPING THE BOAT

So far, we have been concerned with keeping the boat moving through proper trim and steering. This exercise will help the helmsman and crew to stop the boat wherever they want. Control in stopping a boat is as important as control when moving. At the end of this exercise, the helmsman should be able to stop the boat within six feet to windward of an object in the water.

In Part One, we were concerned with getting the boat moving. We started with the sails luffing and the boat at right angles to the wind (on a beam reach). To stop the boat, we have to be able to position the boat so that the wind cannot possibly fill the sails. This is done by easing the sails out as far as possible when the boat is on a close reach.

It might seem that the best way to stop the boat is to point it into the wind-head to wind-so the sails just luff. Although the boat will definitely stop when head to wind, the helmsman has the least control of the boat on this point of sail. Control is a primary goal of all helmsmen.

For example, suppose someone's hat blew into the water while the boat was sailing, and the helmsman and crew managed to get the boat turned around and headed back to the point where the hat was lost. If the helmsman headed the boat up until it was head to wind, the boat would stop. However, if the boat stopped a few feet short of the object, the crew would have to get the boat turned away from the wind, start sailing again, and repeat the exercise until the timing of the stop was exactly right.

I will never forget sailing in one major championship in E-Scows on the New Jersey shore. The skipper of the boat I was sailing on had a favorite hat which had followed him for years. As soon as we had rounded the leeward mark to the finish in a race that we were doing well in, his hat, for the first time, blew off his head. He reached to grab it-almost going overboard-but missed. The hat was now in the water. Was

losing the race worth the hat? It seemed foolish at the time to hesitate even for an instant to go back for a hat. But the helmsman reeled around, barely missing another competitor, came up on the breeze; leaning overboard, two of us dived for the hat, picked it up, and on we went. Reflecting on the race later that night, the skipper said, "We might have lost a couple of places in that race, but it would have been tragic for the rest of the summer without my hat."

The following weekend he showed up again with the same hat, this time with a strap underneath his chin.

While you may never have to pick up a treasured hat in the middle of a race, learning how to make a controlled approach toward an object while under sail will reward you in many situations, for example, when approaching a pier. The key is always to make the approach on a close reach. On this point of sail, the boat can both sail fast and be stopped quickly. A good way to practice is to throw a cushion overboard, and then make a wide circle and head back to it.

EXERCISE:
STOPPING THE BOAT

1. Sail toward the object on a close reach.

2. As you near it, let the sails luff to slow the boat gradually until you are stopped with the object just to one side, either windward or leeward.

3. If you stop short of the object, simply trim the sails a little to pick up speed.

Do this exercise until you can stop the boat beside the object every time. This maneuver becomes the heart of a very important exercise that we will describe in the next chapter—making a man overboard rescue.

SUMMARY

In this part, we have introduced the points of sail. These are the angles, relative to the direction of the wind, that a boat can sail. Remember that the point of sail chosen depends on your destination.

If you want to sail upwind, your boat must be close-hauled and you must come about a number of times until the destination is reached. Downwind destinations are attained by running with (in the same direction as) the wind.

If a destination is across the wind, reaching is the necessary point of sail. The boat is easy to control on a reach. The wind comes over the side and the crew eases the sails until they luff and trims them until the luffing just stops.

When there is any doubt as to whether a sail is properly trimmed, ease it to find out. The rule is "when in doubt, let it out. " The coordination of helmsman and crew is essential on all points of sail.

The drills on the water in this part further developed the mechanics of sailing the various points of sail and refined tacking and jibing. The final exercise-stopping the boat-will become an integral part of more complex maneuvers in Parts Three and Four.

PART THREE

Safety and Seamanship

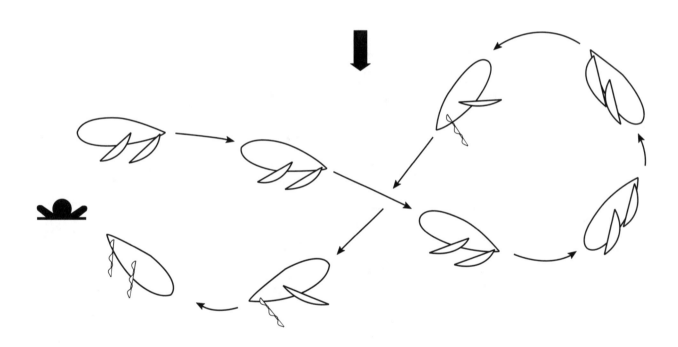

SAILING KNOWLEDGE

Sailors enjoy one of the best safety records of any recreational activity. The U.S. Department of Transportation (Safety Branch) has rated sailing as the safest of all sports. By and large, sailors have themselves to thank for this impressive record. Sailors take the time to prepare for potentially hazardous situations by knowing both their own limitations and those of their boat and equipment. However, even the most knowledgeable sailor can be surprised by a gust of wind or by a wave. For this reason, a good sailor anticipates difficult situations and prepares for them.

High wind and large waves (heavy weather) lead to the majority of unsafe situations aboard a boat. Anticipation and preparation are required of the skipper and crew. We will look at the causes, prevention, and then rescue of a man overboard. The rescue is an important drill; with luck you'll never need it, but be prepared. Further guidelines for heavy-weather sailing are covered in Part Six.

THE SAFETY HARNESS

A safety harness is an important protection against falling overboard. It is a simple web harness that fits around the upper body. There are two steel D rings secured to the front. Attached to these rings is a tether with a quick release shackle at one or preferably both ends. The shackle allows the wearer to attach and detach quickly, using only one hand.

The purpose of the safety harness is to keep a person on board by attaching the individual to a strong part of the boat: the base of a stanchion, the pulpit or stern rail, or a safety line ("jackwire" or "jackline") attached to strong deck cleats. Experts recommend that a person not shackle a safety harness to lifelines, the mast, or rigging because the rigging can fail in extreme conditions.

This crew member is prepared for heavy weather in a safety harness with a tether approximately six feet in length. The tether should not be hooked to lifelines.

DECK SAFETY

Certain areas of the boat are less safe than others. As a crew member moves forward out of the protection of the cockpit, there is an increasing need to hook on with a safety harness. Keeping a low stance with knees bent also reduces the chances of being thrown from the deck. There are times when crawling along the deck while holding on to a secure hand hold is the only safe way to move around the boat. Even with a safety harness, an important rule for all sailors is "One hand for the boat and one hand for yourself. " This simply means hold on to something solid. Move about a boat in rough weather as if you're eighty years old (apologies to you spry octogenarians).

The afterdeck, sidedeck, and foredeck are areas of reduced safety.

Some afterdecks have lazarettes for storing equipment. If a hatch to one of these is left open, a crew member may slip and fall. into the opening. A more common

Areas of reduced safety on deck. Lifelines, stanchions, grabrails, and shrouds are excellent handholds.

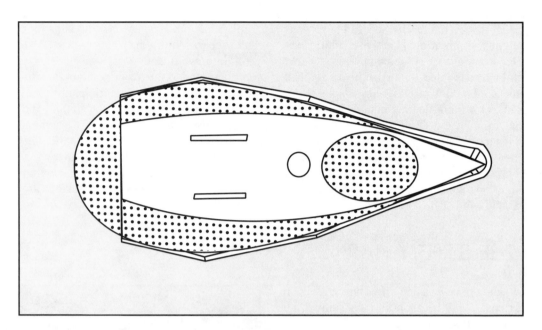

The safety line is led from the cockpit to a cleat on the bow. The safety line is sometimes called a jackline.

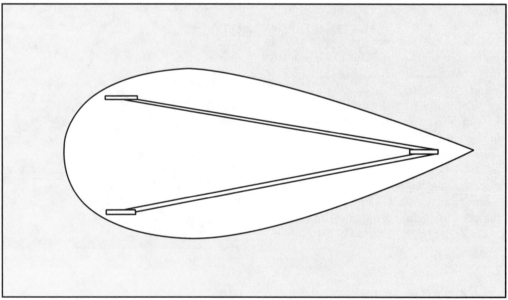

problem is failing down the forward hatch on the foredeck. Further, a sailor moving around on the afterdeck can fall overboard if the boat suddenly pitches.

A crew member moving along the sidedeck to the foredeck should do so along the windward side. It is easier to move on the windward side because the sails are set to the leeward side. Moving past the leeward shrouds requires bending and ducking, while on the high side there is ample room to pass.

The foredeck can be hazardous because there is only a small surface to work on.

Anytime a crew member has to move forward or work on the deck in heavy weather, a safety line should be led from the cockpit to a cleat on the bow. This gives the sailor a secure place to attach the safety harness tether and allows him to move forward without having to detach it at any time. Safety lines should be led down both sides of the boat.

HYPOTHERMIA AND CLOTHING

Although the possibility of drowning by falling into the water from a sailboat is a great concern, another real threat is hypothermia, a condition that exists when the body's core temperature drops below 95 degrees F. The loss of body heat results in loss of dexterity, loss of consciousness, and eventually loss of life.

Hypothermia is not only a danger in very cold water. In fact, the only time it is not a threat is when the water temperature is over 91 degrees. It is rare to experience water this warm in the United States. For example, the water off the coast of California in the summer rarely exceeds 70 degrees. Even the shallow, sun-drenched waters of the Bahamas reach only 85 degrees in the summer. Waters in the United States are cold enough to be a threat year-round.

In 65-degree water, the norm in summer throughout most of the United States, the average person without protective clothing could lose consciousness in just two hours. Survival time is greatly reduced if the individual is swimming, for example, from an overturned boat to shore.

Hypothermia can easily occur on deck when the air temperature is between 30 and 50 degrees. It is important to take precautions. I once spent a day on the water when the temperature never went above 35 degrees and I was so excited about being out on the boat that I didn't realize how cold I was until the day was over. Two hours later I started shivering and was sick for two days.

Hypothermia is a progressive problem. The body passes through several stages before an individual lapses into unconsciousness. Each of these stages provides signs to a rescuer of what immediate treatment is appropriate. The treatment of the victim depends on the level of hypothermia.

The extent of an individual's hypothermia can be ascertained from the following symptoms:

mild hypothermia
> feeling cold

> violent shivering
> slurred speech

medium hypothermia
> loss of muscular control
> drowsiness, incoherence, stupor
> and exhaustion

severe hypothermia
> collapse and unconsciousness
> respiratory distress and/or cardiac
> arrest probably leading to death

The first stage occurs when the body temperature drops to 95 degrees-just 3 degrees below the body's normal temperature. The body, in an attempt to reduce heat loss and at the same time replace the heat that has dissipated into the surrounding water, restricts circulation by reducing the flow of blood to the arms and legs. With less blood flowing, there is less heat drawn away from the body core and lost into the surrounding water. At the same time, the muscles involuntarily start to shiver as a means of generating more heat. These visual symptoms can be seen in a small child at the beach-blue lips (from reduced blood flow) and shivering.

Mild hypothermia is dealt with the same way you would treat a shivering child at the beach. The person is removed from the elements (wind and water), wrapped in a warm towel, and given warm fluids. Just as with a child, *no alcohol.*

In a state of medium hypothermia, an additional drop in the body's core temperature results in more violent shivering and a loss of coordination and manual dexterity. Simple tasks, such as grasping a thrown line, become difficult. The victim is less aware of his or her mental condition. If the limbs are cold and stiff, damage may result from trying to remove clothing. At this level, simply wrapping the individual in a blanket or towel is virtually useless because the body cannot generate enough heat to rewarm itself. The person has to be reheated by application of external direct warmth. The most practical and accessible source of heat aboard a boat is another human being. Simply sharing a sleeping bag

MINIMUM INSULATION FOR IMMERSION IN COLD WATER	
Water Temp. (F)	**Insulation (Foam Neoprene)**
60° or higher	3/16" vest or V8" jacket
50-60°	3/16" jacket, pants, boots, and gloves
40-50°	3/16" jacket, pants, hood, boots, and mittens
below 40°	1/4" jacket, pants, hood, boots, and mittens

or a blanket will provide the proper amount of heat at the right temperature.

Do not administer fluids to someone who is not totally coherent. Having to deal with a choking victim will take away from the essential treatment of warming the individual.

Do not massage the victim's arms and legs. Massage will cause the circulatory system to take cold blood from the surface into the body's core, resulting in further temperature drop. And, due to numbness, the victim cannot discern if the massage is too rough. Damage to skin tissue and nerve endings can result.

Do not administer alcohol, which causes loss of body heat, or coffee or tea. Stimulants may have the same effect as massage.

Even if the victim is breathing and does not require mouth-to-mouth resuscitation, emulating the rescue breathing technique by timing the rescuer's breathing rate with that of the victim will allow warm air to enter the victim's lungs and supply direct heat to the body core.

Severe hypothermia requires the same treatment as the medium stage. An added risk, however, comes from the chance of respiratory distress or cardiac arrest. A person in a severe stage of hypothermia may appear dead, without apparent pulse or breath. This should not stop the rescuer from using mouth-to-mouth or cardiopulmonary resuscitation (CPR) to revive the victim. These techniques are beyond the scope of this learn-to-sail text, but courses in first aid and CPR should be a high priority for all sailors, especially those in cold water.

As the core temperature continues to drop, the shivering stops and the muscles become rigid. Loss of consciousness soon follows and, if the victim does not receive prompt medical attention, the result can be fatal.

Hypothermia in severe stages is a medical emergency. Medical assistance is a must.

CONSERVING HEAT IN THE WATER

Conservation of heat is the foremost objective for a person in the water. To accomplish this, limit body movement. Any action generates heat, which is absorbed by the water and taken away from the body. Movement, such as treading water, will also cause the water warmed by the body to be moved away, and new, colder water will take its place. This exchange of water accelerates the cooling of the body.

A person without a personal flotation device (PFD) has to tread water to keep afloat. This uses up precious body heat and further exposes the high heat loss areas to the cold water. Heat loss, therefore, is greatly accelerated. A prudent sailor dons a PFD as soon as sailing conditions deteriorate. If someone who has fallen overboard does not have one, then a PFD must be thrown to the victim immediately. (See Sailing Skills in this part for Rescuing a Man Overboard.)

The PFD allows the person in the water to assume the heat escape lessening position-H.E.L.P. This position, commonly referred to as the fetal position, permits the victim to float with little effort and to concentrate on reducing heat loss. The areas of greatest heat loss-those requiring the greatest protection-are around the head, armpits, sides of the chest, groin, and backs of the knees.

Some survival suits and float coats are approved PFDs that provide life-saving insulation. In 60-degree water, a full survival suit considerably extends survival time.

A person without a flotation device should restrict movements to just those required to keep the head out of the water, since over 50 percent of the body heat loss in water is through the head. If possible,

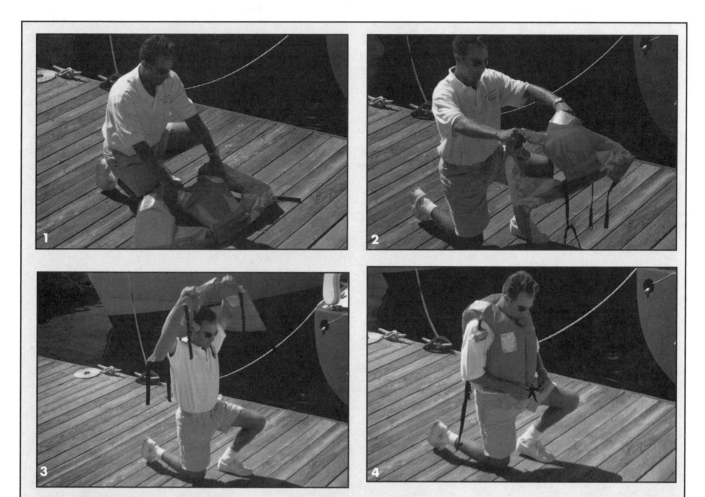

To don a PFD while in the water:

1. Place the PFD in front of you, inside out with the collar toward you.

2. Place arms in armholes.
3. Raise arms, bringing PFD over the head.

4. Lower arms, allowing PFD to be pulled down into place. Fasten zipper.

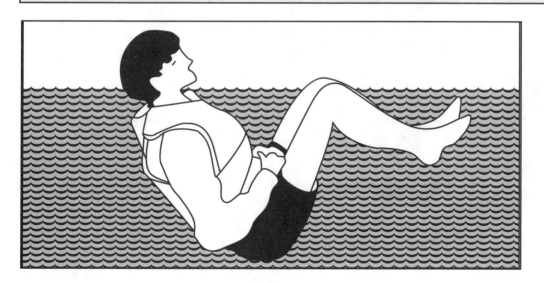

Heat Escape Lessening Position (H.E.L.P.)

get out of the water (possibly into an over-turned boat). Water conducts heat away from the body twenty-five times faster than air. Never attempt to swim to shore from an overturned boat. The combination of increased circulation from swimming and exposure of high heat-loss areas (head, neck, and groin) to the water will greatly increase the risk of hypothermia. Always *stay with the boat.*

A huddle should be formed to trap water warmed by heat loss.

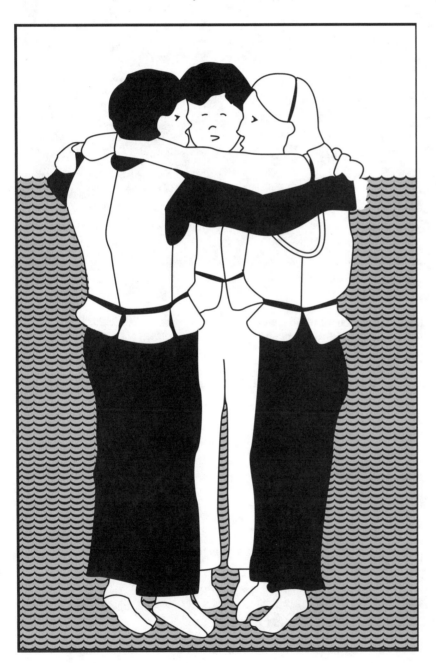

Another word of caution: "Drownproofing, " a rescue swimming and breathing method taught in the sixties and seventies, will accelerate the progression of hypothermia. Do not use drownproofing techniques.

A group of people in the water together should form a huddle. In this position, the water warmed by the heat loss of the group is trapped in the huddle. Once the water has been warmed, it draws less heat from the individuals into the water. This is the same principle behind the protection provided by a diver's wet suit. Small children should be kept in the center of the huddle. They are greatly protected by the relatively warmer water there.

THE RIGHT CLOTHES

The best way a sailor can prevent hypothermia out of the water is to wear the right clothes and stay warm and dry. The chill factor gets worse rapidly as the wind increases.

In no other sport is there a greater variety of clothing, ranging from nothing at all (as I found sailing in St. Tropez) to wearing every stitch of clothes you own. On one race from Chicago to Mackinac Island I was shivering in my bunk waiting for the next watch at 3:30 A.M. One of the crew came below to wake our watch and told us, "Put on everything you have. " I was already wearing everything I had, and it was a cold morning.

One of the secrets to sailing well is to be comfortable while on the water. Although foul-weather gear is an expensive investment, it's worth it.

Wear sneakers or nonskid shoes with soft soles at all times. Although I generally don't wear socks on shore, I always wear them while sailing to give me better traction. It is a bad habit to sail barefoot, since you may lose your balance.

There are many styles of boots. On off-shore yachts, calf-high boots are best. For dinghy sailing, wear boots that fit tightly around the ankle. These are particularly comfortable for hiking.

The warmest sailing clothes are thermal

polypropylene underwear and socks under wool or pile pants and shirt, goose-down vests or jackets, topped off with foul-weather pants and a waterproof parka.

Wind takes heat right away from the body. Even a light breeze can reduce the air temperature between the layers of clothing. Ideally, the outer layer of clothing should act as a windbreaker, keeping the wind and water away from the body.

The goal is to contain as much body heat as possible. Many sailors wear towels around their necks to keep water from trickling in. Gloves can be useful, particularly on long passages. Plan your sail in advance so you can take the right clothes with you. In boats that are particularly wet, a wet suit will keep you warm and comfortable and give you some flotation. A wet suit or dry suit should be used on wet boats when the water temperature dips below 72 degrees. In a wet suit, a thin layer of moisture that develops under the rubber suit gets warmed by your body and acts as insulation. Wear foul-weather gear over your wet suit in particularly cold weather.

Headgear (a hat or visor) is helpful in sunny weather because it shades you from the sun and helps keep you cool. In cold weather, a hat is important since a great deal of body heat escapes from your head. I find the best for cold weather are wool ski hats because they stay on your head and are designed for warmth.

An oiled woolen sweater is particularly good in cold weather since it resists water. I generally wear a T-shirt underneath my sweater to absorb perspiration. Wear sneakers, deck shoes, or boots with soft soles at all times. But be careful. If you end up in the water, all of this clothing will soak up water and restrict your movements. To counteract all of this weight it is best to wear a life jacket (PFD) so that you will stay afloat in the water.

A float coat is a jacket with flotation material sewn into the panels. Float coats are popular because they keep you warm and provide flotation if you do go into the water. Some sailors use a float coat with a strobe light sewn into a pocket in case they

fall overboard at night. Some sailors sew a safety harness into their coats as well. Short jackets can be annoying, as they ride up and leave part of your back exposed. Longer float coats are best since they stay down to keep you covered.

There are many excellent brands of foul-weather gear on the market. Find an outfit that fits you comfortably, slightly loose so that it is easy to move around in, yet able

Insulated sailing gear comes in all sizes and colors.

Raising the hoods on this foul weather gear (left) gives head to toe protection. A windbreaker with a high neck (right) offers comfort in less severe conditions.

to keep you dry in all kinds of weather. There really is no substitute for a good set of foul-weather gear. Pick a foul-weather jacket with a good hood and front designed to prevent rain from trickling in. Traditionally, foul-weather gear is bright yellow, orange, or red so that a person can be easily spotted if he falls in the water. I favor sweaters or chamois shirts instead of heavy jackets underneath my foul-weather gear, since they permit better movement.

Remember, the pleasure of sailing is directly proportional to your comfort. Proper clothing for different weather conditions makes it that much more enjoyable.

SEASICKNESS

Seasickness is generally less dangerous than hypothermia (although a severe case of motion sickness can be incapacitating), and its symptoms are easier to spot. Motion sickness afflicts many sailors, particularly at night. Some people are more prone to it than others, but no one ever escapes it entirely. A primary contributor to motion sickness is becoming overheated or chilled. It is important to wear the right clothing to maintain normal body temperature. Early symptoms of motion sickness are nausea, overheating, or feeling uncomfortable just moving around. Swallowing helps, although chewing gum doesn't since it creates too much saliva.

The first thing to do when you start feeling ill is to get some fresh air. Try to be active but relaxed. Don't be uptight about it. Fighting it off can make it worse. Often when you are feeling seasick you may not have eaten for a while; it may help to eat saltine crackers and drink a noncarbonated beverage. There are pills you can take, although they may make you drowsy. The motion sickness medicine used on the NASA space shuttle is the disc Transderm Scop (scopolamine), a prescription drug. Transderm Scop helps provide protection against motion sickness by delivering the drug scopolamine through the skin at a consistent, controlled rate. The adhesive disc is worn behind the ear and delivers the drug for up to three days. Tests show, however, that one out of six users of Transderm Scop experience drowsiness and two out of three users experience dryness of mouth. Other common side effects include vision problems in persons with glaucoma and urinary problems in older men as a result of the drug's effect on the prostate. Avoid overuse! Persons complaining of problems on cruises in the Caribbean have been found to have as many as four patches adhered to their body. Even replacing the patch daily can result in an overdose, as patches are meant to release a predetermined dosage over a few days. Read the product literature carefully and consult your doctor if you have questions.

If you do get seasick, head for the leeward rail.

YOU ARE WHAT YOU EAT

How well you eat determines how well you sail. The night before you sail, try to avoid exotic foods. Stay away from alcohol. Acidic (gas-producing) and greasy foods help induce motion sickness. Try to eat foods that store energy. Carbohydrates, such as pasta,

This adhesive disc on the author's neck delivers scopolamine through the skin.

potatoes, and bread, are best. It is best to have a good, solid breakfast about two to three hours before you go out so that you will have plenty of stored energy for the day's sail. Eat lightly if you are tense. On the water it is best to drink water and iced tea in hot weather; hot soup is best when the weather is cold. Stay away from carbonated beverages, as they produce gas. Sugary foods are good for short bursts of energy, but in the long run they are fatiguing.

REVIEW QUESTIONS

1. The purpose of the safety harness is to

_____ .

2. If alone in the water, wearing a PFD, an individual can extend his or her survival time by assuming the h _____ e _____ l _____ position.

3. List three *dos* when treating a hypothermia victim.

_____

_____

_____

4. List three *do nots* when treating a hypothermia victim.

_____

_____

_____

Answers in Appendix A, p. 201.

SAILING SKILLS

SAILING A TRIANGULAR COURSE

Each set of on-the-water exercises in this book builds upon the previous exercises. The following exercise will give you an opportunity to consolidate some of the skills you have acquired thus far. Once you can successfully sail a triangular course, you will be able to sail anywhere. This is because all points of sail, as well as coming about and jibing, are required to sail around the triangle.

The course for this exercise consists of three marks set far enough apart to allow five to seven tacks on the upwind leg. The key to success with this exercise is repetition.

By now, the helmsman and crew should be working as a coordinated team. Communications should be excellent and proper commands should be used during every maneuver. On the upwind leg, the helmsman should be able to sail a close-hauled course without having to adjust the boat's course except for changes in wind direction.

When coming about, the helmsman should try to complete the 90-degree turn without oversteering. The turn should be executed fast enough so that the boat does not slow down or stall, but slow enough for the crew to handle the sails properly and safely.

The crew's goal is to respond to the helmsman's commands quickly. When coming up to a close-hauled course from a reach, the crew sheets the sails in as the boat is heading up-not before or after the turn. When coming about, the crew releases the jib just as it starts to backwind and blow through the **foretriangle**—the space between the mast and forestay.

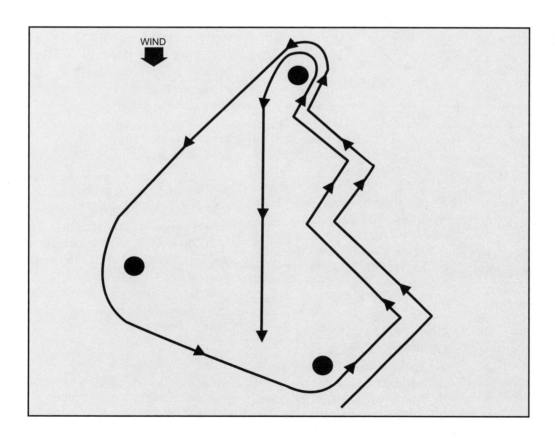

A triangular course. The windward leg is between marks 1 and 2; the reach legs are 2 to 3 and 3 to 1; the downwind leg is from mark 2 back to 1.

EXERCISE: **SAILING A TRIANGULAR COURSE**

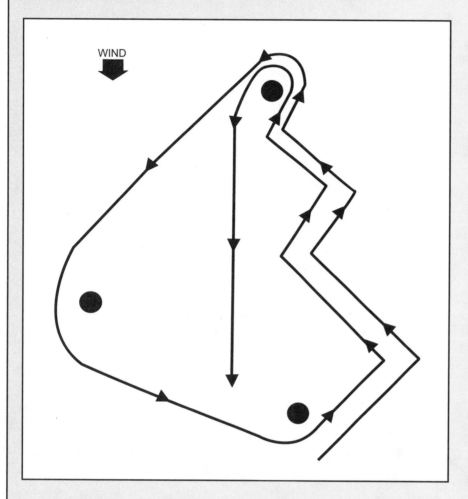

WIND

man makes sure the boat is actually sailing close-hauled by heading up until the telltales luff and then bearing away until the luffing stops.

3. To ensure that the turn is as close to 90 degrees as possible, the helmsman looks to windward to select a landmark for reference. This reference point will be off the windward beam of the boat (90 degrees off the bow).

4. With the command "Hard alee," the helmsman initiates a smooth turn to windward.

5. The crew member tending the leeward jib sheet releases the sheet just as the sail starts to move across the boat. Of course the sailor must be careful not to release the sheet too soon, or the boat will not come about as efficiently as possible. If he is too late in releasing the jib sheet, the sail will backwind and the helmsman will have difficulties in preventing the boat from oversteering.

6. As the boat completes its 90-degree turn, the crew member trims the jib on the new tack and the helmsman again tests that the boat is sailing on a close-hauled course by observing the telltales.

ON THE FIRST LEG, YOU WILL BE SAILING CLOSE-HAULED:

1. Starting from a reach at the leeward mark (**1,** the mark farthest away from the wind), the helmsman will be on the windward side of the boat, the best position for watching the telltales and water ahead. He gives the command to head up to a close-hauled course.

2. The helmsman or a crew member trims the mainsail as the boat comes up to close-hauled. One crew member trims the jib.

3. The helmsman tests to make sure the boat is sailing close-hauled by gradually heading up until the

windward (inside) telltales start to luff and then bearing away until the telltales stream aft.

4. If the wind gusts, the boat may become overpowered. The crew should then ease the mainsail slightly to allow some of the excess wind to be "spilled" from the sail * When the gust passes, the crew retrims the mainsail. The jib remains sheeted tight for upwind sailing.

COMING ABOUT ON THE UPWIND LEG:

1. The helmsman and crew use all appropriate commands and responses.

2. Before coming about, the helms-

BEARING AWAY AT THE WINDWARD MARK:

1. The helmsman gives the proper commands to bear away as the boat rounds the windward mark (**2,** the mark closest to the wind).

2. The crew eases the mainsheet and jib sheet as the helmsman bears away.

3. The helmsman lets the crew know when the boat is on course to the next mark (**3**).

REACHING:

1. The helmsman now steers a straight course to the third mark.

2. The crew ensures the correct trim of jib and mainsail by continually adjusting the sails as the wind direction varies. The crew sets the jib by easing the sheet until the inside telltale luffs and then sheeting in until the telltales are streaming aft. One of the most common. problems experienced by new crew is sheeting the jib too tight. The rule of thumb for preventing this remains "When in doubt, let it out."

3. Trim the mainsail concurrently with the jib, easing it until the sail backwinds from the wind coming off the jib. Retrim until the sail is just full again.

JIBING AT THE THIRD MARK:

1. While approaching the third mark, the helmsman prepares the crew with the appropriate commands for jibing.

2. As the boat starts to turn, one crew member begins sheeting in the mainsail. Optimal timing would have the boom coming to the centerline of the boat just as the wind passes over the stern. The mainsheet is then eased to allow the sail to swing out to the opposite side of the boat.

If this action is smooth and coordinated, the mains" movement will be continuous, without pause in the center of the jibe and without the boom banging into the rigging or the mainsheet taking a great shock as the boom swings out.

The reach back to the leeward mark **(1)** will require the same coordination as the first reach.

HEADING UP TO BEGIN AGAIN:

1. At the leeward mark the helmsman gives the commands to head the boat up to a close-hauled course.

2. Giving the command "trim sheets," the helmsman heads the boat up and the crew trims the mainsheet and jib sheet.

3. The crew trims the mainsail and jib to the close-hauled setting.

4. The crew tells the helmsman when the sails are trimmed for sailing on a close-hauled course.

5. The helmsman tests that the boat is actually sailing close-hauled by sailing toward the wind until the sails luff.

The second windward leg is just like the first.

SAILING DOWNWIND:

1. When the boat rounds the windward mark (2) for the second time, the helmsman bears away to a run, setting a course for the leeward mark (1).

2. As the boat bears away, the helmsman gives the command "ease sheets, " and the crew eases the sheets.

3. The helmsman watches the masthead fly to determine when the boat is on a run. The jib will become blanketed by the mainsail and will no longer fly to leeward.

4. One of the crew releases the old jib sheet, while the other crew member pulls in on the new jib sheet to guide the jib to the opposite side of the boat.

5. The jib sheet is eased until the jib is full and parallel to the mainsail. This is called sailing **wing-and-wing.**

6. Practice jibing while sailing downwind toward Mark 1. Avoid sailing by-the-lee (where the wind is coming from the same side the boom is on) and accidental jibes.

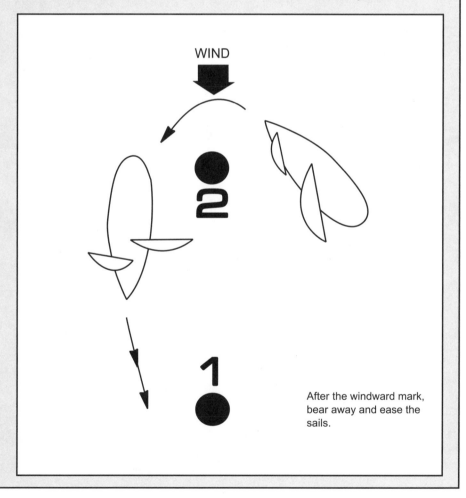

WIND

After the windward mark, bear away and ease the sails.

Winging the jib to windward on a run

RESCUING A MAN OVERBOARD

Man overboard is a serious situation on all boats. Consequently, the best method for returning to someone who has fallen in the water is one of the most hotly debated subjects s in sailing. Of the three popular basic methods, we feel that the following is the most efficient method of rescue and includes some safeguards which make it preferable for new sailors. Others may choose alternate methods, but the objective for everyone is the same-safe, efficient, and reliable recovery of someone who has fallen overboard.

The following method involves sailing a figure eight course with one tack and no jibe. It places the rescuing vessel on a close reach approaching the victim. You will remember from Part Two that a sailboat is easiest to stop with control on a close reach; that's why the following method is recommended for beginners. Crews should practice it many times in all types of weather.

THE FIGURE EIGHT METHOD

1. As soon as the person falls overboard;

a) Someone must shout "Man overboard!"

b) The nearest person must throw a PFD, life jacket, life ring or any other large, buoyant object to the person in the water.

c) Another person must be assigned to

watch the person in the water. This spotter points to the victim and gives verbal directions to the helmsman as to where the man overboard is. The spotter must never take his eyes off the person in the water.

2. The helmsman immediately steers to a beam reach from whatever point of sail the boat has been sailing.

3. The crew prepares a heaving line, boarding ladder, blankets, and jackets.

4. After sailing long enough for the crew to get prepared (about 100 yards), the helmsman commands the crew to prepare to come about.

5. As the boat comes about, the crew trims the mainsail but not the jib. This slows the boat's speed. Not having to tend the jib also frees up one member of the crew to assist the spotter or prepare to rescue the man overboard. The loop formed by the jib sheet in the water also gives the man overboard something to grasp as the boat comes near.

6. The spotter continues to give verbal and visual directions to the helmsman.

7. The helmsman, before getting too close to the victim, will have to test to see if the boat is actually on a close reach by having the crew luff the mainsail. If the mainsail luffs fully, the boat is on a close reach and the helmsman and crew carry on as if this were a stopping exercise. The helmsman stops the boat a few feet to windward of the victim. (The helmsman can also look to see that the masthead fly is pointing 40 to 50 degrees off the bow. This too indicates a close reach, but requires the helmsman to take his eyes off the spotter or the person in the water.)

8. As soon as the boat is stopped to windward of the victim, a line should be thrown and the individual secured to the vessel.

9. Once the person is alongside, the crew must bring him aboard. If he is unconscious or exhausted, he will not be able to help himself, so all crew members will have to haul him up by the armpits. Alternatively, a line may be led under his armpits and pulled up with a halyard. However, if the swimmer is self-sufficient, the crew should lower the boat's swimming ladder (if there is one). Obviously, the boat must be at a dead stop,

10. After the victim is aboard, treat him or her for hypothermia.

Picking up a man overboard

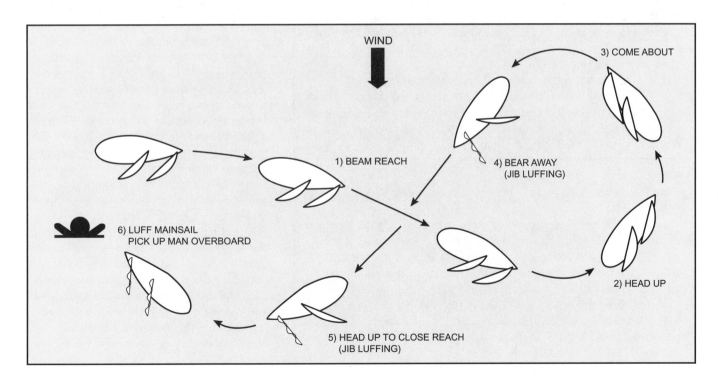

WIND

1) BEAM REACH

3) COME ABOUT

4) BEAR AWAY (JIB LUFFING)

6) LUFF MAINSAIL PICK UP MAN OVERBOARD

2) HEAD UP

5) HEAD UP TO CLOSE REACH (JIB LUFFING)

SAILING IN CONFINED WATERS

A sailboat does not require auxiliary power, although there are times when entering and leaving a crowded anchorage or mooring area can be greatly assisted by an engine. In these exercises, we will develop the skills required to handle a sailboat in confined or crowded conditions.

BOAT SPEED

The single most important factor in handling a vessel in an area with restricted maneuverability is control of boat speed. If a boat is stopped, it cannot be steered any more than it is possible to turn a parked car by turning the steering wheel. The crew will have to keep the sails trimmed properly at all times. The slightest luffing or stalling will result in loss of speed.

The faster you turn a boat, the faster it will stop. I recall one time sailing into a small harbor where a cocktail party was being held on the seawall near its opening. Any maneuvers would have to be sharp and precise. At the time I was seventeen and in a mood to do a little "hot dogging. " I was sailing a 28-foot E-Scow, a boat known to sail at speeds in excess of 20 knots. In entering the marine basin, we were sailing fast on a beam reach. Just before crashing into the seawall where the party was being held, I pushed the helm over as hard and as fast as I possibly could, forcing the boat to round up into the wind. The maneuver was made so sharply that the boat came to a complete stop. One of the crew marched forward to the bow, took the painter (bow line) and wrapped it around the cleat on the dock. We all stood up and took a bow to the cheering crowd. It must have looked spectacular to everyone except the owner, who was hesitant to loan us his boat again.

Once out of the slip, it is important to accelerate as quickly as possible, since speed equals control. Practice the following exercise in open water before trying it in a crowded area.

COMING ABOUT IN A CONFINED AREA

We have learned to come about around buoys. Sailing in confined waters presents a different problem-coming about in front of objects such as boats, docks, and breakwaters. The objective of this next exercise is to be able to judge how close to an object the helmsman can sail the boat and still have sufficient room to come about without hitting the object. Success depends primarily on two factors: boat speed (momentum needed to carry the boat through the turn) and the turning radius of the boat (how much space it requires to turn).

It is important to maintain boat speed and to be able to sail efficiently on all points of sail. Sailing close-hauled when beating out of a harbor or around a breakwater or dock will require the greatest concentration and coordination by helmsman and crew.

Practice this confined waters exercise often, because even sailors with engines on their boats will find this type of maneuver

---

EXERCISE: SAIL TRIMMING

This exercise is designed to illustrate the effects of proper sail trim techniques by comparing them with improper methods. The first part of the exercise is what not to do:

1. The helmsman stops the boat about fifteen feet to windward of a buoy on a beam to close reach with the sails luffing. The buoy serves as a reference point.

2. The crew sheets the sails quickly and abruptly.

The boat will move sideways rather than forward. This is a result of the sail being sheeted in so fast that the boat is not able to accelerate and simply drifts sideways with the wind blowing into rather than around the sail. To see how the boat will respond when the sails are trimmed gradually and to the proper angle relative to the wind, try this:

3. The helmsman brings the boat back to the same position as in step 1.

4. One crew member sheets the mainsail in gradually until it stops luffing. Another will trim the jib concurrently. As the boat starts to move, the crew will continue to trim the sails, making sure that the jib telltales are both streaming aft and that the mainsail is not luffing.

This time, the boat will move slightly to leeward (watch the buoy to determine how much) and then accelerate. As the boat speed increases, the leeway (slipping to leeward) will diminish. This exercise gives dramatic proof of the need for proper sail trimming.

ing necessary should the engine fail when they're coming into a mooring area or anchorage. The difference between making a boat sail and making it sail well is the difference between someone who owns a boat and a sailor.

OBSTRUCTIONS

If an obstruction or another boat is in your path, you must maneuver to stay clear. Always keep a sharp lookout when you approach another boat: don't lose sight of it. As a rule it is best to pass astern, although on starboard tack you have the right-of-way and will be the stand-on boat. A yacht on port tack is obligated to stay clear. Remember that many sailors do not know the rules and are uncertain about what to do. Any time it looks close, stay clear to avoid a collision.

If you encounter a boat that has the right of way (or one that does not but whose crew thinks it does), but are obstructed by other boats or shallow water from passing on either side, there's not much you can do except stop, luff your sails, and wait for the

boat to get out of your way. Sometimes you may be able to turn around and backtrack. Either way, try to stay to windward of the other boat. If it's downwind of you, there's no way that it can drift down onto you.

> EXERCISE: **COMING ABOUT IN A CONFINED AREA**
>
> Practice in open water before attempting this exercise in confined sailing conditions.
>
> **1.** The helmsman approaches a buoy on a close-hauled course. (The buoy should be plastic, or use a plastic drop mark, since we will attempt to turn as close to the buoy as possible and there may be some contact.)
>
> **2.** When approximately one-half boat length from the buoy, the helmsman comes about with the proper commands.
>
> **3.** The helmsman watches the bow closely throughout the turn. If the boat comes too near the mark after the boat is past head to wind (over halfway through the turn), the helmsman straightens out the vessel's course slightly to avoid contact with the buoy.
>
> The helmsman must judge how close the boat is able to turn to the buoy. Repeat the exercise until the bow passes within a few feet. This is as close as the boat should come to the buoy.

SUMMARY

The emphasis of the Sailing Knowledge part of Part Three has been on safety and seamanship. From preparation to execution, the skipper of a sailing vessel must keep the safety of crew and vessel as his or her primary concern.

We have discussed hypothermia. In the cold waters of the United States and elsewhere, this is a subject that should never be taken lightly. Adequate clothing, sensible diet, and attention to deck safety are your insurance against medical emergencies on the water. The use of safety harnesses and

PFDs goes a long way toward ensuring the safety of the crew.

The Sailing Skills part of this section continued this safety theme. Recovering someone who has fallen overboard is a drill we all hope we'll never have to use. However, the helmsman and crew must still be properly prepared.

Finally, the sailing exercises (around a triangular course and in confined waters) test skills acquired so far. We are now only one lesson away from completing the ASA Basic Sailing standard.

Basic Seamanship Skills

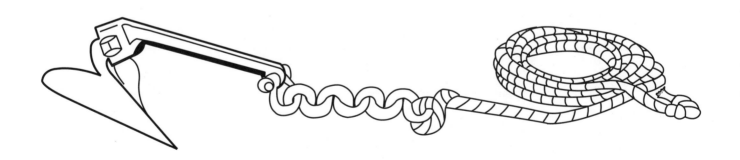

SAILING KNOWLEDGE

In this section, our concern is with special seamanship skills: chart reading, anchoring, heaving to (a way of stopping the boat while underway), and docking under sail. All of the skills taught so far will be practiced and polished in the sailing exercises, but in addition the new skills will make the handling and sailing of the boat more controlled and much safer.

DAYSAIL PLANNING

Before you go sailing, the following factors (other than the boat) have to be considered:
• weather
• season and time of day
• clothing
• the crew and their abilities

WATCH THE WEATHER

Before I go sailing I call the National Weather Service to get their report. I find that they are generally accurate in most parts of the country. Special continuous weather broadcasts are available on VHF radio channels. A marine weather radio will receive these broadcasts. Radio stations, particularly in cities along the coasts, have regular boating forecasts. Forecasters usually mention the barometric pressure, which indicates variation in air pressure. The direction and rate of change of the barometric pressure is important when forecasting weather. Weather changes are caused by the movement of pressure systems. A steadily failing barometer normally indicates unsettled or wet weather. A rapidly falling barometer usually forecasts the development of strong winds or a storm. A slowly rising barometer is normally associated with lighter winds.

Clouds are also helpful weather indicators. In general, thickening and lowering cloud layers are a sign of approaching wet weather. When layers of clouds show holes and openings or are frayed and indistinct at the edges, you can expect improving weather or a delay in the development of foul weather. An old adage says "Red sky at night, sailors delight; red sky at morning, sailors take warning. "

There are many helpful indicators, including the following:

• bright blue sky: good sailing
• dark, gloomy sky: wind
• bright yellow sky at sunset: wind
• sunrise from a gray horizon: fair day
• weak and washed-out sun: rain in the future
• sunset with diffused and glaring white clouds: storm
• ring around the moon: rain
• soft clouds: fine weather with light to moderate wind
• hard-edged, oily clouds: wind
• small, inky clouds: rain

Be familiar with the coastal warning displays issued by the U.S. Weather Service. These indicate foul weather. The following displays are normally shown at marinas, yacht clubs, and some Coast Guard stations (the Coast Guard is moving away from using storm signals):

Small craft advisory. One red pennant displayed by day and one red light above a white light at night. Indicates wind and sea conditions dangerous to small craft.

Gale warning. Two red pennants displayed by day and a white light above a red light at night. Indicates conditions dangerous to all boats.

Storm warning. A single square red flag with black center displayed by day and two red lights at night. Indicates very dangerous conditions.

Hurricane warning. Two square red flags with black centers displayed by day and a white light between two red lights at night. Indicates the most dangerous conditions.

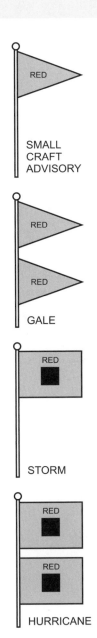

Daytime signals

SEASON AND TIME OF DAY

If your daysail is to last three to four hours, it naturally would be started during daylight. In the summer, a pleasant evening sail can be started at 6 P.M. and be over by sundown. In the fall or winter (if you live in an area where winter sailing is possible), you should start just after noon so you can have the boat back and tied to the dock before sunset. Evening sails are fun, but sailing in the dark shouldn't be attempted by a new sailor until boat-handling skills and knowledge are more developed.

CLOTHING

In warm weather wear light clothing, but keep in mind that the sun, particularly on hazy days, can give you severe sunburn. The sun's rays are intensified as they reflect off your deck and sails. Therefore stay covered for a good portion of the day. It doesn't take long to get sunburned. I have seen the rays burn through T-shirts. Use a sun screen lotion with a high SPF (sun protection factor). It is better to use too much sun screen than too little. Constant exposure to the sun and wind also ages your skin and increases your chances for skin cancer. Sun screens will help counteract this.

THE CREW AND THEIR ABILITIES

New sailors cannot wait to take their friends sailing. However, this usually results in a crew consisting of one not very experienced sailor and a group of novices. The workload and responsibilities of the skipper in this situation increase dramatically with each nonsailor who comes aboard.

A new skipper should take along at least one other experienced sailor on a daysail. There is always someone at the local sailing school, sailing club, or marina who has some experience and who would enjoy the opportunity to sail.

While they are putting on the sails and preparing the boat, the skipper and the experienced guest should take some time to discuss their duties and responsibilities once they are underway. In this situation, it's all too easy for each person to defer to the other, the end result being that nobody knows who's in charge. In a difficult situation that calls for decisive commands and authority-say, when a collision or a thunderstorm is threatening-confusion like this could be disastrous. It's also a good idea for everybody on board to agree on a common terminology. Sailors of different generations, backgrounds, and levels of experience often find themselves speaking remarkably different languages when they're sailing, and this, too, can lead to trouble.

CHART SYMBOLS

It is not our intent to teach navigation. However, even on a daysail, you need to be able to read the symbols on a nautical chart to determine the depth of the water, the hazards in the area (such as wrecks or rocks), and the composition of the bottom under the water in case you wish to anchor.

Chart symbols are bits of concise information on a nautical chart. The placement of the symbols is accurate and important. They give the skipper a clear map of the bottom over which the boat is sailing. The full list of chart symbols is found in the publication Chart No 1, "Symbols Abbreviations and Terms," that is the key to all chart symbols and an essential part of any vessel's sailing equipment.

SOUNDINGS

Soundings, or water depths, are listed in fathoms (one fathom equals six feet), feet, and meters. Nautical charts are being converted to the metric system and an increasing number of charts are now labeled in meters. The vertical reference plane—or datum–for soundings is mean lower low water, which means that charted depths are generally conservative. However, the actual water depth can be less than that charted and the prudent mariner allows a safety margin.

A common and embarrassing error is to read four feet as four fathoms and to find the boat in four feet of water and not twenty-four feet (4 fathoms). A skipper who reads a chart in fathoms, when it is actually in feet, will find that a boat does not sail well when it is sitting on the bottom, aground.

Running aground is easy to do. If you are sailing in new waters that you have not been in before, it is helpful to have a chart on deck and keep track of the course you are steering and your position on the chart. On the bright side, if you run aground you become a warning mark for other vessels that are passing. Never laugh at a boat that has run aground; you may be the next to hit the bricks.

Even the famous America's Cup helmsman, Dennis Connor, once ran aground off Newport, Rhode Island, cutting between a series of rocks and the mainland. Although the chart showed that passage was risky at low tide, Connor and his crew took a chance. The crew was forced to stay on the rocks for at least twenty-five minutes while the tide rose. In the meantime, thirty-eight other competitors all sailed by. Connor's boat was named *Lobo*, and today local watering holes in Newport have a special drink called "Lobo on the rocks" in honor of the occurrence.

DISTANCE

Distance on a nautical chart is measured in **nautical miles.** A nautical mile equals 1.15 statute miles (the miles used on land and on inland charts). Unlike the statute mile, which has evolved from the whims of kings

Sounding - Symbols for Water Depths

#	Symbol	Description	#	Symbol	Description
1	SD	Doubtful sounding	10		Hairline depth figures
2	65	No bottom found	10a	8₂ 19	Figures for ordinary soundings
3	(23)	Out of position	11		Soundings taken from foreign charts
4		Least depth in narrow channels	12		Soundings taken from older surveys (or smaller scale chts)
5	30 FEET APR 1972	Dredged channel (with controlling depth indicated)	13	8₁ 19	Echo soundings
6	24 FEET / MAY 1972	Dredged area	14	8₂ 19	Sloping figures
7		Swept channel (See Q 9)	15	8₂ 19	Upright figures (See Q 10a)
8	2₁	Drying (or uncovering) heights above chart sounding datum	16	(25) (2)	Bracketed figures (See O 1, 2)
9	17 119	Swept area, not adequately sounded (shown by purple or green tint)	17	6	Underlined sounding figures (See Q 8)
9a	29 23 3 30 8 21 7	Swept area adequately sounded (swept by wire drag to depth indicated)	18	3₂ 6₁	Soundings expressed in fathoms and feet
			22		Unsounded area
			(Qa)	6 5 21	Stream

and politicians, the nautical mile is not an arbitrary measure. The circumference of the earth is measured in degrees. If measured through the poles (north and south), the degrees of the circumference are referred to as *latitude* (degrees north and south from the equator). *Longitude* (east and west) is the measure of the earth's circumference around the equator.

One degree of latitude is equal to sixty nautical miles. Annapolis, Maryland, is about 39 degrees north latitude. Therefore, Annapolis-the home of the U.S. Naval Academy-is approximately 2,340 miles north of the equator (39 degrees of latitude times 60 nautical miles per degree of latitude).

One sixtieth of one degree of latitude (called a minute) is one nautical mile. The scale for this measurement (the latitude scale) is found on the side of a nautical chart. One nautical mile can be divided into tenths or sixtieths (one second of arc is one sixtieth of one minute). Most charts, however, will be in tenths of nautical miles, because a sixtieth is too small a distance with which to be concerned on a boat.

AIDS TO NAVIGATION

Aids to navigation (ATONs) are devices found on waterways, such as buoys and beacons, that identify the locations of channels where safe passage is assured, warn boaters of dangers and obstructions, and help boaters determine their positions. This section provides an introduction to ATONs. Other courses offered by ASA and USCGAUX provide more information on navigation and ATONs.

The United States has an excellent system of ATONS. Indeed, the density of buoys and beacons in U.S. waters is quite high compared to those of most other countries.

BUOYS

Buoys are floating ATONs. Depending upon their use, buoys are identified by color (green, red, green/red bands, red and white striped, or yellow), shape (can or conical), and usually by either a number or letter(s). Buoys may be lighted (green, white, or red) or unlighted. Numbering (or lettering) and light rhythms on buoys help the boater to identify a particular buoy on a nautical chart.

Unlighted green buoys that resemble vertical cylinders are called CANs and have odd numbers. Unlighted red buoys that look like cylinders with conical tops are called NUNs and have even numbers.

Storms, wave action, and damage caused by collisions can move a buoy, so prudent boaters should not rely on buoys alone to determine their positions. Report any buoys or other ATONs that may be out of position, damaged, or defective to the USCG.

Do not moor your vessel to a buoy or other ATON. This practice is prohibited, among other reasons, because it may prevent other boaters from observing the ATON and cause an unsafe situation!

Do not pass too close to buoys. They may be very close to the danger they mark.

Channel with buoys and daymarks

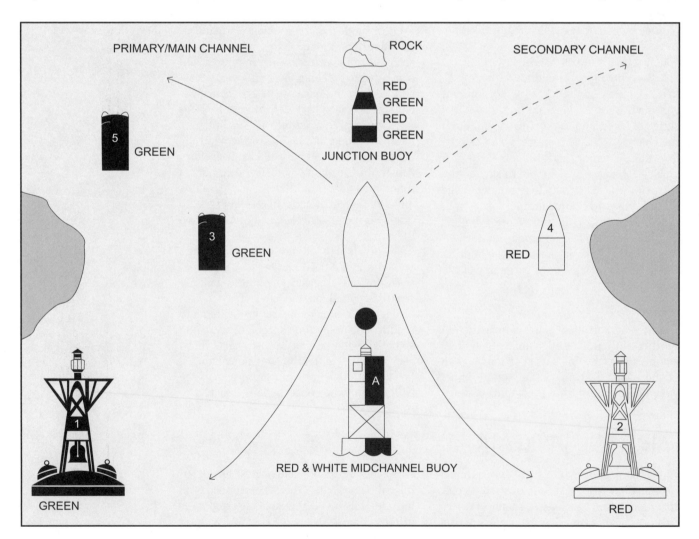

Daymark #4 is attached to a structure marking the entrance to this harbor.

Moreover, buoys are anchored to the bottom with chains and may shift location (within a so-called watch circle) as a result of wind and current action.

BEACONS

Beacons are fixed ATONs. Daybeacons, used in shallow water, have one or more signboards (daymarks) on them. Depending upon their use, daymarks are identified by color (green, red, green/red bands, red and white stripes, or yellow), shape (square, octagonal, or triangular), and usually by either a number or letter(s). Green daymarks are square and have odd numbers. Red daymarks are triangular and have even numbers. Octagonal daymarks have eight sides and are marked with letters. Daymarks may be mounted on posts or on groups of pilings tied together (dolphin). Daybeacons may have lights that correspond to the daymarks.

ATON SYSTEMS

There are two general ATON systems used in the United States: the U.S. Aids to Navigation System and the Uniform State Waterway Marking System (USWMS). The waters of the United States and its territories are marked by the U.S. Aids to Navigation System. The U.S. Aids to Navigation System has two variations, the

† 1 (25) ♂(25) Rock which does not cover (height above MHW)	**11** Wreck showing any portion of hull or superstructure (above sounding datum)
Uncov 2 ft ✿*Uncov 2 ft* *(2) ✿(2) **2** Rock which covers and uncovers with height above chart sounding datum (see Introduction)	**12** Wreck with only masts visible (above sounding datum) ⚓Masts
	13 Old symbols for wrecks
3 Rock awash at (near) level of chart sounding datum Dotted line emphasizes danger to navigation	**13a** PA Wreck always partially submerged
	14 Sunken wreck dangerous to surface navigation (less than 11 fathoms over wreck) (See O 6a)
	15 (5⅓)Wk Wreck over which depth is known

Chart danger symbols

Intracoastal Waterway Aids to Navigation System and the U.S. Aids to Navigation System on the Western River System. There are slight differences between these systems. ASA publishes an insert card, ASA-152, on ATONs, which displays the various types and colors of ATONs.

Intracoastal Waterway System

This system is used on the Intracoastal Waterway (ICW), an inland waterway running parallel to the Atlantic and Gulf coasts from

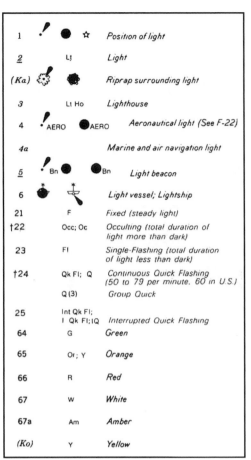

Lights

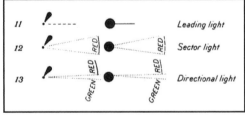

Limit symbols

Gloves and a firm grip will reduce the possibility of injury during anchoring.

Manasquan Inlet, New Jersey, to Brownsville, Texas. ATONs marking these waters follow the same coloring and numbering system as the U.S. Aids to Navigation System, except that some portion of each ATON is marked with a yellow square, a yellow triangle, or a yellow band. When following the ICW in a southerly direction from New Jersey to Florida and/or westerly to Texas:

Yellow Square: Keep the ATON on your left.

Yellow Triangle: Keep the ATON on your right.

Horizontal yellow bands are found on safe-water daymarks and buoys. These identify aids as marking the ICW.

Note that the shape of the yellow marker (not the shape of the buoy or daymark) determines the side to pass on when in the ICW.

The Western River System

This system is used on the Mississippi River and its tributaries above Baton Rouge,

Louisiana, as well as on certain other rivers that flow toward the Gulf of Mexico. Buoys and daymarks are shown in the figure.

The USWMS

The USWMS supplements and is generally compatible with the U.S. Aids to Navigation System. This system was developed in 1966 to provide an easily understood navigation system for operators of small boats. Although the USWMS is intended for use on lakes and other inland waterways that are not depicted on nautical charts, it is authorized for use on other waters as well. This system has specific variations from the U.S. Aids to Navigation System evident in the figure. (Note: black buoys in the USWMS are being phased out in favor of green buoys to achieve greater harmonization with the U.S. Aids to Navigation System.)

TYPES OF ATONS

The U.S. Aids to Navigation System uses two basic types of ATONs: lateral marks, including preferred-channel marks, and nonlateral marks.

Lateral Marks

Lateral marks are buoys or beacons that indicate the port and starboard sides of a route to be followed. Both are used in conjunction with a conventional direction of buoyage. "Red, right, returning," is a helpful phrase in figuring out how to use lateral marks. When returning from seaward (proceeding in the conventional direction of buoyage) keep red buoys or daymarks on your starboard (right) side as you pass them and green buoys on your port (left) side. When proceeding toward the sea, reverse the rule, leaving green buoys or daymarks on your starboard side as you pass them and red buoys on your port side.

In U.S. waters, returning from seaward and proceeding toward the head of navigation is generally considered to be moving southerly along the Atlantic coast, westerly along the Gulf coast, and northerly along the Pacific coast. In the Great Lakes, the conventional direction of buoyage is gener-

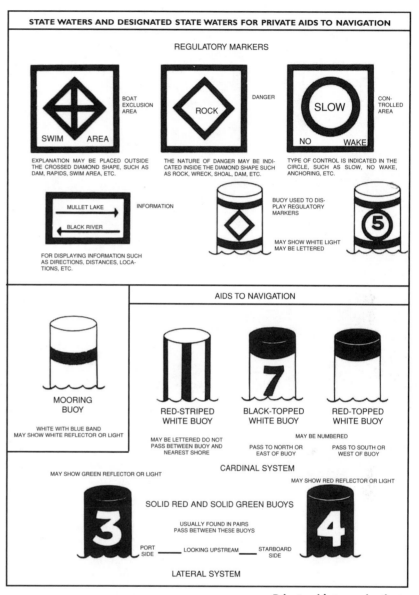

Private aids to navigation

ally considered westerly and northerly, except on Lake Michigan, where southerly movement is considered as returning from the sea. These general principles are not always sufficient to enable boaters to know the direction of buoyage in a particular area. The nautical chart should always be consulted.

Preferred-channel marks, which are colored with green and red bands, mark channel junctions or splits. Preferred-channel marks may also indicate wrecks or obstructions. Normally, preferred-channel marks

Communication between bow crew and helmsperson is essential during anchoring.

may be passed on either side, but your intended route should dictate how you pass the mark. If you wish to follow the preferred channel, be guided by the color of the topmost band on the mark. That is, if the topmost band is red, leave it on the right, if green, leave it on the left when proceeding in the conventional direction of buoyage. Always check your chart to determine if there is sufficient water depth in the preferred or alternate channels. Channel depths vary greatly. This is important with all craft, but particularly to sailboats, which because of their generally deeper drafts require more water for safe passage.

Nonlateral Marks

As the name implies, these marks have no lateral significance, but are used to supplement lateral ATONs. Nonlateral marks include information and regulatory marks used to provide warnings or regulatory information, isolated-danger marks to warn of specific dangers, lighthouses, range lights to

mark the centerlines of certain channels, safe-water (fairway) marks, and special marks to alert the boater to special features or areas, such as spoil areas, pipelines, water intakes, anchorage areas, and so on.

Information and regulatory marks provide warnings and regulatory information. These marks use orange diamonds, circles, squares, or rectangles on a white background. For example, an open-faced diamond means danger, a circle denotes restrictions of various types (e.g., no-wake area), and a diamond containing a cross means that boats are excluded.

CHARTING OF ATONS

The locations and descriptions of most ATONs are shown on nautical charts. This is designed to help boaters determine their positions. In some cases, such as inlets subject to frequent shoaling and consequent repositioning of buoys, buoys are not charted and a note is appended to this effect on the chart.

ANCHORS AND THEIR USES

The combination of anchor, chain, and rode (rope) is commonly called ground tackle. This entire system keeps the boat securely fastened to the bottom. The chain and rode are as important for keeping the vessel from dragging as the anchor itself.

Anchors hold by one of two means: weight or digging into the bottom. A pleasure boat does not have the crew or the machinery to pull up a very heavy anchor like the ones found on naval vessels and commercial ships, so small craft anchors have to be designed to hold by digging into the bottom.

The proper anchor varies with the type of bottom one is anchoring in. Wise sailors carry more than one type of anchor so that they're prepared for any anchoring situation. The two most popular cruising anchors are the Danforth and the plough.

The **Danforth** is an all-purpose anchor, and it will hold in any bottom soft enough to allow the flukes to dig in. If the bottom is too soft (soft mud), however, the flukes will simply drag through the mud and the anchor will not hold.

The flukes of the Danforth have sharp edges to dig into harder mud or soft clay, and a wide flat surface to resist dragging once the anchor is buried in the bottom. Suited for hard mud, sand, and soft clay, the Danforth, or an anchor of similar design, is the choice for the weekend sailor and cruiser alike.

The **plough** anchor is so called because the shape of the fluke is like that of a plough share. This heavy-duty cruising anchor digs into harder surfaces than the Danforth anchor can penetrate; it also grabs into rocks. The plough is able to dig through some weeds and into the bottom. A plough must be heavier than a Danforth to provide the same holding power for the same size boat.

The **rode** is the rope line. When anchoring you should normally let out approximately four to seven times as much anchor rode as you have depth in water. In other words, in ten feet of water you should let out forty to seventy feet of anchor rode.

Danforth anchor

Plough anchor

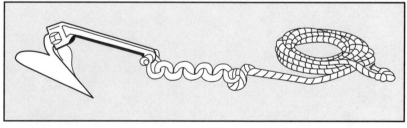

Ground tackle

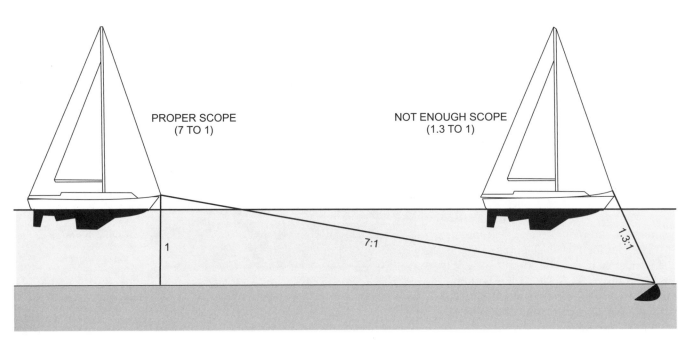

PROPER SCOPE
(7 TO 1)

NOT ENOUGH SCOPE
(1.3 TO 1)

1

7:1

1.3:1

Anchor scope

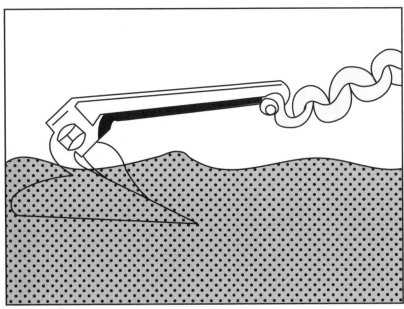

How anchors dig in

The rode should be marked at regular intervals. If the winds are heavy or the seas high, more anchor rode may be required.

The **chain** connects the anchor to the rode. A chain will absorb shock from a pitching boat in heavy seas, allowing the anchor to stay dug into the bottom. Also, a chain keeps the rode from chafing on the bottom, particularly important when the anchor is passing over jagged coral or rocks.

The anchor, rode, and chain combine to hold a boat in place. The most common anchoring errors are not letting out enough rode and using an anchor that is too light or not suited to the type of bottom. To make sure the ground tackle holds together, tighten with a wrench the pins in the shackles joining the anchor to the chain and rode, and wire them closed.

THE ANCHORAGE

A safe anchorage must have:
• shelter
• room to swing on the anchor
• sufficient depth of water
• good holding ground (bottom)

SHELTER

The ideal anchorage is out of wind, waves, and traffic; however, it is difficult to have all of these advantages at once. Therefore, compromise may be necessary. The best place to anchor is in the lee of an island or shore. You are in the lee of an island when the island is between you and the wind. To be in the lee of something (or to leeward of it) is to be protected from the wind. A lee shore, however, is to leeward of the boat (on the side of the boat away from the wind).

ROOM TO SWING ON THE ANCHOR

If we pay out seventy feet of rode to maintain sufficient (7: 1) scope, a wind shift will cause the boat to swing through a very large circle. The result could be embarrass-ing or even dangerous if the boat is anchored too close to a pier, the shoreline, or another boat that is not swinging in the same size circle.

The boat's swinging circle can be reduced by setting more than one anchor. For now, we are concerned with basic anchoring skills. Advanced anchoring (setting two anchors) is covered in the ASA Bareboat Chartering and Advanced Coastal Cruising standards. For now, simply allow enough room for the boat to swing through 360 degrees. Seventy feet of rode will result in a swinging circle of approximately 140 feet in diameter.

SUFFICIENT DEPTH OF WATER

We have learned that the amount of rode let out to maintain scope depends on the depth of water. If the water is too deep, it is possible there will not be enough rode aboard to maintain a scope of 7: 1. If the water is too shallow at any place in the swinging circle of the boat, or if a tide change reduces the water depth, the boat

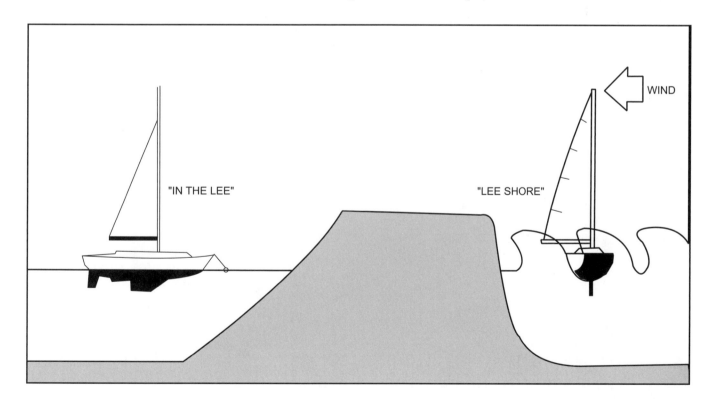

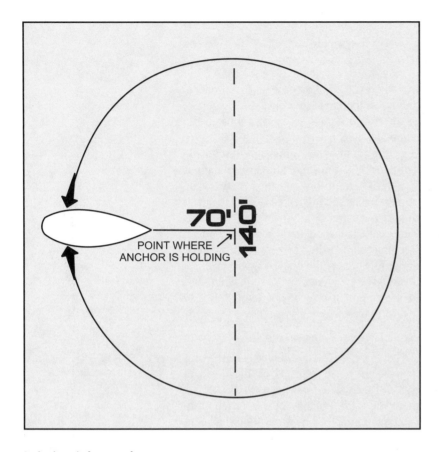

Swinging circle at anchor

may ground (come in contact with the bottom).

Note: Grounding occurs when a boat is left aground and dry by an outgoing tide. Running aground is the act of hitting bottom when in shallow waters; it will be covered in Part Six. If a vessel runs aground on a falling tide, it is in double trouble.

In tidal waters, the scope of the boat's anchor rode may be sufficient at low tide. At high tide, the water will be deeper and more rode will have to be paid out in order to maintain proper scope. It may therefore become necessary to post an anchor watch to correct the scope during tide changes and to warn the crew if, for any other reason, the anchorage becomes unsafe. This rarely becomes a concern on a daysail, as the boat is normally anchored only for a short times such as a lunch break, when there is usually someone on deck to assess the situation.

GOOD HOLDING GROUND

The type of bottom will affect the anchor's ability to dig in. If the bottom is too soft,

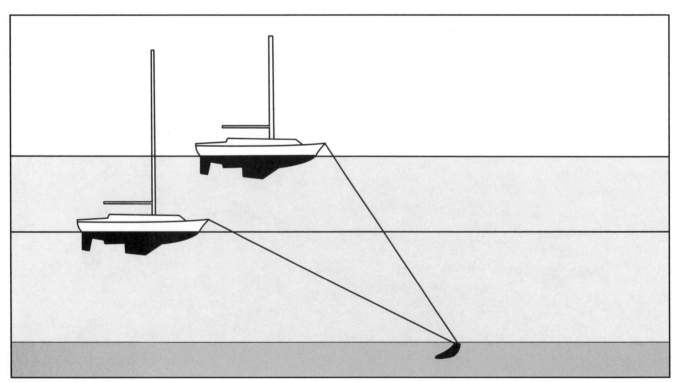

Rising tide reduces scope.

the anchor will just slide through. If it is too hard, the flukes will not be able to grab.

In areas like the Florida Keys, quite often it's a matter of simply looking down through the crystal clear water to see if there is sand, weed, or coral under the boat. Most water, however, is not that clear. Therefore, our best reference is the nautical chart. The chart symbols for a suitable bottom type are

S–sand   **M**–mud   **C**–clay

Chart symbols for usable but less than desirable anchorages are

Oz–ooze (very soft mud or sludge)
Rk–rocks or rocky bottom

Selecting a suitable anchorage is a matter of practice, patience, and wisdom to know when to leave an anchorage before it deteriorates and becomes unsafe. Proper selection, based on the four factors we have discussed, will lessen the chances of anchoring in a dangerous location.

KNOTS

In the Sailing Skills section of this part, we will be practicing docking under sail. Some docks will not have mooring cleats. Therefore it may be necessary to tie to a piling or rail when docking. The **clove hitch** and the **round turn** and **two half hitches** are used to secure a vessel to a piling.

The clove hitch is used for temporary docking or for securing fenders to a lifeline before docking. A clove hitch will undo if left for any length of time. For anything more than a few minutes, secure the clove hitch by making one or two half hitches on the line. But before leaving the boat unattended, always replace a clove hitch with a round turn and two half hitches, which is a more secure knot.

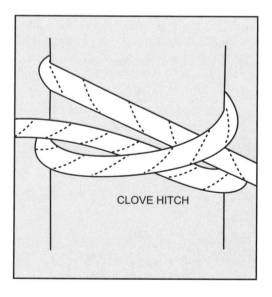

CLOVE HITCH

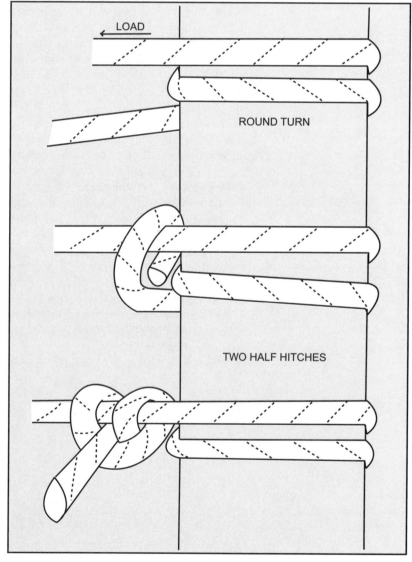

LOAD

ROUND TURN

TWO HALF HITCHES

DOCK LINES AND THEIR USES

The proper use of dock lines can simplify the docking and undocking of a boat and protect the boat during rough weather. Below are the lines necessary for docking.

Bow lines secure the bow to the dock. The inshore bow line runs from an inshore chock to a cleat on the dock. The offshore bow line runs through the offshore chock to a separate cleat on the dock.

Stern lines secure the stern. The inshore stern line runs from a cleat through an inshore chock to a cleat on the dock.

Spring lines are used to control fore and aft motion of a boat at a dock. Spring lines can also be used to aid in maneuvering a vessel for docking or undocking. The forward spring line runs from the aft end of the boat forward to a cleat on the dock. The after spring line runs the other way, from the bow aft (see illustration p. 157). When maneuvering away from a berth, use the after spring line to turn the boat. With all of the bow lines and the forward spring line let go, and the engine put slow astern, the bow will swing away from the dock.

Be familiar with the types of line and the job each is best suited for. The most common types of lines are listed below.

Nylon has superior strength as well as a stretch characteristic with high recovery quality. It is rot and mildew-proof, easy to handle, and highly resistant to abrasion. It is excellent for anchor and mooring lines, although it loses about 10 percent of its strength when wet.

Dacron retains its full strength when it is wet and has only slight stretch under loads. It is as strong as nylon with similar characteristics. It is used for sheets, halyards, and other running rigging.

Polyethylene is made in a variety of colors and has little stretch. Its floatability makes it popular for ski tow ropes and dinghy painters. Polyethylene is adversely affected by heat and friction.

Polypropylene has a higher melting point than polyethylene, is more abrasive-resistant, and not as slippery. It is used for ski tow ropes and where low stretch is important.

Cotton is soft, pliable, and easy to handle except when wet. Cotton lines are used mostly in small sizes for flag halyards and lanyards.

Lines should never be left in a heap, whether on deck or down below. A line is always coiled so it will be ready in a hurry without kinks or tangles. To coil a line, hold one end (or the part near where the line is cleated) in one hand, and with the other hand make two-foot-long loops, which you then drop into the first hand. Don't twist the line as you coil it, or it will kink. When all but the last 4-6 feet of the line has been coiled, finish the coil off by wrapping half the remaining line around the middle of the loops three times, forming a figure-8. Then push the bight (middle) of the remainder through the top hole in the open "8" and pull the bight over the top, and slide it to the middle again. Tighten it and hang the coil up with the remaining bit of line.

REVIEW QUESTIONS

I. Soundings are measured in units of _____, _____, and _____. Soundings are being converted to the metric system and will be given in _____ in the future.

2. When entering a harbor, green buoys are kept to which side?
a) port
b) starboard

3. A junction buoy indicates where a river or channel
a) crosses the road.
b) stops.
c) splits into two routes.

4. Identify what each of the following buoys means:

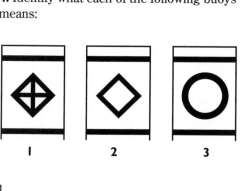

1. _____

2. _____

3. _____

5. Label the three parts of the ground tackle.

6. list two functions of the chain in the ground tackle system.

a) _____

b) _____

7. What are four prerequisites of a good anchorage?

a) _____

b) _____

c) _____

d) _____

8. What is the best kind of rope to use for

a) dock lines _____

b) sheets _____

c) anchor rodes _____

d) halyards _____

e) ski tow lines_____

9. Spring lines are used to control the _____ and _____ motion of a boat at a dock. Spring lines can also be used to aid in _____

Answers in Appendix A, p. 201.

SAILING SKILLS

ANCHORING

Anchoring is an art. The helmsman and crew have to orchestrate their efforts with the wind, current, and vessel. Earlier in this part, we looked at the anchor and the anchorage. By the end of this exercise, you should be able to select a suitable anchorage, set the anchor with a scope of 7:1, retrieve the anchor, and properly stow the ground tackle.

To check whether the anchor is dragging, take simple sightings on objects ashore or observe the relative position of other boats in the anchorage. Use a compass to take bearings. If the bearings begin changing, your anchor is dragging. For more on how to handle a boat that is dragging anchor, see Part Six, Running Aground and Other Nuisances.

Another way to determine if an anchor is dragging is to place your hand on the rode. If it is bounding, the anchor is dragging over the bottom. The vibrating of the rode indicates that the anchor is skipping over the bottom.

EXERCISE: **VESSEL AND CREW PREPARATION**

1. The crew takes down the jib and clears it from the foredeck. This will give the crew room to work on the foredeck and will prevent the sail from being damaged when the anchor is raised and lowered. It also keeps the crew from slipping on the sail.

2. The crew then lays the anchor on the foredeck.

3. The end of the rode not attached to the anchor-the bitter end-is then tied around the mast. This is to prevent the ground tackle from being lost overboard should the crew lose control of it.

4. The rode is then coiled into a basket or onto the foredeck to make sure that there are no snags or tangles when the rode pays out.

A coiled line will invariably knot and tangle unless it is properly flaked, or laid out on deck in long loops. This reduces the tendency of the anchor rode to snarl.

5. One crew member positions himself to signal the helmsman when the anchor is on the bottom.

6. When the deck is clear, the anchor rode is flaked, and everyone is prepared, the helmsman makes a first approach to the selected anchorage. The helmsman and crew survey the site: the number of boats already in the anchorage, location of docks and channels, and overall suitability.

The helmsman should not attempt to anchor on this first pass. Once the skipper is sure the anchorage has shelter, swinging room, sufficient water depth, and good holding ground, the final approach can be planned. After the first approach is complete, the helmsman heads the boat back into open water and turns to make the final approach.

The rode should be carefully coiled so it does not kink when running out.

EXERCISE: **THE FINAL APPROACH**

The anchoring technique is the same whether the boat is under sail or power. If under power, simply reverse the engine (see Part Five, p. 159) instead of backing the mainsail.

If there is any confusion, or if the anchoring is not going well, the helmsman can abort the final approach and return for another try. It is better to start again than to try to salvage a poor situation.

1. The helmsman steers on a close reach course to a point two or three boat lengths downwind of the spot selected.

2. At this point, the helmsman heads the boat directly into the wind to stop its forward motion. This is different from the stopping drills previously practiced.

3. As the boat stops (and not before), the crew should lower-not throw-the anchor. As the anchor is being lowered, the crew backs the boat down by backing the mainsail.

4. As the boat drifts backwards, one crew member continues to ease the anchor rode. The others will indicate to the helmsman in which direction the anchor is lying in order to keep the helmsman backing the boat directly away from the anchor.

5. The boat should drift backwards after the anchor is on the bottom.

6. When a scope of 4:1 is reached, the crew snubs the rode around the deck cleat to set (dig in) the anchor.

7. Once the anchor has been set, the crew continues to pay out the rode until a scope of 7:1 is reached.

8. Once the scope is let out, tug on the anchor line to make sure that the anchor is secured to the bottom. Then secure to the deck cleat.

9. Once the crew is certain the anchor has been properly set, the mainsail will be lowered to prevent the boat from sailing.

A

C

D

To anchor, this bow crew, A. points the bow into the wind and drops the jib, B. secures the halyard, C. folds and removes the jib from the deck, D. carefully lowers the anchor into the water and E. pays out rode while the helmsman backs the boat.

EXERCISE: **RECOVERING THE ANCHOR**

1. Before raising the anchor, raise the mainsail, for once the anchor breaks free of the bottom, the boat has to be able to maneuver. Even if the boat will be maneuvered under power, it is wise to have the mainsail hoisted in case the engine fails.

2. The crew then leads the anchor rode to a winch and wraps it around three or four times. With the foredeck crew guiding the helmsman toward the location of the anchor with hand signals, the crew winches the rode and anchor aboard.

3. As the anchor breaks free, the helmsman bears away and sails to open water, while the crew coils or flakes and stows the ground tackle. The crew should dunk the anchor repeatedly to clean any mud or clay from its flukes. Mud is difficult to clean from the deck and sails, and it may be tracked into the cabin if the crew is not careful.

HEAVING TO

It is sometimes necessary to stop a boat in order to make repairs, fix meals, or reef the sails (see Part Six, Reefing Systems). **Heaving** to is a technique for laying a boat across the wind so that it makes slow progress to leeward. The major safety concern when hove to is to check that there are no obstructions to leeward in your path of drift.

Once the boat is hove to, the jib will be backed (trimmed on the windward side of the boat), the mainsail will be either luffing or partially luffing and the tiller will be lashed to the leeward side of the vessel.

With the tiller to leeward, the boat tends to steer into the wind. As the boat heads up, the wind catches the backed jib and pushes the bow away from the wind. These two actions cancel each other, and the net result is a slow zigzag course with very little progress.

EXERCISE: **HEAVING TO**

The maneuver and commands for heaving to are similar to those for coming about.

1. With the command "Ready to heave to, PP the helmsman instructs the crew to prepare. When ready, the crew responds "Ready."

2. The helmsman brings the boat about with the command "Hard alee," as the tiller is pushed to the leeward side of the boat.

3. As the bow of the boat passes through the wind, the crew eases the mainsail but leaves the jib sheeted to weather.

4. As the boat slows, the helmsman pushes the tiller to the new leeward side of the boat. This causes the bow to head toward the wind. With the jib backed, the motion will be stopped and the boat successfully hove to. A little trimming of the mainsail might be regained to balance the boat and provide a little headway.

TO GET UNDER WAY AFTER HEAVING TO:

5. The crew releases the windward jib sheet.

6. The helmsman centers the tiller or wheel.

7. The crew trims the mainsheet.

Repeat the maneuver until everyone on board understands the procedure.

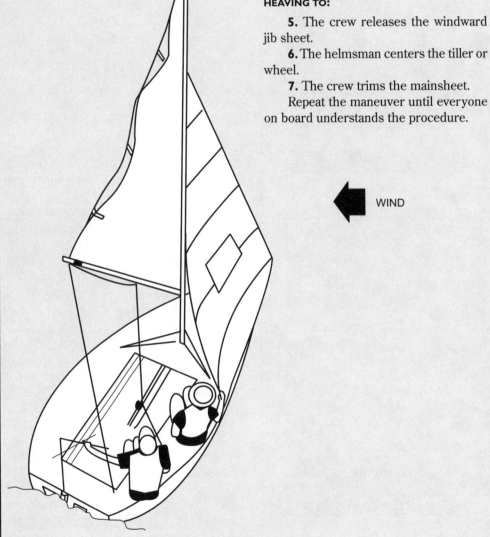

WIND

Hove to

DOCKING UNDER SAIL

Docking under sail requires the same reaching approach as picking up a marker (Part Four) or the man overboard drill (Part Three). It also requires the same control of boat speed. Remember that a boat under sail has no brakes. The momentum of the boat will continue to carry it forward even after the sails have been eased and are luffing.

Wind and current are determining factors in whether to approach the dock on a close reach or broad reach. If the slip is upwind, the approach will be easier than if the slip is crosswind or downwind. Let us first concentrate on the easier approaches. Techniques learned in the early exercises will make the more complicated situations easier to handle.

As a precaution, the end of the slip should be padded with a fender or rubber bumper. Even veteran sailors misjudge distances, and accidents do happen. It is easier to repair a damaged ego than the bow of a sailboat.

CREW PREPARATION

Before you approach the dock, dock lines must be secured to the cleats on the boat and led through the appropriate chocks. Using a beam spring line (as opposed to a bow or stern line) will allow a boat to stop at a dock or in a slip without the bow being pulled into the dock.

The crew, positioned on the sidedecks outside the lifelines and holding onto the shrouds, should be prepared to step ashore. This is normally the safest position for stepping onto or off the boat because it

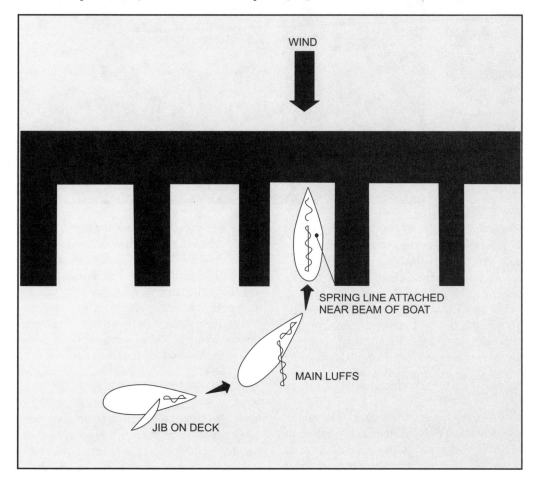

Docking in a slip under sail

WIND

SPRING LINE ATTACHED
NEAR BEAM OF BOAT

MAIN LUFFS

JIB ON DECK

On first approaching a dock, A. the jib comes down, B. the boat sails toward the dock on a close reach and C. the mainsheet is eased allowing the mainsail to luff and slow the boat. Bow crew prepares to step onto the dock from the boat's beam.

is the widest point of the boat (and therefore nearest the dock) and the shrouds provide excellent handholds.

It is important when docking to use chocks or blocks and cleats as well as good nylon line. Big waves or heavy winds when you are off the boat can break lines or pull the boat away from the dock if it is not secured correctly. Avoid using lifelines or running rigging to tie a boat up.

DOCKING IN A SLIP

A slip is just an enclosed dock. The enclosure creates a complication. If he makes an error in judgment while approaching an open dock, the helmsman can turn the boat back into open water and try again. When approaching a slip, however, the helmsman is faced with a dead-end street and nowhere to go. Forward motion can be slowed by backing the mainsail or by zigzagging through the water. Any turning motion slows the boat, and repeated turning (zigzagging) before entering the slip is an excellent method for reducing speed.

The only time a boat should be docked when heading downwind is in a slip. On a dock, it is a simple matter of approaching from the opposite direction to overcome an unfavorable wind. And the only way to dock safely in a downwind slip is to take all of the sails down before turning the boat down-

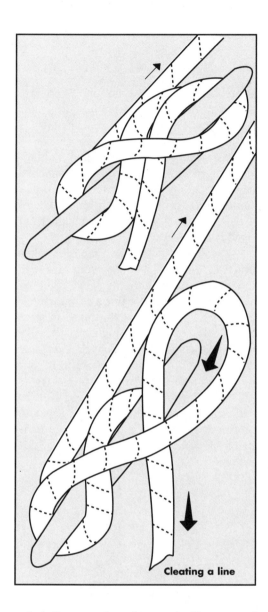

Cleating a line

EXERCISE: **DOCKING UPWIND (no current)**

Practice this first exercise approaching a pier, as opposed to a slip, to allow yourself greater escape possibilities. Winds in and around docks can be affected by buildings and land masses and will challenge the helmsman more than winds in open water. So, make a pass at the dock to determine how the wind is blowing off the dock and whether there are any drastic changes in wind direction. Then make a second approach to complete docking.

1. As with all other boat-stopping exercises, the helmsman, for control, approaches the dock on a close reach under mainsail alone.
2. The crew luffs the mainsail two or three boat lengths from the dock. If the boat is moving too slowly, the crew retrims the mainsail to accelerate.
3. As the bow nears the dock, the helmsman heads up into the wind, parallel to and at least six feet from the dock. The dock provides a reference point for judging the speed of the boat and the stopping distance required.
4. Just before the boat comes to a stop, the helmsman bears away and returns to open water. The crew sheets in the mainsail.
With the stopping distance of the boat determined, the second approach is made.
5. This time, the helmsman steers parallel to and about three feet out from the dock.
6. Just before the boat stops its forward progress, the crew steps ashore and secures the dock lines to the cleats on the dock.
This procedure will work on all docks where the wind direction is off the dock. If the wind is blowing onto the dock, the procedure is similar however, the helmsman will stop the boat on a beam reach four to six feet from the dock and the wind will carry the vessel onto the dock.

wind. Crew work and control of boat speed become very important during this maneuver.

As soon as the boat turns downwind, it will start to accelerate. A crew member with a dock line attached to the beam of the boat must step ashore at the first possible moment and take one wrap of the dock line around a dock cleat to stop the boat before it reaches the end of the slip. Do not tie off the dock line at this point; let it slip controllably until the boat is fully stopped.

SECURING THE VESSEL

Once the boat has stopped alongside the dock or is in the slip, the crew ties off the bow and stern lines with **cleat hitchs**. The crew then rigs spring lines forward and aft to keep the boat from pivoting in the slip. Longer lines to more remote dock cleats may be necessary to allow lines to stretch in areas of extreme tides. Take a look at how your neighbors have set their lines in unfamiliar areas.

MOORING

A mooring is a buoy connected to an extremely heavy anchor or weight (such as an engine block). Many yacht clubs, marinas, and harbors have moorings where you can tie your boat temporarily or permanently for a fee. Picking up a mooring has three advantages over anchoring. First, you don't have to go to the bother of using your anchor. Second, the mooring's anchor probably is never going to drag. And third, because the mooring's anchor is so heavy and deeply imbedded in the bottom, less scope is needed on the rode and, therefore, the boat will swing around in a tighter radius than it would on its own anchor.

A mooring consists of an anchor, a chain, a mooring pendant, and a buoy. Usually, each mooring has a distinctive mark (generally a number or color) so you can tell one from the other. Moorings are usually located out of the main channel and rapid currents.

Landing a sailboat at a mooring takes practice. Your goal is to stop your boat with the bow directly into the wind right up against the mooring, so that a crew member can take hold of the pendant and secure it to the bow cleat. Moorings are always attached through the bow chock and onto a cleat so the boat swings around it. If your boat sails past the mooring, do not try to hold onto it from the stern. Instead, let it go and sail around until you make a better, more controlled landing. The maneuver is much like anchoring. Once again, practice is the key.

EXERCISE: **MOORING**

1. The skipper checks to be sure the boat may be kept at the mooring.
2. If so, the crew lowers and removes the jib.
3. The helmsman approaches the mooring from downwind.
4. The crew picks up and secures the mooring line.
5. The crew lowers and flakes the mainsail.
6. The crew double-checks all the mooring lines and secures the halyards.

SUMMARY

In this part we have learned about planning a daysail. We have studied the aids to navigation and learned how a skipper uses a local chart and Chart No. 1 to find the safest sailing waters.

In Sailing Skills we learned how to anchor and how to heave-to. There is nothing quite like setting an anchor and having lunch off a secluded beach. Heaving-to is a way of stopping the boat so that repairs can be made or so that you can have lunch if you do not wish to anchor or if there is no suitable anchorage nearby.

Finally, we looked at the skills required to dock a boat under sail and secure a boat to a mooring. These are valuable skills for all sailors. Whether or not you have an engine aboard, you will eventually need or want to dock your boat under sail.

In the next part we will begin to learn about cruising.

Basic Coastal Cruising I

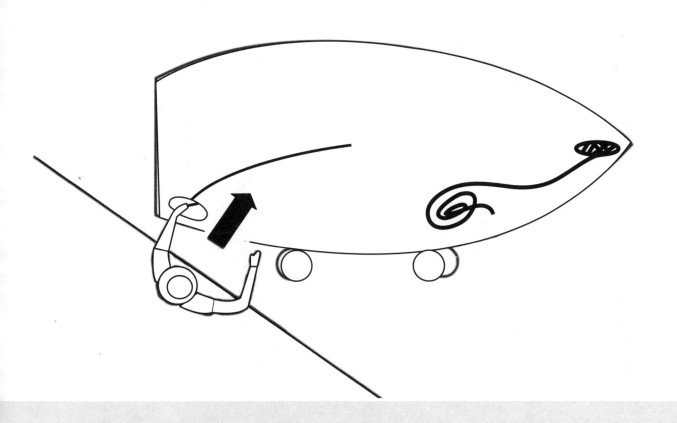

SAILING KNOWLEDGE

The first four parts of this book were designed to teach a person to sail a 16 to 26 -foot sailboat. This part and the next build on that knowledge and introduce the new sailor to some of the skills and knowledge required to cruise a small sailboat.

The word cruise conjures up a different notion in every individual. For our purposes, a cruise is a journey by boat from a home harbor to another harbor or anchor-age. A cruise may take as little as an afternoon or it may take weeks or years.

In this part we will add some new sailing terms. As you prepare to venture farther from home, it is essential to know the language of the sea. When there is a lot of activity on the boat, you don't want to run the risk of misinterpreting an instruction or command. Precise and accurate terms must be learned and used at all times.

TERMS AND DEFINITIONS

A **self-bailing cockpit** is one that allows the water to run out as it enters, automatically. It is no different from the drain in a kitchen sink. The floor of the cockpit is above the waterline of the boat and the **through-hull fitting** is below the waterline. The drains in the cockpit **sole** (floor) allow any water to drain out the through-hull fitting.

Earlier in the book we discussed the purpose and action of the rudder. What we haven't considered is how the rudder attaches to the boat. There are two methods, depending on whether the rudder is suspended from the **transom** (flat surface across the stern) or placed under the boat.

If the rudder is mounted on the transom (as is usual on smaller boats), it must be connected with hinges, like a door. The parts of the hinges are called the **pintle** (the pin) and **gudgeon** (the opening into which the pin fits). Most rudders use a stop just above the pintle and gudgeon to prevent the rudder from popping out. All rudders should have a fixed system. If the rudder is suspended through the hull, it is done so on a post called the **rudderpost.** The rudderpost is an integral part of the rudder and must pass through the hull and into the cockpit. Some boats have swing rudders which tilt up in shallow water. They should be secured in the lowered position.

The tiller attaches to the top of the rudderpost or to the top of the rudder if it is mounted on the transom. A steering wheel

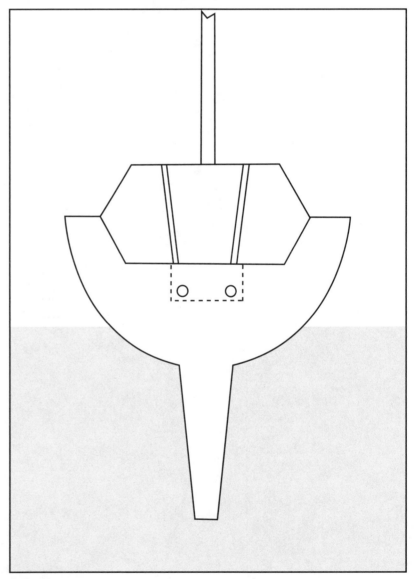

Self-bailing cockpit

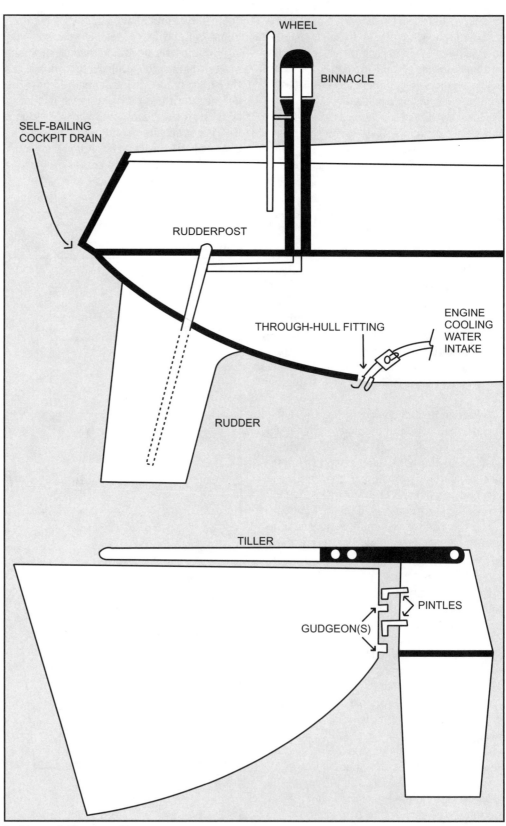

Rudder and tiller assembly

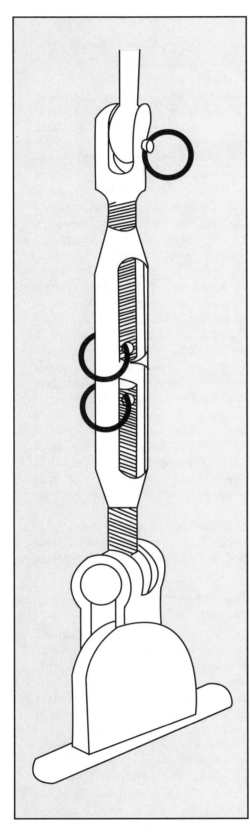

attaches to the rudderpost under the cockpit by one of many mechanical means; however, the top of the post is still exposed in the cockpit as an attachment point for the emergency tiller, if the steering wheel should fail.

The shrouds, forestay, and backstay support the mast. The strong metal fittings that attach these wires to the mast are called tangs. The other end of each shroud and backstay is attached to an adjustable device called a turnbuckle. The turnbuckle allows the shrouds and stays to be adjusted to the proper tension. Proper tensioning, or tuning of the mast, is a subject for an intermediate cruising course.

The shroud and backstay turnbuckles attach to the boat's hull by means of chainplates. These stainless steel straps are fastened securely to the boat's hull and form a secure base to keep the mast standing. The forestay is attached to the stem fitting, an integral part of the bow construction.

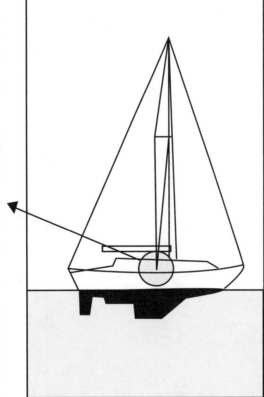

RUNNING LIGHTS

All boats must show the correct lights at night and at other times when visibility is restricted, whether at anchor or under way. It is against the law to sail at night without them.

The **masthead light** is a fixed white light over the fore-and-aft centerline of the vessel. Attached to the mast, it is visible from ahead around to an angle of 22.5 degrees abaft the beam on both sides. A masthead light is also called a **bow** or **steaming light.** It indicates a boat moving under engine power. Note: the masthead light should be extinguished on a sailboat when the engine is not operating.

Sidelights are red and green lights visible on the port and starboard sides respectively from directly ahead to an angle of 22.5 degrees abaft the beam. On a boat under power, the sidelights must be lower than the masthead light.

The **sternlight** is a white light placed as near the stern as possible and visible astern from an angle of 22.5 degrees abaft the beam on either side.

Vessels under 65.5 feet may have sidelights combined in one lantern on the centerline and may have sidelights and sternlights combined in one lantern at the top of the mast, but they may use them only when under sail. Vessels under 23 feet should carry sidelights and a sternlight if practical, though they are not required by law. There must at least be a bright flashlight or other white light aboard, ready to be displayed in order to prevent collisions.

If practical, a sailing vessel less than 7 meters in length shall exhibit the lights described above, If not, however, an electric torch or lighted lantern should be readily at hand and exhibited in sufficient time to prevent collision. This same provision applies to vessels powered by oars.

At anchor, all vessels are required to show one **360-degree white light** unless anchored in a recognized small craft anchorage (see Part Four, Chart Symbols, p. 112).

Most boat manufacturers install lights as a matter of course, and these are usually installed to Department of Transportation specifications.

INTERPRETING ANOTHER BOAT'S LIGHTS

For the new sailor, it is important not only to know what lights should be displayed on a sailing vessel but to be able to interpret the lights on another boat at night. The color and position of lights indicate whether another vessel is under power, sailing, or anchored. The lights also indicate the direction the other vessel is moving-to the right or left, toward or away from you.

Remember, the Rules of the Road apply at night. A helmsman must be able to discern what course another vessel is taking,

Lights that may be used under sail only. Only boats smaller than 65.5 feet may use the combination masthead light.

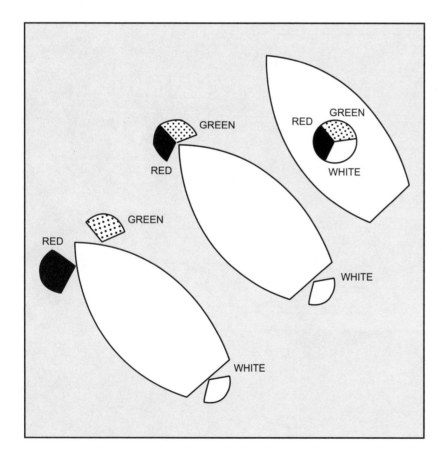

what rule applies, and what action, if any, is to be taken.

Let us look at the lights shown by recreational vessels under 65.5 feet in length. For pleasure boats, there are only three colors of lights with which to be concerned: white, red, and green.

The red light is shown from forward to just past the beam on the port side. To help recall which side is red, try this aid: Port wine is red. The starboard sidelight is green. The sternlight, which completes the circle of light, is white. If a vessel is propelled by sails alone, it will show just these three colors on the appropriate sides of the boat.

A powerboat (or sailboat under power) will show the following lights: sidelights, masthead light (higher than the sidelights), and sternlight.

The above description of required lights illustrates the key lighting requirements for sail- and powerboats. However, there are many other light configurations that apply to vessels of particular types, such as tugs, barges, vessels constrained by draft, and pilot vessels. It is possible to learn a great deal about the nature and activities of an unknown vessel when only its lights can be seen through the darkness. These are fully described in the International/Inland Navigation Rules and should be studied by boaters.

Running lights

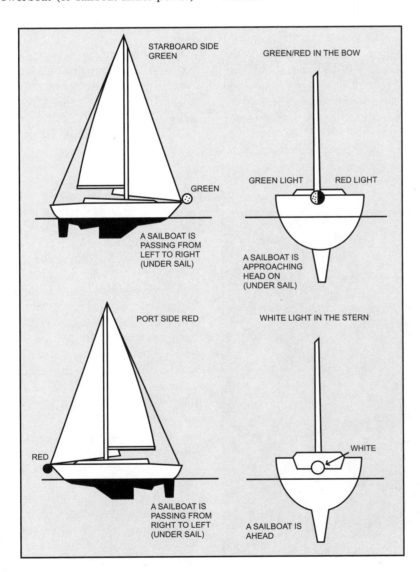

STARBOARD SIDE GREEN

GREEN

A SAILBOAT IS PASSING FROM LEFT TO RIGHT (UNDER SAIL)

GREEN/RED IN THE BOW

GREEN LIGHT   RED LIGHT

A SAILBOAT IS APPROACHING HEAD ON (UNDER SAIL)

PORT SIDE RED

RED

A SAILBOAT IS PASSING FROM RIGHT TO LEFT (UNDER SAIL)

WHITE LIGHT IN THE STERN

WHITE

A SAILBOAT IS AHEAD

DUTIES OF SKIPPER AND CREW FOR CRUISING

In Part Two we discussed the duties of the skipper-the safe operation of the vessel and the safety of the crew. The crew's duty is to assist the skipper in the safe operation of the vessel.

The skipper is responsible for the safety of the crew and must be able to delegate tasks and responsibilities to those who have the capacity to carry them out. Some of the tasks, such as steering the boat, are not necessarily part of the skipper's role, although in tough situations the skipper may want to assume the duties of helmsman.

If a crew member does not know how to do something on the boat, it is the skipper's responsibility to instruct that person in the required techniques. Among the skipper's most difficult decisions are whether to set sail in the first place and whether to head for home when the weather turns bad. Although these decisions may be made after a discussion with the crew, the decision and responsibility ultimately rest with the skipper.

The crew's duty to assist in the safe operation of the boat includes cleaning up dock lines and other boat equipment without being asked and taking a hand in the operation of the vessel. Tending sheets, steering, assisting with the anchor, and cooking, as well as assisting with the navigation, are all part of the crew's responsibilities.

A good crew member will always be invited back for the next sail. One way to ensure a second invitation is to bring along refreshments for an afternoon's sail. A crew member who packs some extra sandwiches, soft drinks, or other staples shows respect for the skipper and owner, who picks up the tab for the expensive parts of sailing.

If the crew pays for some of the fuel or puts money toward the slip fees or other costs, the crew is, in effect, **chartering** the boat. This means that the skipper has to be licensed by the U.S. Coast Guard. Skippers and boat owners should be careful not to get caught in this situation.

BOAT ETIQUETTE

Sailing is more enjoyable for everyone when basic good manners are observed. Below are some fundamental rules of boating etiquette.

- Do not throw any garbage overboard.
- Arrange your mooring before landing; this is easily done by a phone call before setting sail or by hailing people on shore.
- Do not tie up to government buoys or navigational aids (this is a law).
- Anchor in areas that are clear of traffic and away from narrow channels. Many harbors have specific anchorage areas marked by special buoys. Stay clear of other anchored boats.
- Follow the right-of-way rules and stay clear to avoid confusion. Stay clear of boats with fishing lines or boats that are sailing in races.
- Ask permission from the owner or skipper before boarding another boat.
- Always offer assistance to a boat in distress.

The most important thing in sailing is to enjoy yourself.

RULES OF THE ROAD UNDER POWER

A sailboat is only defined as a sailboat under the Rules of the Road when propelled by the wind alone. If the engine is running and in gear, the vessel is considered a powerboat and must follow the powerboat rules. The three basic right-of-way situations for powerboats are:

1. Two powerboats approaching each other should pass port side to port side (give way to the right), just like two cars on the highway.

2. When two powerboats are crossing, the vessel that has the other vessel to its starboard side is to keep clear. When getting out of the way, the helmsman of the vessel giving way must not attempt to cross ahead of the other vessel by speeding up. The best action is to alter course and pass astern or to slow down and wait for the other vessel to pass.

3. When one boat is overtaking another, the overtaking vessel shall keep out of the way of the vessel being overtaken. Thus, for example, a sailboat (operating under sail alone) is required to keep out of the way of any vessel it is overtaking.

Whistle (horn) signals are also required in meeting, crossing, and overtaking situations between powerboats in sight of one another. Although the precise meaning of these horn signals differs depending upon whether Inland or International Navigation Rules apply, the rules are generally similar. Briefly, for Inland Rules:

One short (1 second) blast indicates that you intend to leave the other boat to port.

Two short blasts indicate that you intend to leave the other boat to starboard.

Three short blasts should be sounded to indicate that you are operating in reverse.

Under the Inland Rules, these whistle signals indicate intention, and a response to these whistle signals is required by the other vessel. Under International Rules, these are signals of action (e.g., one short blast means that you are altering course to the right), and no response is required. Under Inland Rules, the response consists of the same signal (e.g., one or two blasts) if the proposed maneuver is agreeable to the other vessel or five or more short blasts-the danger or doubt signal-to indicate that a dangerous situation exists. Under no circumstances should "crossed" signals be sounded (e.g., answering one short blast with two short blasts or the converse).

International Rules require unique signals when overtaking in a narrow channel or fairway. If you are in the overtaking vessel in this circumstance, you must sound two prolonged blasts and one short blast to indicate that you intend to pass the other vessel on your port side, or two prolonged blasts followed by two short blasts to indicate that you intend to pass the other vessel on your starboard side. If the vessel being overtaken is in agreement, it should sound one prolonged, one short, one prolonged, one short, blast in response or, if not in agreement, sound the danger signal of five or more short blasts.

Under both Inland and International Navigation Rules, a boat nearing a bend or an area of a channel or fairway where other boats may be obscured by obstructions is required to sound one prolonged (4-6 seconds) blast. Additionally, under Inland Navigation Rules, a powerboat leaving a dock is required to sound one prolonged blast.

The above sound signals are widely misunderstood and many boaters either fail to use these signals or use them incorrectly. Nonetheless, they are required by the navigation rules and you may be cited for failure to sound them correctly. Moreover, if you do not properly sound these signals and then get into an accident, the failure to observe the rules may have consequences in terms of the liability for damages.

The navigation rules also require sound signals when operating in circumstances of reduced visibility. For example, a sailboat (without engine running) is required to sound one prolonged blast followed by two short blasts at intervals of not more than 2 minutes when operating in or near an area of restricted visibility. More information on sound signals in restricted visibility is provided in part six of this text.

ESSENTIAL SAFETY EQUIPMENT

Sailing is a great way to escape the hassles of the everyday world. People become involved in sailing to gain the freedom and independence of needing only the wind to power a boat. To protect this independence, a sailor has to prepare for almost any eventuality. As we have already seen, the Department of Transportation has prescribed the minimum safety equipment to be carried on sailboats without auxiliary power (see Part One, Federal Requirements for Recreational Boats, p. 27). A prudent sailor would take much more gear to sea.

There are legal requirements as well for safety equipment on boats with auxiliary power. The United States Coast Guard maintains one of the finest search and rescue forces in the world, but there are times when the Coast Guard may not be available to assist a vessel unless there is a life-threatening situation. The required safety equipment enables the skipper and crew to cope with many annoying or potentially dangerous situations.

Here is a list of some of the required safety equipment that should be aboard your vessel:

• **Personal Flotation Devices (PFDs):** the official name for life preservers or life jackets. They are available in a variety of sizes and types. To be acceptable, they must be Coast Guard approved, in good condition, and readily accessible. Here is a brief summary of the various types of PFDs:

Type I (Off-shore life jacket): Type I PFDs will turn most unconscious people from face-down positions to vertical or nearly face-up positions. Type I PFDs come in two sizes to fit most children and adults. The adult size provides a minimum of 22 pounds of buoyancy. Type I PFDs provide more protection than other types, but are bulky and less comfortable. Type I PFDs will keep swimmers afloat for extended periods in rough water and are recommended for offshore cruising where a delayed rescue is probable.

Type II (Near-shore buoyant vest): Type II PFDs will turn some unconscious people from face-down to vertical or nearly face-up positions. Type II PFDs come in several sizes, including infant, child, and adult. The adult size provides a minimum of 15.5 pounds of buoyancy. The Type II is more comfortable than a Type I but does not have as much buoyancy. Type IIs are recommended for inshore and inland cruising on calm water. Use these when prompt rescue is likely.

Type III (Flotation Aids): Type III PFDs are similar to Type II PFDs in terms of minimum buoyancy (although they may not turn unconscious swimmers face up), but are designed for greater comfort. Type IIIs are usually worn where freedom of movement is necessary, such as when waterskiing, sailing in small boats, and hunting and fishing. Type IIIs come in several sizes from small child through large adult.

Type IV (Throwable Device): Type IV Ring Life Buoys, Buoyant Cushions, and Horseshoe Buoys are Coast Guard approved devices designed to be thrown to persons in the water. Type IV throwables are not designed as PFDs for unconscious persons, nonswimmers, or children. Use these only in an emergency. Ring buoys come in 18-, 20-, 24-, and 30-inch diameter sizes and have grab lines. You should attach about 60 feet of polypropylene line to the grab line to aid in retrieving someone in the water. If you throw a ring, be careful not to hit the person.

Type V (Special-Use Devices, Hybrids): There are two kinds of Type V PFDs: special-use devices and hybrids. Special-use devices include boardsailing vests, deck suits, work vests, and others. They are approved only for the special uses or conditions indicated on their labels. Each is designed for the particular application shown on its label. They do not meet legal requirements for general use aboard recreational boats. Hybrid life jackets are inflatable devices with some built-in buoyancy provided by plastic foam or kapok. They can be inflated orally or with cylinders of compressed gas. Inflating a Type V increases its buoyancy In some hybrids the gas is released manually. Others inflate automatically when the PFDs are immersed in water. Hybrids manufactured before February 8,1995, must be worn whenever a boat is underway and persons wearing them are not below decks or in an enclosed space. Otherwise, they are not considered part of the required number of PFDs (see below). Those manufactured after this date need not be worn in order to count toward carriage requirements.

By law, a Coast Guard–approved wearable PFD-that is, a Type I, II, III, or V–must be carried for each person on board. Additionally, if your boat is 16 feet or greater in length and not a canoe or kayak, you must also have one Type IV on board. Life jackets should be readily accessible-not enclosed in the original wrapping materials or in a remote location. Store PFDs in a dry place. PFDs should be fitted to each person aboard. PFDs are important safety equipment and not fenders or seat cushions.

In addition to ratings for type (I, II, III. IV and V), PFDs are rated for buoyancy and a person's size and weight. All rating information is listed on a tag attached to the device. Lay-out all PFDs before getting underway and match them to the people on board.

PFDs come in several colors: red, blue, green, camouflage, and so on. However, from a safety standpoint, international orange is easiest to see in the water, especially in rough seas.

If possible, you and your crew should have some experience in swimming while wearing a PFD.

The safety margin around a boat pulling a skier or other towed device increases as a result of the length of tow line and the rapid speed with which most towing boats travel. Maintain a distance of at least 100 feet on either sided of a towing boat to avoid interfering with the skier.

If your interest in boating expands to include hunting and fishing from a boat, remember that all safety rules still apply. In the excitement of getting off the perfect cast or shot, hunters and fisherman might feel the urge to move into unbalanced positions. Always remain seated.

Studies estimate that as many as 80 percent of boating fatalities could have been prevented if the victims had been wearing PFDs. Make it a policy to wear a PFD whenever there is any risk of falling overboard. Nonswimmers, children, physically challenged, and elderly persons should always wear life jackets whenever they are aboard and not below. In potentially hazardous waters or at night, ensure that everyone is wearing a PFD.

FIRE AND FIRE EXTINGUISHERS

Fire at sea is a frightening prospect. Fire prevention is the first line of defense-for example, using proper fueling practices, avoiding stowage of oily rags in bilges, inspection of fuel tubing for proper fit, inspection of all electrical systems for poor connections and bare wires that could cause a short circuit. But fire extinguishers are essential if prevention measures fail. Fires are subdivided into three major classes: Class A-ordinary combustible material, such as paper or wood; Class B-gasoline, oil, grease, and other flammable liquids; and Class C-electrical fires. Fire extinguishers are also classified in terms of their suitability of use for the various classes of fires. For example, carbon dioxide is suitable for use on all three classes of fires. Water is only suitable for use against Class A fires.

MINIMUM NUMBER OF FIRE EXTINGUISHERS REQUIRED

Vessel Length	No Fixed System	Approved Fixed System
Less than 26 feet	1 B-1	None
26 feet to under 40 feet	2 B-I or 1 B-II	1 B-1
40 feet to 65 feet	3 B-I, or 1 B-II and 1 B-I	2 B-I or 1 B-II

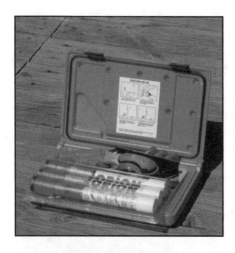

Safety equipment: running light, bell, air horn, PFD, throwabe cushion, fire extinguisher, flares

Fire extinguishers must be Coast Guard approved, in serviceable condition, and mounted in fixed brackets.

Fire extinguishers come in two basic types of canister: portable and approved fixed systems (for machinery spaces). Portable systems are further classified among type and size. A B-I extinguisher, for example, contains 4 pounds of carbon dioxide or 2 pounds of dry chemical or 2.5 pounds of Halon. A B-II extinguisher contains 15 pounds of carbon dioxide or 10 pounds of dry chemical or 10 pounds of Halon. Required fire extinguishers for powerboats (including sailboats equipped with auxiliary engines) depend upon the vessel length and whether or not an approved fixed system is installed. The table on p. 145 provides a brief summary of the minimum requirements.

Fire extinguishers should be checked frequently to ensure that they are properly stored, are undamaged, have adequate pressure, and (in the case of Halon or carbon dioxide extinguishers) have appropriate weight. Do not "try out" an extinguisher to see if it will work. If an extinguisher has been discharged, replace or refill it promptly.

Fire Preparedness

All crew and guests aboard should know the location of and how to use all fire extinguishers and should inform the skipper whenever a fire or related symptoms occur (e.g., heat, the smell of burning wire insulation, smoke). You should conduct periodic fire drills to ensure that your crew are ready to help if necessary

In the event of fire, get everyone into PFDs (in case evacuation is required). Stop the boat immediately if possible; wind from the boat's motion could fan the flames. Position the boat so that the fire is downwind if possible (e.g., head the bow into the wind if the stern is on fire). If time permits, instruct a crew member to get on the radio to advise rescue authorities of the boat's problem and position. React quickly and decisively to attempt to put out the fire. Fire extinguishers usually have a device (locking pin) to keep them from being discharged accidentally. Remove the locking pin, point the nozzle at the base of the fire, and squeeze the handle to discharge the contents while sweeping the nozzle from side to side. Be careful. Smoldering materials may ignite. Dunk cushions and other smoldering materials on the downwind side of the boat to prevent reignition. If the fire is controlled and rescue authorities have been contacted by radio, make sure that you call to let them know that help is no longer required.

If fire starts in the engine compartment, shut off fuel to the engine(s) and discharge the fixed engine-fire-suppression system (if not automatic). Do not open engine hatches immediately, as a fresh supply of oxygen may restart the fire. After an engine fire is extinguished, do not attempt to restart the engine(s) without a careful assessment of the possible cause of and damages resulting from the fire.

If it appears that the fire cannot be controlled, prepare to abandon ship. Account for all persons aboard, ensure they are all wearing PFDs. Break out a life raft or tender if available, and depart the vessel.

• A **horn, whistle, or bell,** audible for one mile, must be carried on all vessels over 39.4 ft. but less than 65.5 ft.

• Vessels less than 12 meters (39.4 ft.) need not carry a whistle, horn, or bell. However, the navigation rules require sound signals to be made under certain circumstances, and you should carry some means for making an efficient signal.

• A vessel operating at night must show the required **running lights.**

• **Visual distress signals** (flares) suitable for day and night must be carried on all boats in coastal waters.

The two most common types of flares are, aerial and hand-held. Both types burn at high temperatures to produce brilliant light and smoke. Avoid injury and damage to the boat by holding or launching flares downwind and away from the boat.

SAFETY EQUIPMENT RECOMMENDED BY ASA AND USCGAUX

The ASA and USCGAUX recommend that boats heading out on long cruises or into rough weather carry the following equipment. Of course, some of this gear-flashlights, for example-should be on any boat that is used for cruising.

Anchors: A well-equipped cruising boat should carry two anchors with no less than 200 feet of cable, rope, or chain on each. When the usual means of propulsion on a sailboat-the wind or motor-fails, it may be necessary to stop the movement of the boat. A vessel can be easily carried onto a lee shore by waves and current, even after the wind has stopped blowing. A well-set anchor will prevent a boat from going aground. The second anchor may be slightly smaller than the first. A lighter anchor is often used if the boat is only stopping briefly, perhaps for lunch.

One anchor is not enough to hold a boat in very strong winds, so a second anchor should always be carried to be set as a reserve. On a cruising boat the anchor should be stowed neatly on deck. If an anchor is stowed below deck or in a cockpit locker, it must be easily accessible in an emergency and, therefore, should not be stowed under sails or other gear. Anchor rodes must be kept neatly coiled or flaked into a basket.

Bailer or manual bilge pump: Boats tend to collect water in the bilge (lowest part of the hull) from rain, condensation, or from stray waves that find their way into the cabin. Although a plastic bucket will serve as a bailer, a hand-operated bilge pump is required to remove large quantities of water in a short time. Two buckets should always be carried as a backup.

Flashlight and extra batteries: A flashlight is invaluable for looking into dark corners or for illuminating the sails at night. The flashlight should have a focused beam for distances and be rubberized to protect it from corrosion. Spare batteries and light bulbs should be kept in a safe, dry place. Plastic Ziploc bags are great for storing small items that have to be kept dry.

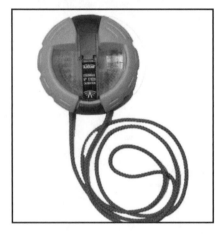

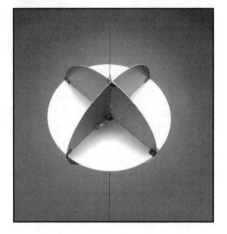

VHF marine radio, bulk-head-mounted compass, hand bearing compass, radar reflector, tool kit

First aid kit. A good first aid kit is needed for dealing with common problems, among them sunburn, scrapes, bruises, minor burns from the galley stove, seasickness, and bug bites. Here is a minimum inventory.

first aid manual
adhesive bandages in various sizes
3-inch sterile pads
triangular bandages
1-inch and 3-inch rolled bandages
tweezers and blunt scissors
cotton balls or cotton wool
antiseptic
sun screen (min. SPF15)
calamine lotion
motion sickness pills (or scopolamine patches)
aspirin or substitutes
eyewash cup

Tool kit and spare parts: Every boat should have a tool kit and spare parts. The kit should contain:

large and small screwdrivers
Phillips screwdriver
wrench for every type of fastening, nut, or bolt on the boat
sailmaker's needle and thread to sew sails and lines
sail ties
coil of nylon line
assorted shackles, nuts, bolts, and screws
vice grips
hammer
sharp knife and sharpening tool (a seaman's best friend)
high-quality duct (silver) tape
lubrication spray
hacksaw and several sharp blades

Tools should be kept well lubricated with spray to prevent rust.

Navigation charts and equipment: Even for a short daysail in familiar waters, it will be necessary to refer to a large-scale (the most detailed) chart of the area to determine the location of any hazards (see Part Four, Chart Symbols, p. 112). The latest editions should be kept on board and these should be corrected with information from the *Local Notices to Mariners,* published by the Coast Guard. Buoys and other ATONs are sometimes relocated, navigational hazards are discovered, and other pertinent information may have changed since the chart was issued. In addition to charts, a copy of the local *Coast Pilot,* Chart No. 1 (the chart symbols), and the *Light List* should be on board at all times. These publications are available from stores that sell charts and other navibation books. Also carry a compass!

Other safety items:

Soft wood plugs, tapered and of various sizes to plug any leaky valve or through-hull fitting.

A **VHF radio** to receive weather reports, to transmit emergency information, and for general ship-to-ship and ship-to-shore communications. At the very least, a boat should have an inexpensive weather radio.

An Emergency Position Indicating Radio Beacon (EPIRB) is a small, battery-powered radio transmitting buoylike device. When activated by immersion in water or a manual switch, an EPIRB transmits a distress signal that can be detected by SAR units, which can increase the speed of location and rescue. The recently introduced 406 MHz EPIRBs are more expensive but preferable, due to their ability to transmit a code identifying a database of information specific to your vessel (if the unit is properly registered).

Every boat less than 16 feet long should carry an alternate means of propulsion, such as a paddle, oar, or small outboard engine. Even if this second means of propulsion is impractical for getting all the way home, it can be used to move the vessel to a safer location. Safety often requires moving a distressed boat out of a shipping channel or to shallow water where secure anchoring is possible.

Personal safety equipment:

Safety harnesses, one for each person. One or more for each person on motor cruisers as may be needed when on deck. Wear a safety harness on deck in bad weather or at night. Make sure it is properly adjusted.

Rescue equipment for man overboard:

Life buoys, at least two. One life buoy should be kept within easy reach of the helmsman. For sailing at night, it should be fitted with a self-igniting light.

Buoyant heaving line, at least 100 feet, with breaking strain of 250 pounds. This should be kept within easy reach of the helmsman.

Inflatable life raft, large enough to carry everyone on board. It should be stowed on deck or in a locker opening directly to the deck and should be serviced annually; or

Rigid dinghy with permanent, not inflatable, buoyancy and with oars and oarlocks secured. It should be carried on deck. It may be a collapsible type; or

Inflatable dinghy, built with two compartments, one at least always kept fully inflated, or built with one compartment, always kept fully inflated, and having oars and oarlocks secured. It should be carried on deck.

In sheltered waters the equipment listed below is usually adequate.

Distress flares, six with two of the rocket/parachute type.

Daylight distress (smoke) signals.

Tow rope, of adequate size to tow the boat.

Water-resistant light.

Fog horn.

Name and sail number of the boat should be marked on all pieces of large equipment and on the vessel itself. If you're sailing offshore, display the number and name so they may be easily read from an aircraft flying overhead.

REVIEW QUESTIONS

I. Identify the following parts of the boat on the diagram.

self-bailing cockpit _____
through-hull fittings_____
pintle _____

gudgeon _____
rudderpost _____
tiller _____
turnbuckle _____
chainplate _____

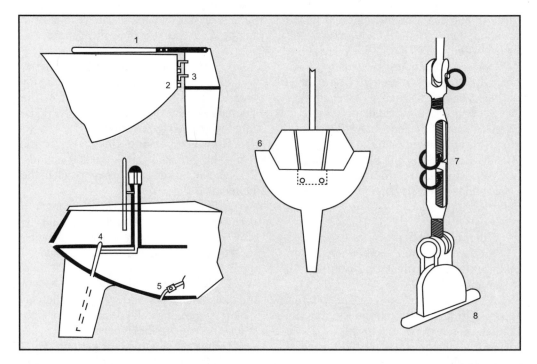

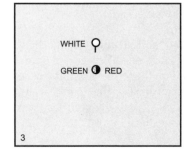

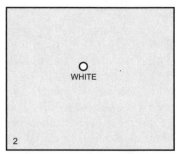

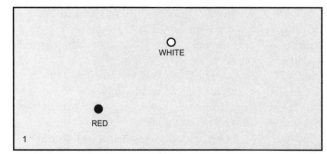

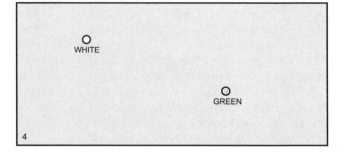

2. In what directions do the lights on the bottom of page 160 indicate a powerboat is heading?
a) left to right _____
b) right to left _____
c) toward us _____
d) away from us _____

3. Circle the vessel that may stand on (hold its course) in each of the following situations and indicate which direction the other boat should turn to avoid a collision.

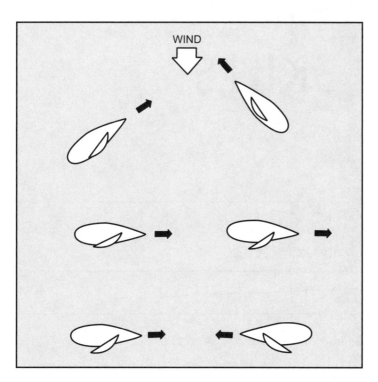

4. Under the Inland Navigation Rules, a power-driven vessel that proposes a port-to-port passage in a head-on situation should sound _____ blast(s). If in agreement, the other vessel should sound _____, if not, it should sound _____.

5. A power-driven vessel nearing a bend or an area of a channel or fairway where other vessels may be obscured by an intervening obstruction should sound _____.

6. A _____ PFD can turn most unconscious wears face-up in the water and is recommended for open, rough, or remote waters.

7. An auxiliary-engine equipped sailboat between 26 and 40 feet in length without an approved fixed fire extinguisher installed is required to carry _____ fire extinguishers on board.

8. Burning oil or gasoline is a Class _____ fire.

9. On discovering a fire in the engine compartment, you should,
a) Ensure that all crew members put on PFDs
b) Stop the boat
c) Shut off fuel to the engine, if possible
d) All of the above

10. Water is only suitable to extinguish a _____ fire.

Answers in Appendix A, p.201.

SAILING SKILLS

As you move up from small daysailers to auxiliary-powered sailboats, you will find that at least a minimum knowledge of out- board motor operation is essential to your pleasure and security on the water.

ENGINE OPERATION-OUTBOARDS

Outboard motors are mounted on the tran- som of sailboats, either by a bracket or in a stern lazarette. To raise and lower bracket- mounted motors follow the manufacturer's instructions.

REFUELING

To prevent a fire or explosion, take the fol- lowing precautions when refueling.

1. Moor the boat securely.

2. Shut off the motor and make sure all passengers are ashore.

3. Don't smoke. Extinguish all open flames and close all windows and hatches.

4. Don't use electrical switches.

5. Don't overfill the tank. Ground (touch) the nozzle against the filler pipe.

6. Wipe up any spills and turn the blow- er on for five minutes.

7. Check for vapor odor; when clear, start the motor and reload your passengers.

Improper maintenance of an outboard engine will lead to frustration and loss of sail- ing time. The proper gas and oil mixture and clean spark plugs go a long way in ensuring the efficient operation of the motor.

STARTING THE ENGINE PRIOR TO
LEAVING THE DOCK/MOORING

Before starting:

1. Check the gas tank by shaking or lift- ing the can to determine how much fuel is in the tank (don't rely on gauges-they have a tendency to stick).

2. Check the fuel line to make sure the 0 ring is in place and intact. Connect the fuel line to the motor.

3. Pump fuel into the carburetor by squeezing the priming bulb until the bulb feels firm.

4. Place the gear shift in neutral.

5. If the motor is attached to a two po-

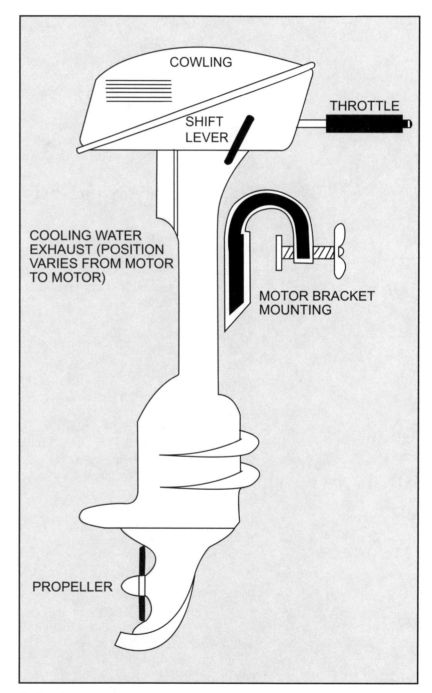

Outboard motor

sition motor mount, make sure the motor is in the down position to allow for proper water intake for the cooling system.

6. Set the throttle to the start position.

7. Pull out the choke.

Starting procedure:

1. Pull the starter cord slowly until you feel resistance.

2. Check behind you to make sure no one will be hit by a flying elbow.

3. Pull the starter cord with a short, quick motion. Do not pull the cord more than about 18 to 24 inches. If the starter cord is pulled too far and too hard, it will eventually be pulled from the starting coil.

4. Once the engine has started and is running well, the choke is pushed in slowly (first) and the throttle turned to the idle position.

5. The engine operator will check to see if there is cooling water flowing from the back of the motor. If not, the motor must be turned off immediately.

6. While the boat is tied securely to the dock, check the transmission by first putting the motor into forward and then into reverse. It is better to discover the transmission will not shift while in the slip or mooring rather than when you're already halfway down the channel.

If the starter cord breaks off, the motor can still be started. Put a figure eight knot in the end of the starter cord and wind it around the flywheel.

TROUBLESHOOTING THE ENGINE

BATTERY AND STARTER MOTOR

- Battery run down. Recharge or start engine by hand.
- Battery terminal loose or corroded. Tighten or clean.
- Battery lead faulty.
- Starter switch, solenoid, or starter motor faulty.
- Starter motor brushes dirty. Clean or replace.
- Bendix gear jammed. Loosen starter motor to free.
- Starter motor not engaging. Starter motor turns but engine does not. Caused by a faulty or dirty Bendix gear.
  Starter motor turns engine too slowly to start it:
- Battery run down.
- Battery lead or terminal faulty.
- Starter motor faulty.
- Engine oil of wrong grade. Drain and replace.

DIESEL ENGINES

Fuel faults: Detach fuel pipe at injection pump to see whether fuel is reaching it. If not, suspect one of the following:

- Fuel tank low or empty. Refill and bleed engine.

- Fuel tap turned off.
- Fuel pipe or filter blocked. Clear and bleed engine.
- Fuel tank vent blocked.
- Fuel pipe fractured or leaking. Repair and bleed engine.
- Fuel lift pump faulty.

If fuel is reaching the injection pump, suspect one of the following:

- Stop control not released.
- Injection pump faulty. Control rod may be sticking.
- Injector faulty. Normally requires expert adjustment.

Warning: The spray from an injector is powerful enough to penetrate the skin.

Mechanical faults:

- Injection timing wrong.
- Compression poor. Normally the result of wear.
- Valve faulty.
- Air cleaner blocked.

Engine stops: This may be caused by a fuel system fault. In rough seas dirt or water may be stirred up from the bottom of the tank, or air may be drawn into the fuel pipe if fuel is low. It may also be caused by a mechanical system fault:

- Valve sticking.
- Governor idling setting incorrect.
- Injection timing too far advanced. Retard.

Engine loses power: This may be caused by a fuel system fault, a mechanical system fault, or overheating. In addition, it may be caused by the following:
- Propeller fouled.
- Stern gear bearings seizing. Regrease.

Engine misfires: This may be caused by a fuel system fault or overheating. Also suspect one of the following:
- Injector pipe fractured.
- Piston ring sticking.
- Valve sticking.

In diesel engines overheating may also be caused by a faulty injector.

Bleeding the fuel system: Air may enter the fuel system of a diesel engine as a result of running out of fuel, leaks in pipes or connections, disconnection of pipes, or changing filters. The following procedure is generally applicable to most diesel engines. However, the exact procedure varies from model to model.

1. Trace fuel pipe from lift pump to fuel filter. Open bleed screw on inlet side.

2. Operate priming lever until fuel, free of air bubbles, emerges around screw.

3. Open bleed screw on outlet side of filter and repeat procedure above.

4. Trace fuel pipe to injection pump. Open bleed screw and repeat procedure above.

If the engine runs for a few minutes and then stops, there is probably still air in the system, so the whole procedure must be carried out again. If there is air in the system, the engine may in fact run satisfactorily until stopped, then fail to start.

GASOLINE ENGINES

Fuel faults: Detach fuel pipe at the carburetor to see whether fuel is reaching it. If not, suspect one of the following:
- Fuel tank low or empty. Refill.
- Fuel valve turned off.
- Fuel pipe or filter blocked. Clear.
- Fuel tank vent blocked.
- Fuel pump faulty.

If fuel is reaching the carburetor, suspect one of the following:
- Engine flooded. Remove spark plugs and turn engine several times.
- Fuel contaminated with water. Drain fuel tank and clean fuel pipes and carburetor.
- Choke defective. Check valve and cable.
- Jets blocked. Clear.
- Carburetor faulty.

Mechanical faults:
- Intake manifold air leak. Check by squirting oil around intake connections. Tighten manifold.
- Cylinder head gasket leaking. Replace.
- Spark plug loose. Tighten.
- Compression poor. Normally the result of wear.
- Valves faulty.

Ignition faults: Check for spark at plugs. If none, suspect the following:
- Plugs fouled. Clean tip with sandpaper.
- Plug gaps incorrect. Reset or replace.
- Porcelain cracked. Replace plug.

Check for spark at plug leads. If none, suspect the following:
- Plug lead loose or faulty. Tighten or replace.
- Distributor cap wet or dirty. Clean and dry.
- Distributor cap cracked. Replace.
- Condenser faulty. Replace.
- Rotor arm not making contact with carbon brush in distributor cap. Adjust.

Check for spark at HT lead. If none, suspect the following:
- HT lead loose or faulty. Tighten or replace.
- Ignition coil faulty. Replace.
- Contact breaker points out of adjustment. Reset.

Engine stops: This may be caused by a fuel system fault or an ignition system fault.
- LT lead loose. Tighten.
- Contact points dirty. Clean.
- Ignition switch faulty.

Engine loses power: This may be caused by a fuel system fault. It may also be caused by one of the following:
- Fuel mixture too lean.
- Carburetor flooding.
- Valve faulty.

- Ignition timing incorrect. Advance or retard.
- HT lead shorting.
- Propeller fouled.
- Plug leads crossed.

Engine Overheats:
- Header tank low or empty. Refill with fresh water.
- Drive belt slipping or broken.
- Seawater intake closed or blocked. Check that water is coming out of the system.
- Water pump faulty.
- Thermostat sticking.
- Engine oil low. Refill.
- Air in cooling system.

In gasoline engines overheating may also be caused by the following:
- Fuel mixture too weak.
- Ignition timing incorrect.

OUTBOARD MOTORS

If the engine will not start, suspect one of the following:
- Fuel tank empty or supply turned off.
- Fuel line blocked or kinked.
- Fuel system not primed. Squeeze priming bulb until hard.
- Fuel tank vent closed.
- Engine flooded. Release choke, shut off fuel, turn engine over several times, and wait one or two minutes.
- Engine not choked.
- Spark plug fouled or faulty. Clean or replace.
- Throttle low.

If the engine lacks power, suspect one of the following:
- Fuel line blocked or kinked.
- Carburetor out of adjustment.
- Spark plug faulty.
- Engine overheating.

If the engine will not idle, suspect one of the following:
- Spark plugs dirty or faulty.
- Carburetor out of adjustment. Adjust idling speed.
- Fuel mixture incorrect.

If the engine overheats, suspect one of the following:
- Water intake blocked.
- Water pump faulty.
- Prolonged low speed running.

Outboards dropped in the water must be serviced quickly because corrosion sets in within about three hours. If you think sand may have been drawn into the engine or if there is any sign of binding when the flywheel is turned, do not turn the engine over.

1. Rinse motor with fresh water.
2. Remove plugs and dry them.
3. Clean carburetor, preferably with kerosene.
4. Turn engine over several times with plug hole facing downward.
5. Squirt oil into cylinders.
6. Refit plugs and carburetor.
7. Try to start engine.

If engine fails to start, remove plugs and repeat procedure. If all attempts fail, take the engine to a dealer.

HANDLING A VESSEL UNDER POWER

Getting a vessel safely away from a dock or out of a slip involves more than just proper technique. It requires awareness and coordination of the entire crew. A predetermined sequence of events as well as clear, concise instructions from the helmsman will ensure a seamanlike exit from any dock.

Determine the wind's direction and strength. Remember that the wind will push the bow away faster than the rest of the boat. Plan the best route for leaving the dock. Be alert to hazards, especially moving boats.

Before taking a boat away from the dock, review how the boat is tied up. It will be left this way at the end of the on-the-water session.

DEPARTING FROM A DOCK-WIND OFF THE DOCK

When the wind is blowing off the dock, it will push the bow away from the dock. The helmsman takes advantage of this to simplify leaving the dock.

1. The helmsman tells the crew to "Prepare to cast off."

2. The crew removes the spring lines and takes the hitches out of the bow and stern lines. The crew leaves the bow and stern lines wrapped once around the dock cleats to prevent the boat from moving until the helmsman gives the command. When this is done, the crew replies, "Ready."

3. With the command "cast off the bow line," the crew casts off the bow line from the dock and steps aboard at the shrouds, the widest and closest part of the boat to the dock.

4. With the command "cast off the stern line," the crew will cast off the stern line from the dock while the helmsman puts the gear shift lever into forward (slow speed) and steers the boat away from the dock.

5. Both the helmsman and the crew member on the dock should make sure the stern does not hit the dock, and as soon as possible, the crew member should step aboard at the stern of the boat.

6. Once clear of the dock, the crew removes and stows fenders and dock lines in their proper places.

DEPARTING FROM THE DOCK-WIND TOWARD THE DOCK

When the wind is blowing toward the dock, the bow of the boat will be pushed into the dock faster than the stern. Therefore, backing away from the dock will be easiest.

A crew member should always have a fender ready to place between the boat and the dock. It is important to have instantly available one fender that is not tied in place.

1. The helmsman tells the crew to "Prepare to cast off. " Once the spring lines have been cast off, the bow of the boat will start to drift into the dock.

2. When the crew has undone the half hitches in the bow and stern lines and there is one wrap of each remaining on the cleat, the crew responds, "Ready."

3. The helmsman instructs the crew

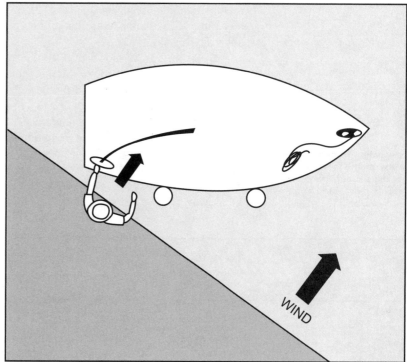

A crew member on the dock casts off the stern line and watches that the stern does not hit the dock.

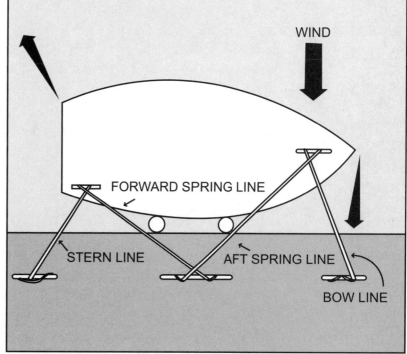

The boat is properly secured to the dock with bow and stern lines, and forward and aft spring lines.

member on the stern line to 'Cast off the stern line." The sailor does this and steps aboard.

4. As the bow is blown into the dock, one of the crew has to move a fender forward to protect the bow from being damaged.

5. As the stern starts to swing clear of the dock, the helmsman puts the engine in reverse and commands the bow crew member to "Cast off the bow line." This time, the sailor on the bow line does not push the bow away from the dock, casts off, and

boards the boat.

6. The boat continues to back away from the dock until it is in open water. At that time, the helmsman shifts into forward and proceeds away from the dock.

DEPARTING FROM A SLIP

1. The helmsman instructs the crew to "Prepare to cast off."

2. The crew releases the spring lines and unties the hitches in the bow and stern lines. Then the crew replies, "Ready."

3. On the command "Prepare to reverse," the crew releases the bow and stern lines and starts to walk the sailboat out of the slip. (Remember to use fenders and lines to protect the boat rather than relying on your strength.)

4. Just before the beam (widest part) of the boat passes the end of the slip, the crew steps aboard on the beam.

5. The helmsman continues to back the boat out until it is clear of the slip.

6. After clearing the slip, the helmsman shifts the engine into forward and throttles up until the boat starts moving forward. Don't turn the helm until the boat is moving forward.

Every sailboat handles differently under power. The best way to discover how a particular vessel will respond in a tight situation (especially in a crowded marina) is to practice in the open water. Boats with inboard engines turn faster in one direction

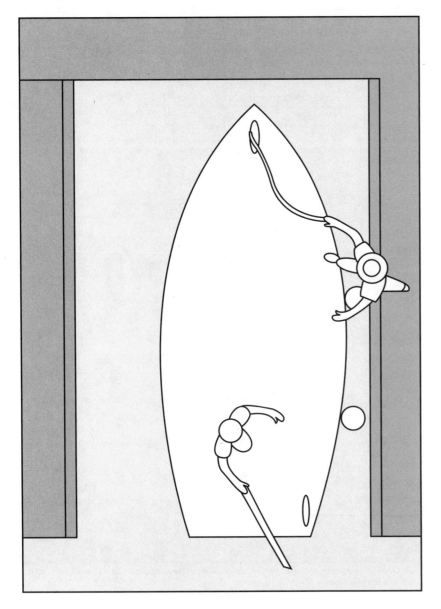

Departing from a slip: A crew member steps aboard at the shrouds (the most stable part of the boat) as he casts off.

EXERCISE: **POWER**

The purpose of this exercise is to gain a feel for the boat's movement through the water. It will also show how the boat responds to easy and abrupt turns.

1. In open water, clear of other boats, bring the boat up to half speed.

2. First turn the boat to starboard, straighten it out, and then slowly turn to port.

3. Repeat the exercise, this time at full throttle.

EXERCISE: **FIGURE EIGHT AT HALF THROTTLE AND FULL THROTTLE**

The purpose of this exercise is to illustrate the area required to turn a vessel to port and to starboard. You will find the turning radius increased and stability reduced (resulting in increased heeling) as your speed increases.

1. Using two buoys or markers as in the original sailing exercises, turn to starboard in a complete circle at half throttle.

2. When the boat crosses its wake (the trail from the stern), turn the boat to port, completing a figure eight in the water. You should note if your boat turns better in one direction than the other (due to propeller rotation). This will be useful to know in tight maneuvering situations.

3. Repeat the exercise at full throttle and note the larger turning radius required.

The direction of rotation of the propeller will also have an effect on how well the sailboat stops. If the propeller turns to port in reverse, the stern of the boat will be pulled to port as forward motion is lost.

FIGURE EIGHT REVERSE

Repeat the figure eight exercises in reverse and notice the difference in handling. Be careful to hold the tiller or wheel tightly, since reverse gear puts a lot of pressure on the rudder.

EXERCISE: **FAST STOP**

The objective of this exercise is to determine how long it takes to stop the boat.

1. As the boat passes a marker or buoy at full throttle, throttle down, shift to neutral, then to reverse, and slowly throttle up. Be sure to shift into neutral at very low engine speed, for otherwise the transmission will break down.

2. When the boat comes to a stop, throttle down and shift to neutral.

The helmsman and crew should take notice of how long it takes the boat to stop.

3. Repeat this exercise going upwind, downwind, and across wind. Notice how the wind helps stop the boat upwind and virtually keeps the boat from stopping downwind. Across the wind, as the boat slows, the bow begins to blow away from the wind. The helmsman must keep this in mind when docking in a crosswind slip.

than the other due to the rotation of the propeller. It's important to determine which direction your boat favors.

Although these exercises are designed for beginners, any sailor who steps aboard an unfamiliar boat should use them to test its maneuverability and handling characteristics.

When getting underway, we start from a stationary position and therefore have more control than when docking. In docking we must be prepared before we approach the dock.

The key to all maneuvers under power is controlled speed. The approach must not be so fast that the boat cannot be stopped before it hits the dock, nor so slow that the helmsman loses steerage. As when leaving the dock, consider wind and current when planning the approach.

The stopping exercises were designed to test the distances required to stop a sailboat upwind, downwind, and across the wind. Your are now ready to practice docking at an open upwind dock.

Some docking facilities are designed in

EXERCISE: **LANDING AT AN UPWIND DOCK**

Preparing to dock:

1. Once the sails are lowered, the crew ties dock lines to the bow and stern docking cleats and also readies spring lines. As in docking under sail, a dock line rigged to the widest part of the boat will be used to stop it at the dock without pulling the bow into dock.

2. If the dock is unfamiliar the helmsman makes an initial approach to survey the placement of dock cleats and determine how high the fenders need to be set. This done, the helmsman returns the boat downwind.

3. The crew sets the fenders, keeping one fender free to be quick-ly placed between the boat and the dock should anything unexpected happen.

The boat then makes the final approach:

4. The helmsman approaches parallel to and about three feet away from the dock, while two crew members position themselves holding on to the shrouds, each with a dock line in his hand.

5. The helmsman puts the boat into neutral three to six boat lengths from the point where the boat will be docking. When the boat is about one boat length away, the helmsman steers slightly closer, to within one foot of the dock.

6. To stop the boat, the helmsman shifts into reverse at low revs (otherwise you might lose the coupling or transmission).

7. The crew steps (do not jump) from the boat as soon as it is safe to do so. The crew stops the boat with the after spring, uses the stern line to keep the stern in.

8. As soon as the boat has come to a stop, the helmsman shifts the engine to neutral.

9. The crew centers the boat in the docking space, then completes the cleat hitch on each dock line.

10. Once the boat is secured, the crew secures the spring lines on the dock cleats.

line with the prevailing winds so that the winds blow either along or off the dock. This makes docking easier. Some docks may not be so well designed, and the helmsman may have to dock across the wind or, in the worst case, downwind.

Preparing to land at a dock under power is similar to preparing to land under sail, except that you must lower the sails before entering the docking area. The main-sail should be tied to the boom, but the sail cover should never be put on the mainsail until the boat is securely tied at the dock. If the motor fails, the crew must be able to raise the sail and maneuver out of trouble.

SUMMARY

Part Five has brought us closer to being a skipper-the decision maker. We have learned the care and handling of a sailboat under power. A motor prevents the sailor from being left at the total mercy of the elements. If the wind dies, all we have to do is "hoist the iron genoa" (start the motor).

Learn to take good care of your motor. Always use the proper fuel mixture, warm the motor before putting the transmission in gear, and check the lubrication levels regularly. Do these things and, when you need to use the motor, it will be there to assist you.

Abide by the rules governing the operation of power-driven vessels. Remember, a sailboat under power is a power vessel, whether the sails are raised or not.

PART SIX

Basic Coastal Cruising II

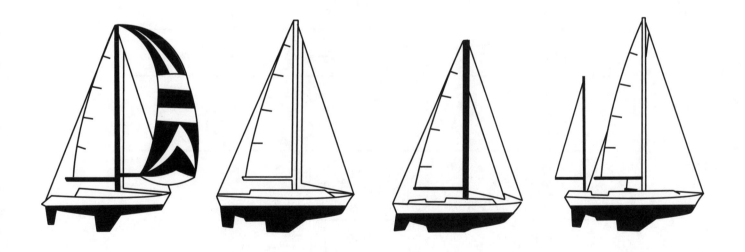

SAILING KNOWLEDGE

As you advance from daysailing to cruising, the boat you sail may change as well. You may move on to a larger **sloop**-rigged sailboat. Others will choose a more traditional rig such as a **ketch, yawl,** or **schooner.** The boat may be of a different construction–steel, fiberglass, or aluminum. The keel may change from the fin shape that we have seen so far to a full-length keel on an offshore cruising yacht.

In this part, we will discuss the selection of sails on a cruising boat. Sails, like tires for a car, come in different designs, sizes, and materials. Cruising sails have qualities different from those of some racing sails, while other characteristics are the same.

The ASA Basic Coastal Cruising standard states that you should be able to perform as a helmsman and crew member on a 20- to 30-foot boat in moderate weather and in local waters. You should be able to anchor the boat, reef the mainsail, change the foresail, and safely negotiate the boat in and out of its slip under sail or power. In short, you should be able to sail.

SAIL SELECTION

Contrary to popular belief, new sailboats are seldom sold with sails included. It may seem strange for a sailboat to be sold without sails, but the selection of a sailmaker is a personal choice.

Cruising sails are usually cut from slightly heavier sailcloth than racing sails, and the seams are reinforced. Racing sails may also be constructed from more exotic and expensive materials such as Mylar and Kevlar.

Sails can be divided into four main categories: mains (and **mizzens**), **foresails** (what we have been calling jibs), **staysails,** and **spinnakers.** We have already discussed the mainsail at great length. The mizzen, the furthest aft sail on a yawl or ketch, is simply another type of mainsail and is handled in the same manner.

The foresails (jibs and genoas) are set from the headstay. The difference between a jib and a genoa is size. A genoa, when it

Different sailing rigs

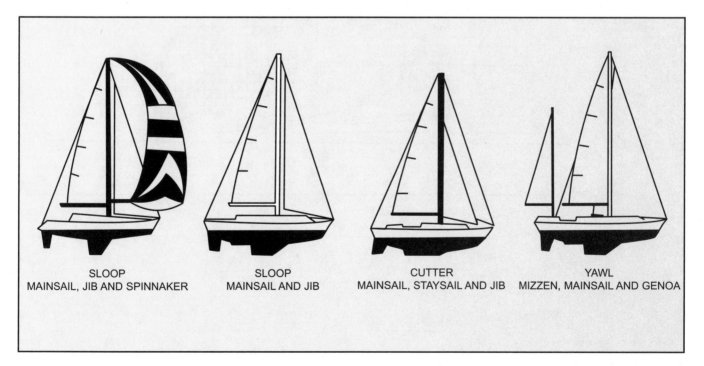

SLOOP
MAINSAIL, JIB AND SPINNAKER

SLOOP
MAINSAIL AND JIB

CUTTER
MAINSAIL, STAYSAIL AND JIB

YAWL
MIZZEN, MAINSAIL AND GENOA

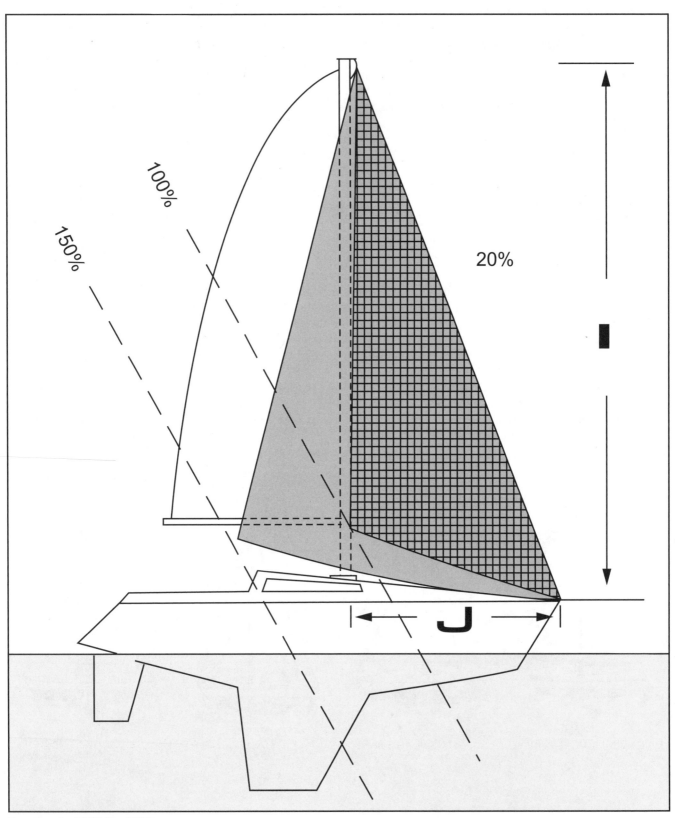

Foretriangle, 100% jib, 150% genoa

100% jib

is set for close-hauled sailing, will overlap the mast, while a jib is smaller and will not. Genoas and jibs are named according to size, and two systems are used. They may simply be numbered 1, 2, 3, etc. (1 being the largest). If the foresails are labeled according to their foot length relative to the distance between the mast and forestay, then percentages are used-100 percent, 120 percent, 150 percent, etc. The number 1 genoa, with the largest overlap, is 150 percent.

Sails are sometimes rated according to how much wind they will withstand without stretching. This is a measure of the strength of the sailcloth used and the construction of the sail. The wind the sail is designed to withstand is usually stronger than the strongest wind in which a new skipper can control the boat. Therefore, a new skipper doesn't have to be concerned with a sail's rating. In strong winds, the skipper should choose a smaller and heavier sail based on the handling characteristics of the boat and the ability of the skipper and crew.

A sloop-rigged cruising sailboat should have a minimum sail inventory of a mainsail with two sets of reef points (see Reefing Systems, p. 173), a regular number 1 genoa (150 to 170 percent), and a working jib (80 to 100 percent). This minimum selection of sails will allow the boat to sail in light winds (using the genoa), while still being able to cope with stronger winds (using the jib and a reefed mainsail).

WEATHER

Armed with some simple facts, the knowledgeable sailor can predict most weather. Thus, the skipper can take appropriate action-in crew preparation, destination plans, and sail reduction-to ensure the safety of the crew and vessel.

WEATHER REPORTS

First, a prudent sailor must know where to get accurate weather information before going sailing. There are many reliable sources for the large-scale weather picture, but local weather forecasting is a matter of being able to read the weather signs. What is experienced at the local weather station or at the airport may not be the same as what you experience on the water.

The primary source of marine weather information is the marine weather bands on VHF radio. Channels W1 and W2 broadcast continuous weather reports, updated regularly every three to six hours. Listen to the VHF before setting out, then monitor it on a regular basis throughout your sail. The broadcast contents vary, but in general they contain:

• a description of weather patterns affecting the broadcast area, including coastal waters

• regional and state forecasts with the outlook for three days ahead

• marine forecasts and warnings for coastal waters

• observations from selected National Weather Service and Coast Guard stations

• radar summaries and reports

• local weather observations and forecasts

• special bulletins and summaries concerning severe weather

• tide reports

Another source of weather information is commercial radio stations. Most stations in coastal areas (including lakes) broadcast a marine weather forecast periodically. The frequencies of these commercial stations and the broadcast times of weather reports are available from a local boating almanac (source of local marine information). Keep the published broadcast schedule on the boat beside the AM/FM radio.

Although no longer required, some Coast Guard installations and marinas at harbor mouths still display storm-warning flags to warn sailors of what to expect past the calm of the sheltered harbor. They have boats on the water reporting local weather that may not be covered in the more general forecasts. Reports transmitted through the local Coast Guard station are often available. Depending upon the size of the station, you may get a recorded message; or you might get lucky and be able to talk directly to someone. Look in the federal government listings in the phone book under Department of Transportation for USCG Weather Information.

If the small craft warning flags are flying, only experienced sailors should go out. The higher wind warnings mean no small craft should sail that day.

All airports have a weather reporting service. Large airports will use a telephone recording, while in smaller communities you may be able to talk to the meteorologist on duty. If this is the case, you may be able to learn some things not included in the official forecast such as an approaching storm front which has just appeared on the local radar. Airport weather information is also listed under the Department of Transportation heading in the phone book.

WIND FORCES

The Beaufort scale is one way to measure and describe the wind velocity. Most U.S. weather reports refer to wind velocity in **knots** - nautical miles per hour.

Beaufort Scale (expressed as "force X" such as "force 5").

0 calm: sea like a mirror

1 light air: Ripples with the appearance of scales but without foam crests; wind 1-3 knots

2 light breeze: small wavelets, short but pronounced; crests have a glassy appearance and do not break; wind 4-6 knots; wave height 1 foot

3 gentle breeze: large wavelets with crests beginning to break, foam of glassy appearance, occasional whitecaps; wind 7-10 knots; wave height 2 feet

4 moderate breeze: small waves, becoming longer; fairly frequent whitecaps; wind 11-16 knots; wave height 3 feet

5 fresh breeze: moderate waves, taking a more pronounced long form; many whitecaps formed (chance of some spray); wind 17-21 knots; wave height 6 feet

6 strong breeze: large waves beginning to form; the white foam crests more extensive (probably some spray); wind 22-27 knots; wave height 10 feet

7 near gale: sea heaps up; white foam from breaking waves beginning to be blown in streaks; wind 28-33 knots; wave height 13 feet

8 gale: moderately high waves of greater length; edges of crests beginning to break into spindrift; foam blown in well-marked streaks; wind 34-40 knots; wave height 18 feet

9 strong gale: high waves; dense streaks of foam; crests of waves beginning to topple, tumble, and roll over; spray may affect visibility; wind 41-47 knots; wave height 22 feet

10 storm: very high waves with long overhanging crests; great patches of foam blown in dense white streaks; the whole surface of the sea taking on a white appearance; the tumbling of the sea heavy and shocklike; visibility affected; wind 48-55 knots; wave height 29 feet

11 violent storm: exceptionally high waves (small and medium ships may be lost to view behind the waves); sea completely covered with long white patches of foam; everywhere the edges of the wave crests blown into froth; visibility affected; wind 56-63 knots; wave height 36 feet

12 hurricane: air filled with foam and spray, and the sea completely white; visibility greatly reduced; wind speed 64-71 knots; wave height 45 feet.

WHAT CAUSES WEATHER

Before we discuss the visual signs that precede thunderstorms, line squalls, or other types of severe weather, we will look at what causes such disturbances. Weather features such as wind, rain, and storms result from the collisions between air masses of different temperatures.

When a warm air mass meets a cold air mass, the result is a low pressure system. Associated with the low is a series of cold and warm fronts. There are distinctive weather and cloud formations related to each of these fronts. For safety's sake, you must learn which ones can result in severe weather.

Weather associated with a warm front: As a warm front catches up with cooler air, the warmer air rises over the cooler mass. The typical shape is a wedge. As the warm air rises, it cools. Moisture in the air condenses and forms clouds along the wedge.

The first clouds identifying an approaching warm front are hazy thin layers (**cirrus**). These indicate that rain will be

Typical warm front

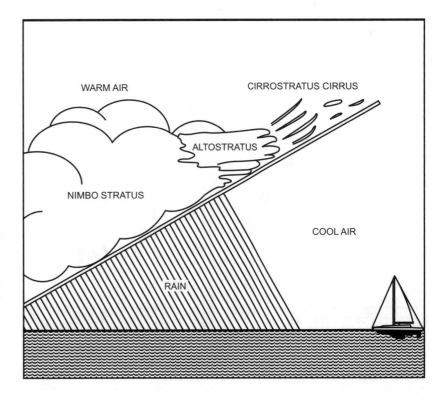

following in less than twenty-four hours. As the cloud layer becomes more defined (**cirrostratus**), the rain is getting closer. With the thicker **altostratus** and **nimbostratus** clouds comes the rain, which is then followed by clear and warmer weather.

Weather associated with a cold front: A cold front tends to produce more severe weather than a warm front. The cooler front forces its way under the warmer air mass. As the warm air is forced up, it condenses rapidly and forms **altocumulus** clouds. These are full and fluffy. As the clouds grow thicker and darker (**nimbostratus** and **cumulonimbus**), the rain comes, and along with it come stronger wind and changes in the wind direction. This weather system can develop into either a thunderstorm or a line squall.

Thunderstorms usually occur along a cold front but can also occur along a warm front. One sign is the formation of large anvil-shaped clouds. There is a discharge of static electricity between the clouds and the earth, causing lightning and thunder. If the wind of the cold front is very strong, it may blow the top off the cumulonimbus cloud before the cloud has the opportunity to build. This results in a quickly passing storm called a **line squall.** The winds of a line squall are short-lived but can be extremely severe. A sign of an approaching line squall is a low rolling cloud. If you see one coming, look for shelter or quickly reduce sail area (double-reef the mainsail) to ride out the storm.

Fog is formed when warm moist air comes into contact with cooler water or land. The warm air may be the leading edge of a warm front. In colder climates (from San Francisco to Vancouver and from Maine to north of Nova Scotia), fog (and rain) on the water are quite common. The colder northern Great Lakes-Superior and Huron-are also very susceptible to fog.

Fog may appear as a whitish haze on the horizon or may form in pockets in harbors and inlets. Fog may fully encompass some sailing areas, while other areas within a few hundred yards remain quite clear.

NAVIGATING IN FOG

In fog the greatest danger to any vessel is collision with either the shore or another vessel. The following procedures are all designed to minimize one or both of these risks. It is also especially important in fog to handle the boat cautiously.

Slow down. As well as giving you more time to take avoiding action, slowing down in a motor boat will also make it easier to hear the sounds of other vessels.

Keep a good lookout. This includes "listening out" too. Every available person should be posted on deck, away from engine and other noise, to look and listen. In particular, someone should be posted at the bow. Sounds can be deceptive in fog; the source of a sound may not lie in the direction from which it appears to be coming.

Make sound signals. For the appropriate signals for a power-driven vessel,

Typical cold front

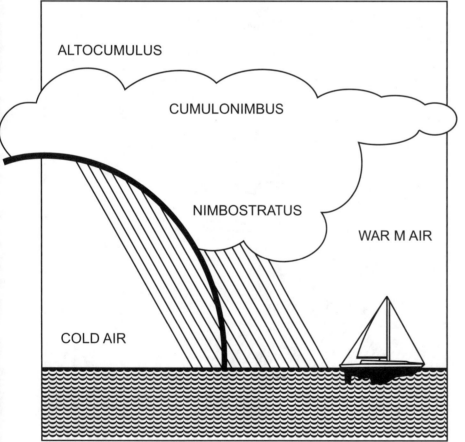

ALTOCUMULUS

CUMULONIMBUS

NIMBOSTRATUS

WARM AIR

COLD AIR

sailing vessel, and vessel at anchor in restricted visibility, see the chart below.

Hoist a radar reflector. The larger it is and the higher it is, the better. In any event it should be at least eighteen inches from comer to comer and not less than twelve feet above sea level. It should be hoisted with one straight edge, not a corner, uppermost.

Keep clear of shipping lanes. If you must cross one, do so at right angles to the flow of traffic. The safest place for a small boat is in water too shallow for big ships. If you find yourself becalmed or moving very slowly across a shipping lane, you should start the engine to get clear of it. Stop the engine at intervals to listen, as you would in any other power-driven vessel.

SOUND SIGNALS IN RESTRICTED VISIBILITY

▬ power vessel making way

▬ ▬ power vessel under way but not making way through the water

▬ •• vessel not under command, vessel restricted in her ability to maneuver, vessel constrained by her draft, sailing vessel, vessel engaged in fishing, vessel towing or pushing

▬ ••• vessel being towed

⬚⬚⬚ vessel at anchor. In the case of a vessel more than 328 feet long, the bell is rung in the fore part of the vessel and followed by a five-second sounding of a gong aft.

• ▬ • warning signal to an approaching vessel made in addition to the signal above

⬚⬚⬚ ⬚⬚⬚ ⬚⬚⬚ vessel aground

It is particularly important in fog to keep an accurate record of your course and distance run and to plot your position regularly on the chart. This means steering as straight a course as possible (use a compass), which is easy to forget when you are concentrating on keeping a lookout.

It is dangerous to get too close to the shore in thick fog, even if you know it well and it is free from outlying dangers. It is often better to anchor and wait for the fog to lift, provided you are clear of shipping lanes and other hazards. If you must approach the shore, do so at right angles to the coast and go in slowly, using the depth sounder. On a shore with cliffs, echoes of your fog signals may also give you some warning of when land is just ahead.

General precautions: All members of the crew should wear life jackets, and the life raft should be ready for immediate launching. Keep some flares ready for instant use to draw attention to yourself if there is a danger of collision with a larger vessel.

VISUAL SIGNS

In the absence of an official forecast or to supplement an official forecast, you can tell a good deal about the likely development of the weather in your own area from the barometer and your own observations. Of course, these layman forecasting methods are by no means infallible.

Barometric pressure. Rapid changes of pressure usually indicate strong winds. A rise or fall of eight millibars (mb) or more within three hours is often followed by a gale, perhaps in four to eight hours' time. A less rapid change of, say, five mb may indicate strong winds of less than gale force.

A falling barometer is a sign of an approaching depression, but the worst of the wind may not come until the barometer has begun to rise again.

> *First rise after low*
> *Foretells a stronger blow.*

Gales with a rising barometer are usually more squally than gales with a falling barometer.

Normal barometric pressures vary from area to area, but if the barometer is lower than normal, and steady or falling, unsettled weather is indicated. If the barometer is high, and steady or rising, settled weather may be expected.

Clouds are useful weather indicators. For a description of seven different cloud types and their implications, (see p. 167-168). Cirrus and cumulus combinations are particularly noteworthy:

Mackerel skies and mares' tails
Make tall ships carry low sails.

In general, lower clouds indicate bad weather. If a lower cloud formation (or the wind) is moving at an angle to high clouds, a change of weather can be expected. When you stand with your back to the wind or oncoming lower clouds and if the upper clouds are moving from left to right, the change will be for the worse; if the upper clouds are moving from right to left, the change will be for the better. These directions are reversed for the southern hemisphere.

Wind direction. As a very rough rule, in the northern hemisphere the wind backs (changes direction counterclockwise) with the approach of bad weather and veers (changes direction clockwise) with the coming of an improvement, although it may not come immediately. The reverse is true in the southern hemisphere.

You can also tell the direction of the center of a low pressure system from the wind. If you stand with your back to the wind, low pressure is on your left in the northern hemisphere (right in the southern).

Sunsets. A bright yellow sunset often means wind, a pale yellow sunset rain, and a pink sunset fair weather. A "high" sunset, when the sun sets behind a bank of clouds, often gives warning of bad weather, assuming the cloud is approaching from the west. Conversely, when the sun's rays light the upper clouds after it has gone below the horizon, the sky to the west must be clear.

Deteriorating weather is often preceded twenty-four to forty-eight hours ahead of time by some or all of these signs, indicating the approach of a depression:
• barometer falling
• feathery cirrus at high altitude (mares' tails), followed by cirrostratus, then altostratus becoming a thick gray sheet of cloud
• wind veering (backing in the southern hemisphere). If the wind moderates rapidly, then begins to back one more time (veer in the southern hemisphere), and the barometer starts falling again, be prepared

for a secondary depression following the first one.

Good weather can be expected to continue when the barometer is high and continues to be steady or rises slowly or when small fleecy cumulus (fair weather cumulus or cirrus) dissolve at high altitude.

Sea fog is formed when relatively warm, moist air comes into contact with a relatively cool sea. In winter and spring the water is normally coldest inshore, so that is where fog forms; in summer and fall the pattern is reversed. Fog also forms over cold ocean currents and where tidal streams stir up cold water from below the surface. Sea fog may persist even in winds of 22 to 27 knots and may not disperse until the arrival of a cold front.

Radiation fog, which forms in damp places inland, sometimes drifts out over the coast, but it tends to lift as it comes into contact with the sea and so it is less of a hazard.

Local winds. Sea breezes occur when the heating of the air over land, often marked by small cumulus clouds, draws in air from the relatively cool sea. Such winds reach their peak in the afternoon and die toward evening. Sea breezes may attain 11 to 16 knots but do not generally occur if the pressure system wind is 17 knots or more. They are a summer phenomenon in temperate latitudes. At night the sea breeze may be replaced by a land breeze, not usually so strong.

Winds tend to be influenced quite substantially by the direction and height of the coastline, being channeled up estuaries or around headlands and often becoming more concentrated in strength. When blowing roughly parallel to the coast, or at a slight angle onto it, the wind often increases in strength within about ten miles of land. This is especially marked on the edges of a high pressure system.

INTERPRETING CLOUDS

Other factors must be taken into consideration when interpreting a cloud formation, apart from the mere appearance of the cloud itself. Do not rely solely on the cloud pattern at any particular moment. Cirrus followed by cirrostratus (see below) often precedes a depression, but cirrus or cirrocumulus may also be visible when a depression has passed and better weather is on the way. Wind direction at sea level, unless it is a sea breeze, is important when interpreting cirrus.

High cloud developments are often not visible because of the presence of clouds at a lower level.

Learn to interpret the following cloud formations:

cirrus (mares' tails): high wispy clouds, often an early warning of bad weather if followed by a buildup of cloud, but wind direction is important. Cirrus dissolving means an improvement.

cirrostratus with a solar halo: a sign of bad weather, especially if it follows cirrus. The larger the halo, the sooner the onset of bad weather.

altocumulus: white and gray, formed in round masses, often partly fibrous. Sometimes a sign of rain, especially when masses break off higher than the rest; these can indicate thunderstorms.

altostratus: a gray cloud sheet formed when cirrostratus thickens. Usually followed by rain, it resembles stratus without its blackness.

nimbostratus with long, ragged clouds (fractostratus) below: may follow cirrostratus. It often accompanies rain and strong winds.

cumulonimbus with characteristic anvil-shaped top: thunderclouds bringing heavy rain and perhaps violent squalls. Such clouds may mark isolated storms or may indicate an approaching front.

cumulus: Small fluffy clouds are a fair weather sign. A buildup of small cumulus over land in the morning may bring sea breezes later. If they grow large, thundery showers can follow.

HEAVY-WEATHER SAILING

Throughout this text we have discussed preparing for each situation and then have built exercises to either simulate or create situations requiring particular sailing skills. Severe weather conditions, however, cannot be simulated in exercises.

In the Sailing Skills section that follows we will preview some routines that should be learned in nice weather so that they will be familiar and can be more easily executed in heavy weather. The keys to being prepared for heavy-weather sailing are practice and routine.

CREW PREPARATION

As bad weather approaches, assuming that it has not been possible to reach a sheltered harbor or marina, the skipper of the vessel will start preparing the crew by assigning the following tasks:

• Put on life jackets and foul weather gear.

• Put on safety harnesses.

• Rig safety lines.

• Reef the mainsail (later in this section).

• Change to a smaller foresail (later in this section) or drop it altogether.

• Stow or tie down all loose gear above and below decks.

• Plot your position on the chart. (This is a subject for the advanced reader and goes beyond the scope of this book.)

REDUCING SAIL AREA AND ITS EFFECT ON BOAT HANDLING

To discover the effect of excess wind on a sailboat, let us return to the simple cat-rigged boat from Part One. As the wind blows into the mainsail, lift is produced. This lift pulls the boat to the side and forward.

As the wind speed increases, there is more power developed than is required to propel the boat through the water. This extra force from the increased wind overpowers the boat. The boat heels excessively and the helmsman now has to pull the

Lift pulls the boat forward.

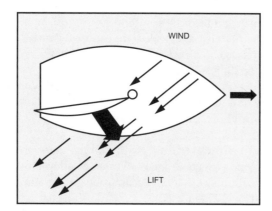

Too much lift creates windward helm and overpowers the boat, causing excess heeling.

The helmsmen is overpowered and uses too much helm to hold a steady course. Note the extreme angle of the tiller.

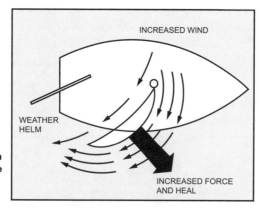

tiller far to windward to keep it sailing in a straight line.

All of this extra force on the sail causes:
• excessive heeling
• weather helm, as the boat wants continually to turn itself into the wind
• added strain on the helmsman, who has to work harder at steering
• added strain on the boat, including more strain on the standing rigging and more strain on the rudder and tiller caused by oversteering to compensate for the weather helm.
• an uncomfortable ride for the passengers and crew. Sailing at an extreme heel is not everyone's idea of a good time.

The quick, short-term solution is to ease the mainsail and spill some of the wind. This works if the wind comes in gusts. If the increase in wind speed is sustained, the remedy is to reduce the amount of sail exposed to the wind so that the boat is propelled efficiently through the water without the added strains and hazards listed above. We reduce mainsail area by reefing.

REEFING SYSTEMS

Looking at the illustration of the mainsail, we see above the tack and clew two reinforced points, the **reefing tack** and **clew.** When the sail is reefed, the reefing tack is secured to the boom by a hook or by a line in the same place the original tack was fastened. What we call the **reefing clew** is an eye, called a **reefing grommet,** set into the leech of the sail. A line called the **reefing line** is led through the grommet, down to the boom, and forward to a cleat (on larger boats, there's a winch to help tighten the line). After the reefing tack is secured, finish taking in the reef by pulling down on the reef line while the sail is luffing. Most cruising boats have two or three pairs of reefing tacks and clews. Each reef shortens the mainsail area by about 25 percent.

After the reef is taken in by securing the tack and pulling down on the leech reefing line, the reefed part of the sail will flap about. To keep this from happening, lead a light quarter-inch line through small holes in the sail, called **reef points,** and around the boom. This line takes the place of old-fashioned short lines dangling from the middle of the sail that you see in pictures of traditional sailing vessels.

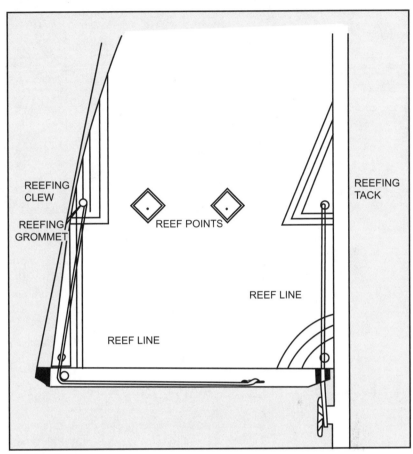

Jiffy reefing

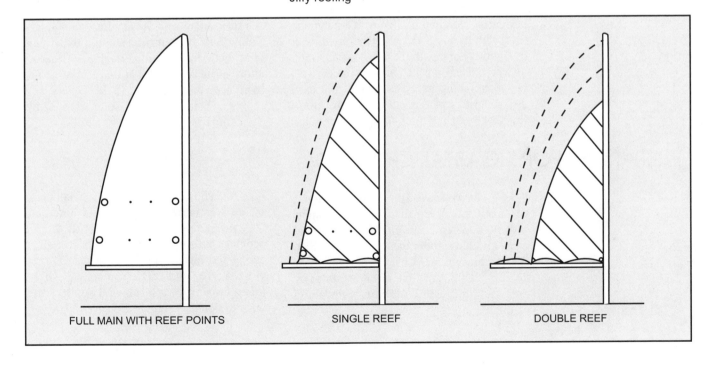

FULL MAIN WITH REEF POINTS   SINGLE REEF   DOUBLE REEF

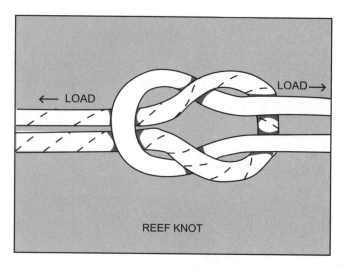

REEF KNOT

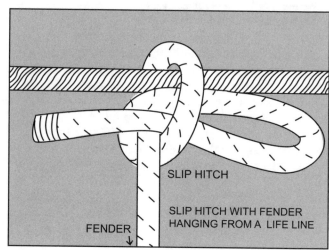

SLIP HITCH

SLIP HITCH WITH FENDER
HANGING FROM A LIFE LINE

FENDER

REEF KNOT AND SLIP HITCH

The reef knot (also called the square knot) is used to tie lines of equal diameter together. A piece of rope through the reef points to secure a sail after being reefed is tied with a reef knot.

The slip hitch is a variation of the reef knot and is not much different from the knot used when tying your shoes. A slip hitch is used when sail ties are nylon webbing, as opposed to rope. A slip hitch is also used on a fender that may have to be moved quickly. When entering an unfamiliar harbor, a fender may have to be adjusted at the last minute. The slip hitch makes this an easy task.

THE MAGNETIC COMPASS

The compass is one of the most important instruments on the boat-if not the most important instrument-because it provides a constant reference point for steering and navigating. Aligned to the earth's magnetic field, with its north arrow always pointing at magnetic north, the compass has 360 degrees clearly marked around the perimeter of the compass card. Around the card are several small posts called **lubber's lines.** The forward, or front, lubber's line lies right over the direction in which the boat is heading.

The compass must be located where the helmsman can see it clearly. In clear weather and during the daytime, most boats sailing near land may be steered by aiming at a buoy or a landmark (an object on shore). But in fog and at night, the helmsman probably won't be able to see any buoys or landmarks, and so must steer by the compass.

PREPARING FOR COASTAL CRUISING

Before you venture from familiar waters, you need to ensure that you are familiar with how to read and interpret a nautical chart and have some basic familiarity with coastal navigation. Coastal navigation is not included in this text, but it is taught by the ASA and USCGAUX in companion courses.

You should also prepare a float plan, which summarizes your planned itinerary, lists the names of persons on board, and provides information about your vessel. A suggested format for this float plan is provided in Appendix B. (You may wish to make up your own form, with some of the information preprinted.) Be sure to leave the float plan with a responsible party (friend, relative, your marina) and with instructions to call the Coast Guard if you do not return at the planned time. (Most maritime law-enforcement agencies-including the Coast Guard-will not act as a repository for your float plan.) Be sure to call this person when you return or if you make changes to the itinerary to let them know that you have arrived safely or changed your plans. Otherwise the Coast Guard or other search and rescue agencies may waste valuable time looking for you.

RUNNING AGROUND AND OTHER NUISANCES

There are three types of sailors in the world: those who have run aground, those who are about to run aground, and those who lie. In 90 percent of the situations, running aground is merely a nuisance and an embarrassment.

Running aground occurs when the navigator misreads the chart, the skipper tries to cut a corner on a harbor entrance, there is **silting** (moving of soft sand and mud) at a harbor mouth, or the tide table is misinterpreted. Running aground can be prevented by avoiding all of the causes listed above, but that is easier said than done.

Listening to the local notice to mariners on the VHF radio (channel 22) will alert a skipper to local hazards such as silting of a channel or **seiches**–changes of water depth caused by strong pressure and/or winds blowing water out of a harbor. Silting is prevalent along the east coast of the United States, and seiches occur regularly on the top end of Chesapeake Bay.

Many pretty anchorages are missed when the skipper of a boat stays in only the deepest water. By all means, avoid running aground on rock and coral-a shipwreck can ruin your whole day. On the other hand, being able to free a vessel after running aground on sand or mud is a skill that all cruising sailors need to acquire and will use.

A vessel runs aground when the depth of water is not sufficient for the draft of the boat. As soon as the boat touches bottom, the helmsman should attempt to reverse direction by coming about or jibing, depending on which point of sail the vessel was on when it started to run aground. This quick maneuver may well save the skipper and crew from having to use the techniques explained below to free the vessel.

Since it is difficult in the short term to make the water deeper (except in tidal water), once you are aground it will be necessary to take other steps, such as:
• heeling the boat
• kedging off, using an anchor
• shifting weight (Put the crew on the boom.)
• taking a tow from another boat
• Waiting for high tide (tidal area only), or
• any combination of the above

HEELING THE BOAT

If sailing off the shoal is not effective, heeling is often a successful solution. When a boat heels to leeward it does not need as much water depth. The skipper of the boat must be quick to assign each member of the crew a job. The largest crew members will all be placed on one side of the boat to make it heel. This effectively reduces the draft and may permit the vessel to be sailed off.

At the same time the engine should be started. A check for lines in the water should be made before the engine is put into gear. This is not the time to add a fouled prop to the predicament.

It may be possible to turn the boat with the aid of the engine until the bow is pointing into deeper water. With the boat heeled and the engine in forward, the helmsman will attempt to drive the boat off the bottom. The helmsman and crew will watch the engine guages to make sure it doesn't overheat. Sand and mud churned up by all the activity may clog the cooling water intake valve. With the sails down and the boat heeled over, it may be possible to motor off in reverse, providing the wind is not too strong.

The boat can be heeled even further by placing some of the crew out on the boom. You can also tie a line into a halyard and secure it to something on shore, to an anchor, or to another boat.

Towing with a bridle (note: deck cleats have been used because the bridle line is too short to reach the mast).

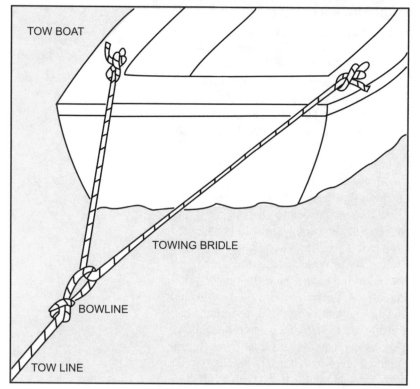

TOW BOAT

TOWING BRIDLE

BOWLINE

TOW LINE

KEDGING OFF

Since an anchor may be used to keep a vessel from going aground in a storm, it seems reasonable that an anchor can be employed to pull a vessel off when it has run aground. This maneuver is called kedging off. To deploy the anchor, row it out in a dinghy. If a small boat is not available, it is possible (but only as a last resort) to have someone swim the anchor offshore by floating it on a PFD or float cushion.

The anchor rode will be led through the bow chock and back to a winch. By winching in the rode, you may be able to pull the bow into open water and refloat the stranded vessel.

TAKING A TOW

When all else fails, the only solution may be to take a tow from a passing boat or from a commercial towing service. Caution must be used to protect the crew of both boats when towing. Don't let anyone stand by the towing line. If it breaks, the recoil can cause severe injury.

The cleats used to tie the boat at night probably aren't constructed or intended to be used for towing. Use them only if you have no other alternative.

Instead, the towed boat should tie one of the dock lines in a loop through one of the bow chocks (or at least under the pulpit), around the mast, in through the other bow chock and then tie the two ends of the rope together using a reef knot or a pair of bowlines. This towing bridle will distribute the towing pull over the greatest area of the boat. The major part of the load will be taken by the strongest part of the boat-the mast.

The towing boat, if it is a sailboat, should rig a line the same way through the stern chocks. A powerboat should attach a bridle around the cabin or at least two deck cleats if that is all there is available. Taking up speed very slowly, the towing boat will then attempt to free the boat that is aground.

The tow line should be attached to the towing bridle with a bowline. Towing puts a great strain on a line, and the bowline knot is easy to untie. Also, the loop formed by the bowline around the towing line helps ensure the tow boat can maneuver properly.

DEALING WITH TIDES WHEN AGROUND

It is easier to get off if the tide is rising. If it is high or falling at a fast rate, speed in getting off is essential. If the boat is stranded by the retreating tide, you should try to make sure, by weight distribution or a line from the top of the mast, that she settles against the uphill slope (if any) of a bank or shoal. The most critical time is as the boat settles on her bilge, when damage may be caused by pounding.

If the tide is flooding (coming in) when the boat goes aground, an anchor should be set offshore to keep the boat from going further aground. The crew can just sit until the boat is refloated by the tide.

If aground on an ebb tide (tide going out), and all attempts to free the boat have failed, follow these steps:

1. An anchor is set further offshore to keep the boat from going further aground.

2. The crew pads the side of the hull to protect against damage if the bottom uncovers (dries) at low tide.

3. The navigator or skipper reads the tide tables to determine when the tide will come back in.

4. The crew then tries to figure out how to prevent the same situation from happening again.

DAMAGE CONTROL

When you're sailing in waters with muddy or sandy bottoms, running aground will not cause much damage. However, you should check for leaks immediately if the impact was a hard one. Minor damage can often be stopped temporarily by covering it on the inside with a bunk cushion or something similar, then wedging it in place with an oar, boat hook, or anything nearby.

SPRINGING A LEAK

One of the most disconcerting things that can happen on a boat is to find water in the bilge after it has supposedly been pumped dry (see bilge pumps, p. 147). This usually means the boat has a leak someplace.

One of the most obvious places is around the through-hull fittings-the valves that let water into the boat for cooling the engine or that let water out from the sink and head. Inspect each fitting to find the problem. It may be as simple as a loose clamp or a broken hose that can be stopped by closing the valve or plugging it with a tapered wood plug (see Essential Safety Equipment, p. 144). Also check the keel bolts for leaks.

If the leak is more serious, plug it with rags, use a sail bag, or even wrap a sail around the outside of the hull. If the leak is at the waterline, heel the boat to the opposite side. If there is any doubt as to the seriousness of the leak, radio the Coast Guard for advice and assistance.

RIGGING FAILURE

If a piece of equipment breaks or is on the verge of breaking, the first step is to remove any pressure from it. There are four major parts of the rig that may fail: the mast, forestay, backstay, and shrouds.

If the mast breaks, the most important concern is to keep the broken section of the mast from damaging the hull. This could mean cutting away the wire supports and the mast. If the sails and mast can be salvaged without any risk to the safety of the crew or boat, they should be.

If a shroud breaks, the helmsman should tack immediately to put the strain on the opposite side of the rigging.

If the forestay fails, the helmsman should immediately bear away to a broad reach or a run. This will cause the pressure on the sails and mast to be forward, taking any additional strain off the luff of the jib. The jib should be left hoisted to support the mast temporarily from the front until a spare halyard can be rigged to the bow and tightened to act as a headstay.

If the backstay breaks, sheet in the mainsheet as hard as possible. The support of the mast normally borne by the backstay will be taken over by the leech of the main sail. Heading upwind will reduce the pressure on the leech. Rig a halyard aft to the stern and tighten. This will act as a temporary backstay allowing you to ease the main.

STEERING FAILURE

If the tiller breaks, the wheel ceases to turn the rudder, or the rudder falls off, the boat can be steered with the sails. In our first exercise in Part One, we found that under mainsail alone the boat tended to head toward the wind. This caused weather helm. Under jib alone, the opposite happens: a lee helm develops and the boat tends to turn away from the wind.

By using these two forces and balancing them when we want to travel in a straight line, we can steer the boat and even come about or jibe. We will practice steering with the sails in the Sailing Skills section that follows.

DRAGGING ANCHOR

If the boat is dragging anchor, the first action is to increase scope (let out more rode) and possibly rig another anchor. If this does not work, the anchor should be hauled up and the vessel re-anchored. If the decision is to re-anchor, the skipper should reconsider the suitability of the anchorage. If the conditions that caused the anchor to drag make the anchorage dangerous to the boat, then the skipper will have to decide whether to select a new site or simply to sail until conditions change. Don't get pinned in an unsafe anchorage.

FOULED PROP

Occasionally a line will get tangled in the propeller. The helmsman should stop the engine immediately (if the engine has not already stalled). Pulling on the line that has committed the impropriety may remedy the situation, but don't count on it. The second option is to send someone over the side to unravel, or as a last resort, cut away the line. The crew on deck should be watching for other vessels or obstacles. It may be necessary to sail to a dock or mooring and secure the boat before cutting the line.

BROKEN HALYARD

If a halyard or shackle breaks while sailing, the next step is to pull the sail down and hoist it again on another halyard, if available.

SERIOUS EMERGENCIES

Most situations are nuisances and nothing more. Prepare for them. Have the proper equipment to handle any of these annoyances quickly and in a seamanlike manner. Don't panic. Sometimes, however, you may find yourself in a serious emergency. Somebody may be badly injured or ill, or the boat may be sinking or her mast may break. If that happens, stay calm, do the best you can to cope with the situation using aids and equipment that you have on board, and call for help. To summon help, use the boat's radio, if there is one, or any of several approved visual signals. These signals are taken from the U. S. Coast Guard's "Navigation Rules."

Official distress signals

REVIEW QUESTIONS

1. Knots have been taught throughout the book. Identify the knots from the following pictures and give one use for each.

KNOT   USE

a) _____ _____
b) _____ _____
c) _____ _____
d) _____ _____
e) _____ _____

2. Which sail would you be most likely to choose for very light wind?
a) 90 percent jib
b) 150 percent genoa
c) storm jib

3. Bad weather comes from
a) high pressure systems
b) low pressure systems

4. More violent weather is usually associated with
a) warm fronts
b) cold fronts

5. What kinds of weather do the following clouds precede?
a) cumulonimbus clouds
b) low rolling clouds

6. Describe the first action to be taken in each of the following situations:

a) You run aground (no tide)._____
_____

b) The boat springs a leak. _____
_____

c) Part of the standing rigging fails. _____
_____

d) The steering fails. _____
_____

e) The prop fouls. _____
_____

Answers in Appendix A, p. 201.

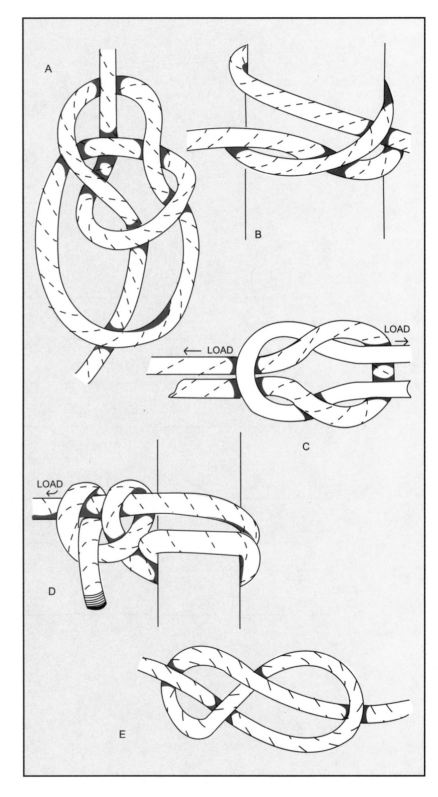

SAILING SKILLS

In this Sailing Skills section, three new skills will be presented: reefing, sailing a compass course, and steering with sails only. The balance of the on-the-water session will be devoted to evaluating your ability to act as skipper and crew. To preview the evaluation, we introduce the ASA Basic Coastal Cruising checklist (see p. 184-185).

You should be able to perform the role of both skipper and of crew for each of the performance objectives on the list. The completed checklist will help you identify weaknesses in your sailing skills. You are not expected to achieve a perfect score. The aim is to perform each maneuver safely and with control. If any item cannot be completed, you will know exactly what has to be practiced. Review the section in the book, and go out and work on those skills in your next on-the-water session. Some items just need practice. But now, on to new skills.

REEFING

Reefing-reducing sail area-can be accomplished in a number of different ways. It is important to reef before there is so much wind that the process becomes too difficult or dangerous. On a windy day, the reef should be taken in before leaving the dock so that the sail is raised in a reduced form. The reef can also be taken in at anchor or when hove to. It is always easier to take out a reef that is not required than it is to put one in when it is too windy. Better safe than sorry.

The crew has rigged first and second reef lines. A reef line should be led any time heavy weather is anticipated.

EXERCISE: **REEFING IN**

Practice this procedure while the boat is docked, moored, anchored, or hove to.

1. The helmsman positions the boat so that the wind is at least 30 degrees off the bow, as when raising sails.

2. The crew checks that the topping lift is secured so that the boom will not fall to the deck as the main halyard is released. The mainsheet and boom vang are then released.

3. Luff the mainsail by easing the sheet.

4. One of the crew at the main halyard lowers the sail until the reefing tack is at the boom.

5. Secure the reefing tack of the sail by the hook or reefing line and rehoist the halyard to the proper tension. Better too tight than too loose.

6. Pull in the reefing line through the leech grommet and cleat it to secure the clew close to the boom. (Use a winch if necessary.)

7. Tie the excess sail area to the boom with fight lines or sail ties led through the grommets in the sail.

8. Sheet in the mainsail.

To undo or shake out the reef, reverse the procedure. It is possible to reef underway by sailing on the jib and letting the main luff.

Reefing greatly reduces sail, making the boat easier to handle in heavier winds.

SAILING A COMPASS COURSE

The helmsman should learn how to use the various indicators that are available to help steer a course.

In very calm water, the helmsman should be able to steer a very accurate course. But if there are waves, steering the precise compass course will be impossible. The boat will wander to either side of the course, perhaps as much as 5 degrees. This is acceptable. Using an object ahead as a guide, the helmsman should try to balance out the wanders to either side so that the boat averages the original compass course as it makes way toward the object. This will take some practice. It is important that the helmsman not simply stare at the compass. Doing so distracts him from the destination and from the sails, weather, waves, objects in the water, and boat traffic around him.

EXERCISE: **SAILING A COMPASS COURSE**

1. While sailing on a reach, the helmsman selects a buoy or a landmark (for example, a water tower or a large building) that lies ahead at a distance of half a mile or more.

2. The helmsman aims the boat directly at the object, and the crew trims the sails properly and keeps a lookout for other boats.

3. The helmsman then looks at the compass to see what compass course the boat is sailing. This is the number just under the forward lubber's line (the front post inside the glass dome).

4. Moving his eyes back and forth between the compass and the object ahead, the helmsman tries to steer a steady compass course.

STEERING WITH THE SAILS

In case your steering equipment ever fails, you should know how to steer a boat by sails alone. Practice this technique in open water, away from land and other boats.

EXERCISE: **STEERING WITH THE SAILS**

1. The helmsman ties the tiller or wheel in a central position.

2. The crew releases the jib and trims the mainsheet. This will cause the boat to head up.

3. The crew releases the mainsheet and trims the jib. The boat will bear away.

4. The crew then trims the mainsheet and eases the jib sheet until the boat is sailing in a straight line.

5. When this has been accomplished, the crew trims the mainsheet, releases the jib sheet, and holds this trim until the boat is head to wind.

6. The crew then trims the jib sheet on the windward side to back the jib. This will force the bow of the boat away from the wind on the new tack. By balancing the sails, steer the boat in a straight line on the new tack.

BASIC COASTAL CRUISING CHECKLIST

This checklist for the Basic Coastal Cruising standard can be used as a guide for what you have learned or are about to learn. It itemizes the minimum skills an individual should possess when taking an auxiliary-powered sailboat on the water.

PRELIMINARIES

Put on life jacket.
Give verbal checklist (Appendix C).
Produce equipment on checklist and
note deficiencies.
Put on sails.
Furl sails neatly.

GETTING UNDER WAY

Check for gas leaks (sniff or smell).
If outboard, check motor secure on
bracket with safety line.
Bilge blower turned on.
Start motor in neutral. Check cooling
water.
One man only on the bow.
All lines on board and shipshape.
Cast off all lines.
Engage motor.

Demonstrate Proper Winch Techniques

When to use winches
Proper wrapping technique on winch
(hand safety)
Removal of winch handle after use

MANEUVERING UNDER POWER

Stop the boat (with bow half a boat length
from mark, using reverse).
Steer straight course on approach.
Use a speed slow enough.

Parallel Docking

Correct approach
Slow speed
Correct distance from dock
Boat stopped without using lines
Bow stopped before mark

Anchoring

Choose good location for anchoring.
Use safe foredeck procedures.
Lower anchor properly.
Pay out good scope for depth and tide.
Check the drag.
Raise the anchor.
Override the anchor.
Use slow speed when hauling in anchor.

BOAT HANDLING UNDER SAIL

Hoisting Sails

Check topping lift.
Hoist and set mainsail.
Tension mainsail luff.
Coil and hang halyard.
Check figure eight used as stopper knot
on halyard and sheets.
Bear off slightly and hoist jib.
Tension jib luff.
Coil and hang halyard.

Lowering Sails

Start motor in neutral.
Bring boat near head to wind.
Check jib sheets inboard.
Check main hatch closed.
Lower jib and secure halyard.
Secure jib.
Attend to topping lift.
Lower mainsail.
Furl mainsail neatly.
Secure halyard and sheets.

SAILING

Beating

Helmsman sails close to wind.
Crew sets sails appropriately.

Reaching

Helmsman sails a compass course.
Crew trims sails appropriately.

Running

Helmsman keeps wind slightly off the
stern.
Crew sets sails as full as possible.

Tacking

Helmsman uses proper commands.
Helmsman selects new heading.
Helmsman executes maneuver smartly.
Crew gives proper responses.
Crew releases sheets at proper time.
Crew retrims sheets correctly.

Jibing

Helmsman uses correct commands.
Helmsman selects new heading.

Helmsman controls mainsheet.
Helmsman executes maneuver smartly.
Crew releases sheets with proper timing.
Crew controls mainsheet.
Crew retrims sheets correctly.

Heading Up

Helmsman sails closer to wind.
Crew trims sails correctly.

Bearing Away

Helmsman sails farther downwind.
Crew trims sails correctly.

Luffing Up

Helmsman brings boat higher up to
wind, without sail adjustment.
Crew eases sheets to cause luff.

REEFING

Boat has sufficient sea room.
Helmsman maintains control.
Crew is safe during procedure.
Complete reefing procedure carried out.

Man Overboard Drill

Hail "Man overboard."
Post lookout.
Toss life ring.
Turn vessel to a beam reach or
downwind.

Use proper approach to victim.
Secure victim.
Bring victim aboard.
Explain one method of bringing victim
aboard when shorthanded.

Securing the Vessel for the Night

Shut off fuel.
Leave motor in neutral.
Run bilge blower if inboard.
Remove key from switch.
Leave proper lines in place and secure.

Making Fast

Bow and stern lines in place
Spring lines in place
Fenders placed correctly
Dock lines coiled where applicable
Halyard secured and away from mast
Lines coiled and hung
Valuables below (winch handles, etc.)
Boat locked
Belongings and garbage ashore

Knots

Tie the following knots:
Reef
Round turn and two half hitches
Bowline
Figure eight
Clove hitch
Sheet bend

SUMMARY

In these six parts we have presented all the basic information you need to sail a small boat. We have not discussed big boat cruising, navigation, or offshore (ocean) sailing, all of which require more experience and training. Sailing is a continual learning process. That is why ASA standards promote continued education.

Now that you have completed the basic instructional part of this book, you are ready to enjoy sailing with your friends and family. For those of you seeking special tips on dinghies, sailboards, and catamarans, continue on to Part Seven. But whatever you sail, you will find every trip a new experience. Learn from each one. There's a new world of fun and adventure ahead of you. Learning to sail is the key to that world.

Special Sailing Information

DINGHY SAILING

There are some principles of sailing that apply equally to a Sunfish or a 12-meter yacht. Mastering one helps you master the others.

Small boats such as dinghies have grown in popularity over the past decades due to their affordability. Recently there has been a huge growth in sailboards, catamarans, and even small cruising boats. The trend is toward easier-to-handle, self-righting boats. Generally, small dinghies are relatively unstable and capsize following the simplest mistake. It is valuable to hone your skills with dinghy sailing before moving up in size. The best large boat sailors are the ones who learned on small boats first.

SAILING TO WINDWARD

Sit on the windward side so you can watch the sails working together and see where you are heading. Keep your back to the wind, face the sail, and sit up on the side of the deck to keep the boat flat.

In very light winds (under 6 knots), sit toward the middle of the boat, allowing it to heel to leeward slightly (see illustration on p. 190). Heeling to leeward helps the sails take shape and the boat sail on its lines.

The centerboard or keel is critical to a boat's performance to windward. If there were no centerboard or keel, the force of the wind would push the boat sideways. Raising the centerboard a few inches will help reduce your helm and your angle of heel in very strong winds. With a force of wind hitting your sail, the larger the centerboard the greater the heeling force. Reducing the area of your centerboard reduces the amount of heel.

TACKING

When tacking, changing sides of the boat can be hard if you are handling both mainsheet and tiller. Take as few steps as possible crossing from one side of the boat to the other. In dinghies only one step is necessary. As you cross you must change hands as well. Hold on to the mainsheet while preparing to tack. Keep your sheet uncleated so it does not get caught on the old leeward side. As you change sides, bring the hand holding the mainsheet back to the tiller behind you, keeping the mainsheet in that hand. For a split second one hand will hold both the mainsheet and the tiller. At this point change hands behind your back. The mainsheet and the tiller will be under control at all times.

Face forward during your tack. You will see where you are going and be able to shift your weight at the right moment to keep your boat on an even keel. Common errors in tacking are holding the tiller over to one

Build your foundation with dinghy sailing before moving up in size. Cat-rigged boats come in many forms, such as the Hunter 90.

Crew and skipper sit in positions where they can watch both sails and see traffic and obstructions.

side too long and not changing hands soon enough.

As you complete your tack, the action of the wind on your sails (whether you are luffing or not) tells you if you are on your new course. You must concentrate on where you are heading and what is happening to your sails.

JIBING

Try to keep the boat flat when jibing. Put the centerboard down halfway. Too little board down will allow the bottom to spin out from under the mast; too much board will cause the board to steer the boat and tip it. Keep your weight aft during the jibe in heavier air so your bow does not dip into the water. Change hands early in a jibe so you do not get twisted.

After the jibe, resume your normal course as soon as possible; staying dead downwind keeps the boat off balance. If the boat is out of balance, head up, heeling the boat slightly to leeward until you are under control. Hold on to the tiller while jibing to keep the boat from spinning out.

ACCELERATING

Part of the fun of sailing small boats is quick acceleration. The heavier the boat, the

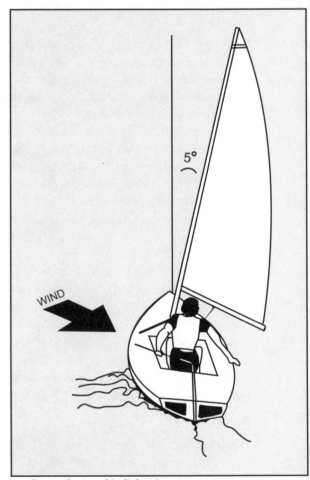

Heeling to leeward in light air.

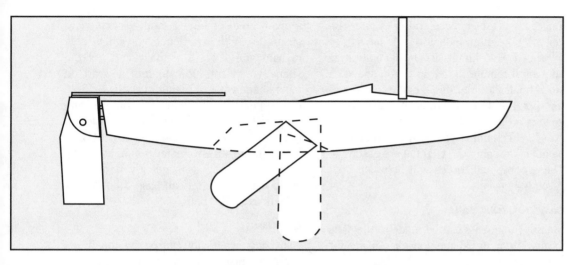

Reduce centerboard area to reduce heel in strong winds.

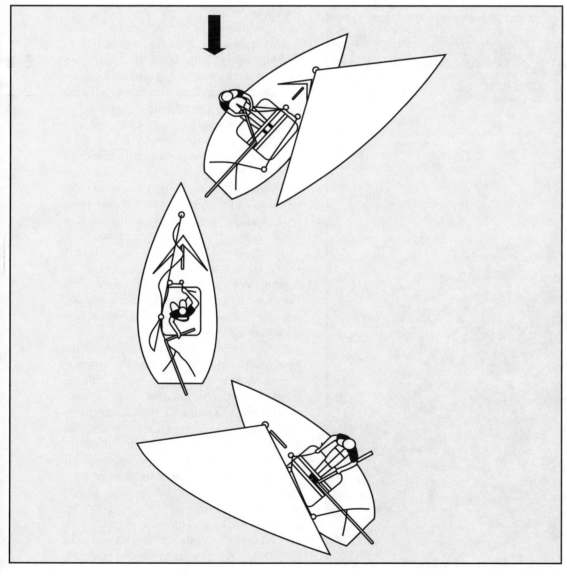

Changing hands during a tack

longer it will take to accelerate. A squarerigger will take minutes before it is moving at full speed. A 12-meter sloop will sometimes take a full minute to get up to top speed. A small boat, like a Sunfish, can easily reach top speed in seconds. To accelerate a boat, keep it on a course as close to a reach as possible. Trimming your sail to the desired point and keeping the boat flat are essential. These combined forces will help the boat reach full speed.

This sailor could flatten his boat easily by shifting his weight to the windward side of the boat.

TRIMMING YOUR SAILS

Many adjustments can be made to the sails to give them any shape you may desire for

a given point of sailing in all various wind strengths. With experience, you will be able to trim your sails effectively and get the shape you want. Adjustments depend on what shape you are trying to achieve. First, it is important that whenever you are trimming sails to never cleat the sheet, especially in smaller boats. If a sudden gust of wind hits with the sheets cleated, you may not be able to ease the sails quickly enough to avoid capsizing. You can ease them at any time if you hold them.

CAPSIZING

Capsizing is usually caused by too much wind for the amount of sail being carried; improper balance by the crew, jibing in a strong wind with the centerboard up too far, not keeping the boat under control, rapidly shifting winds (both in velocity and direction), or simply not paying attention.

Don't let the boat heel too far. Hiking out will help to keep the boat flat, compensating for the angle of heel. Once the boat gets too far over, the rudder will be ineffective. Therefore, it is important to prevent a capsize early.

When capsized, there are several rules of thumb to follow. Of course your pride may be slightly injured, but bodily safety is what counts. Once in the water, stay with the boat. Even if you are unable to right it, never leave the boat. This applies to all members of the crew. You should stay with the boat until you have righted it and are able to sail again, or until another boat comes along to help.

To right the capsized boat, first put the boat head to wind by swinging the bow into the wind. If the mast is pointing into the wind, the boat is likely to capsize once again while it is being righted. Use the centerboard as a lever by standing on the middle of it. Be sure your sheets are uncleated so that as the boat pops up your sails will not fill, causing the boat to go over once again. In a dinghy keep your sheets uncleated at all times.

As your boat comes up, grab the side and continue to pull until the boat is completely upright. Try not to make a mad dash to get on the boat, as you will probably want to; the sharks won't get you yet. Instead, hold on to the side of the boat and rest for a moment to regain your energy. The toughest thing will be climbing back into the boat. When you have rested and feel strong enough, pull yourself into the middle of the boat or over the transom.

If the mast begins to sink and the boat begins to turn turtle (completely upside down), try to place a fife jacket under the tip of the mast to help keep it floating. If the boat does turtle, pulling on the centerboard will slowly bring the boat back. If the mast is wedged tightly in the mud, you may need the assistance of another boat. Have this boat anchor directly upwind and throw a line to you. Eventually, the force of the wind and waves will pivot your boat into the wind, pulling the mast out of the mud and making it easy to right. Training boats are often equipped with Styrofoam, sewn into the head of the sail to stop the boat from turtling.

If the boat is swamped, sit down and begin to bail it out once it is righted. Keep one person in the water to steady the boat. If the rail is awash with one person in, best keep everyone in the water. When the boat is towed by a powerboat, the water proba-

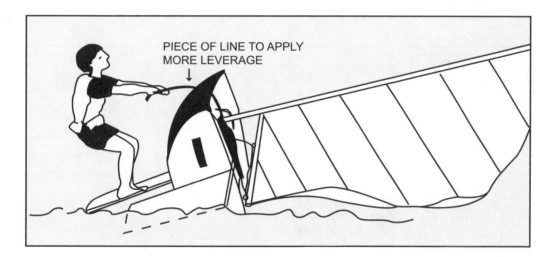

PIECE OF LINE TO APPLY MORE LEVERAGE

Using a centerboard as a lever for righting and a piece of line as shown will help a small (light) person right a boat.

This skipper is using her weight on the centerboard to right her capsized dinghy.

bly will flow out. First let your sails down and secure all equipment to prevent it from floating away. Have the rescuing boat throw you a line. Attach it around the base of the mast. The water will begin to empty out. Have your boat towed straight into the wind at a slow speed. Keep the centerboard up. You may capsize again if the centerboard is down. Water-filled boats are very unstable. Handle with care. Head into the wind a little more if your boat feels unstable. When a swamped boat is being towed, have at least one person in the stern to keep the bow from nose-diving and to balance the boat. As the boat is towed, the bow will rise and the water will pour over the stern. Keep

your fife jacket on. If you weren't wearing one when you capsized, put one on now. You may find swimming more difficult, but at least you will be safe.

Be prepared. Sometimes all the preventative efforts in the world can't keep the boat from capsizing. If you suddenly find yourself in the water, locate your crew and passengers. Double check to see everyone's PFD is on and keeping them afloat. Stay with the boat unless it's drifting toward some hazard like breaking surf or a power plant intake. Anything that floats such as an ice chest or fender might help elevate you and make you more visible for potential rescuers.

Using a jib sheet to right a turtled dinghy.

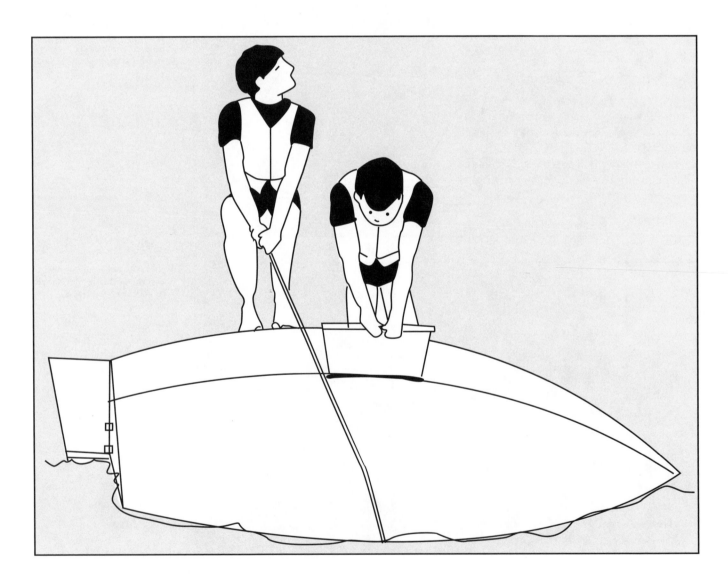

SAILBOARDS

Learning to sail a sailboard can be very enjoyable or extremely frustrating. A successful first attempt requires ideal conditions; it's beneficial to have the use of some type of training equipment and helpful if you have some good instruction.

Under ideal conditions, the wind is less than 8 knots, seas are calm, and the water is warm. The area in which you sail should be relatively free of boat traffic and obstructions. The smaller the area the better, so long as the breeze is not excessively obstructed by buildings.

EQUIPMENT

The basic and most common training sailboard for a beginner has a small sail, usually around 43 square feet. (Stock sails are 56 square feet.) A smaller sail takes a lot of the power out of the rig and reduces the tendency for the beginner to become overpowered. There are several specially designed trainer boards that are wider and more stable and the rig (boom and mast) is made of aluminum and fiberglass, easy to pull out of the water and to hold on to.

INSTRUCTION

Qualified sailboarding instruction is available around the world. Many instructional programs consist of two three-hour lessons. Certified instructors teach the classes using special equipment. Classes start with sailing theory. The instructor demonstrates each step of sailboarding on a land simulator, and each student then practices the steps. The instructor corrects the students' mistakes on land, before they go onto the water, thus saving a lot of time. Later, on the water, students use training boards with small sails.

SAILBOARDING STEP-BY-STEP

There is no substitute for good instruction in sailboarding. However, the steps fisted below give you an idea of what it's all about.

Getting ready: Determine the wind direction and aim the board perpendicular to the wind. Point the mast straight downwind horizontal to the water, so that the mast and the board form a right angle.

Stance: Face the sail with your back to the wind. Place your feet on the centerline of the board. The forward foot should be in front of the mast and the back foot over the centerboard. Bend your knees for more

Sailing takes many forms. Here, an energetic person sails a sailboard.

stability. Keep your feet centered unless tacking or jibing. Straighten your back and keep your hips forward.

Getting started: Be sure the board is crosswise to the wind. Now pull the mast straight up out of the water. To do this, hold the uphaul (a line on the mast) with both hands, reach across with your forward hand (the one closest to the bow), and grab the boom about six inches from the end. Next, move the mast forward using your forward hand, until it is close to your forward leg. Reach back with your back hand and grab the boom. To fill the sail with wind, pull in with your back hand. At the same time, tip the mast and sail toward the nose of the board to keep it from rounding up into the wind.

Control: Hold the rig out of the water by the uphaul. To turn the board away from the wind, tip the mast forward. To turn the board into the wind, tip the mast back. Keep the mast in the center plane. Remember, your body weight and the sail control the board.

Turning: The sail is used to effect all turns including the tack and jibe. To tack, lean the luffing sail back and step around to the bow of the board as it turns into the wind. Stand on the bow with a foot on either side of the center as the sail luffs over the stern. Lean the sail to the left or right to complete the turn, then step back to the centerline of the board.

To jibe, lean the sail forward. As the board turns downwind, step around aft of the sail. Stand on the stern of the board as the sail luffs over the bow. Next, lean the sail to the left or right to complete the turn. As the board moves crosswise to the wind, step back to the centerline.

Tips: If you become overpowered, release the boom with your back hand and pull in with your front hand. This will let the wind out of the sail, just as easing a mainsheet would. If you release the boom with your forward hand, the board will react as if you had cut a shroud (that is, the mast will fall over).

It is important to keep your feet on the centerline. To improve balance, bend at the knees and lean against the sail. If overpowered, let out the sail; if falling backwards, pull in with your back hand to catch more wind.

Advanced technique: Sailing in strong winds requires some special expertise. In high winds you must hang from the boom out over the water and use your body weight to its utmost. This means you will grip the boom farther back and keep your feet much farther back on the board. In extreme winds it is necessary on some boards to change the daggerboard (or centerboard). Use a high-wind centerboard or kick up the adjustable centerboard to reduce the planing surface and move the center of lateral resistance aft when the winds are over 15 knots. Since the partially hoisted centerboard or high-wind daggerboard is small and swept back, it reduces the board's tendency to round up into the wind and makes it possible to bear off and surf on the waves in a strong wind.

Recently sailboarding has grown tremendously in popularity. A new breed of sailboards–short, surfboardlike boards–are being used by sailors to jump and surf waves or just blast around at amazingly high speeds. Design innovations on these high-speed boards keep the entire sailboarding world advancing by leaps and bounds.

CATAMARANS

Catamarans have two hulls of equal length, with the mast supported in the center of a bridge deck between them. Some designs have flexible connections between the hulls and accommodations within the hulls, and some designs have large bridge deck structures with no accommodations at all within the hulls.

Smaller day-racing catamarans fall into several additional groups. One group, whose only function is high speed and maximum performance, includes the Tornado, which has semirounded hulls, pivoting centerboards, and a fully articulating mast with full battened mainsail. This group also includes C class catamarans, among the most sophisticated sailboats in existence and the most close-winded boats afloat. C class catamarans are easily identified by their wing masts and airplane like structure.

Finally, there is a group of day-racing catamarans which might be called "off the beach" boats. Some of these boats, such as the Hobie 14, the Hobie 16, and the various sizes of Prindles, have no daggerboards. Some get their lift to windward from asymmetrical hulls, which work the same way the sails do. Others have kick-up centerboards and rudders. These cats, capable of spirited performance and high speed, are designed for beachability and rugged recreational use.

TRIMARANS

Trimarans have three hulls; beyond that, there is little that is standard. The length of the outer hulls, spacing from the main hulls, percentage of buoyancy, and shape all vary a great deal. There are very few day-sailing trimarans.

WHY A CATAMARAN?

The first advantage in catamaran sailing is high speed; no vessel except for the tiny, speed-oriented sailboards can compare with the potential speed of a catamaran. The second advantage of a catamaran is its great stability. It is easy to board and disembark. It's an easy boat to rig, and you can walk around on it without tipping it over. It is also easy to beach, easy to trailer, and much lighter than many of its single-hulled counterparts.

HANDLING

There are some handling differences between catamarans and most single-hulled boats. The chief difference with the majority of designs is in tacking. Most catamarans, because of their extremely light weight, have no momentum to carry them

through a tack and must be backwinded. In many cases it is necessary to backwind the jib to bring the boat completely around onto the other tack. (The secret is to not release the jib sheet until the main has filled on the new tack.) However you do it, it's slow. In a racing situation this means that the short tacking that might work for a very nimble monohull will probably be disastrous for a catamaran. In catamaran racing, try to make as few tacks as possible.

Catamarans are designed to sail with both hulls in the water or with the windward hull just kissing the water. Hotdogging, or "flying a hull," is a lot of fun and very exciting, but detrimental to the performance of the boat.

Keeping the boat flat is an acquired skill done mostly with the tiller. The secret of keeping the boat flat on a reach is to turn downwind when the hull begins to rise. If you turn upwind, the forces that are lifting the hull in the first place will accelerate. A basic difference in handling a catamaran as opposed to a single-hulled boat is that you turn downwind when the boat becomes overpressed, rather than turning upwind and letting the sail luff. This is because in a single-hulled boat the additional momentum gained by turning upwind heels the boat a little farther, allowing the rig to spill the wind. In a catamaran, the same forces apply. However, if the boat heels farther, the threat of capsize becomes greater; since you are trying to bring the hull back down to the water, you must turn downwind rather than up. In winds too heavy for using the tiller alone, turn by easing the traveler and if necessary the mainsheet.

A catamaran sailor seldom sails directly downwind because a run is the slowest point of sail. When sailing dead downwind, a boat can achieve only a percentage of the true wind speed. On a reaching course you develop your own wind, and you can increase your speed enormously downwind by "tacking downwind." To do so, reach across the wind and turn downwind until you are getting less drive out of the sails. At this point, head back up slightly and maintain that course. Find the best possible downwind course, so that your sails are full but you're not heading dead downwind. This is often about 15 degrees to either side of the true wind. A simple jibe then brings you onto the other tack. Tack downwind toward a mark in the same manner that you would tack upwind. If you have boards, raise them fully to take advantage of your leeway.

Occasionally you may be overpowered going downwind. In smaller boats this usually becomes apparent at about 20 to 25 knots of true wind speed. It is very important that you maintain your control over the boat. In an emergency overpowering situation in heavy wind, the simplest and safest procedure is to sail more of a reach. Your fully battened sail will assist you. When you are going dead downwind and the mainsheet is in as tight as possible, the traveler is centered, and you are ready, release your halyard and pull your mainsail down as quickly as possible. Try to have your mast rotator parallel with the sail during this operation so there is no chance of the sail jamming in the sail groove.

CAPSIZING

Capsizing on a catamaran is no more cause for alarm than capsizing on any other centerboard or nonballasted boat. Swim the boat around so the sails face into the wind. Tie a righting line to the shroud on the dry hull. (If you don't have a righting line on board, undo the mainsheet from the block system and use it.) Be sure to release the mainsheet and jib sheet so the sails won't hold water, which would make righting more difficult. Also, if the sails are left sheeted, the boat may sail away without you when it comes up. Where you stand on the hull as you rotate the boat back out of the water will depend on the type of boat. On some boats with daggerboards you can stand on the board to get more leverage. On some you can't. Find out which kind you have before you get into this situation.

Stand on the submerged hull and lean out against your righting line as far as possible to provide leverage to right the boat. When the boat begins to right and come over to you, duck in between the hulls for maximum safety. Do not drop the righting line until you are aboard, as there is always a possibility that the boat may sail away without you.

JIBING

The broad base, stability, efficient traveler system, and lack of a permanent backstay allow a catamaran to be jibed simply and easily. When jibing in unusually heavy conditions, assist the rig in the jibe in order to take some strain off the equipment. In heavy winds, trim the mainsheet, then assist the rig across the stern by hauling the traveler to center and then allowing it to pay out slowly on the opposite tack. In moderate winds, trim the mainsheet before jibing, then push your tiller to windward and complete your jibe, allowing the traveler to swing across on the new tack by itself.

APPARENT WIND

The apparent wind in catamaran sailing is usually forward of abeam. Since a catamaran's speed is normally a much higher percentage of the true wind speed than that of other boats, the apparent wind is much farther forward. It is not unusual to see single-hulled boats and catamarans on the same downwind course with the catamarans trimmed in much closer than the single-hulled boats. Because the catamarans are moving faster, their apparent wind is farther forward; since sails are trimmed to the apparent wind, their sails will be sheeted in tighter.

The traveler on a catamaran is more important in controlling the sail than it is on many other classes of boat. Most champion catamaran sailors trim their mainsail to the proper shape for the wind speed and direction and then use the traveler to obtain the optimum angle of attack as they sail on reaches. As the boat accelerates, they haul their travelers in toward the centerline; as the boat decelerates, they let the traveler out to maintain the same angle of attack. This is easy to achieve on a catamaran because of the very wide sheeting base and stability.

LAUNCHING, STORING, AND MAINTAINING YOUR BOAT

TRAILERS

Many sailors use trailers both to launch and to store their boats. This is the most versatile form of boat storage and lets you sail on a different body of water every weekend. You can store the boat in your driveway, which eliminates storage costs and the chance of vandalism.

There are two types of trailers. The boom variety emphasizes keel support; the frame type emphasizes hull support. Select a trailer that supports as much of the hull as possible. The trailer should meet local and state trailer regulations, permit dry launching, and provide maximum safety and comfort while being towed.

When pulling your boat and trailer with a vehicle, keep a few things in mind. Be sure your equipment rides well without shifting, chafing, and rattling. Balance is very important when trailering. Too much weight in the rear of the boat will cause your trailer to bob and sway. Check to see if your trailer has a recommended tongue weight and adjust the position of your boat to provide it.

Don't forget that you are really driving two vehicles, not one. Travel slowly and allow plenty of room to brake. An outside rearview mirror is very helpful, and lights on the rear of the trailer are a must.

Before launching a boat from a trailer, set the mast in place and attach the rigging and sails. Don't hoist the sails until you're in the water. Getting under way from a beach is simplified by using an outboard motor.

When launching your boat from a sandy beach, deflate your tires a little, as this will improve traction. Back into the water at right angles to the shoreline. Remember that to turn your trailer to the right, you turn the wheel to the left. To turn the trailer to the left, turn the steering wheel to the right.

RAMP LAUNCHING

In many parks, recreational facilities, and clubs, boats are launched from large con-

crete ramps that lead into the water. Always be aware of the power lines above the ramp and parking lot. You must be especially careful to keep your mast away from these wires.

Launching from a ramp takes great care, since the part that is in the water often develops a large amount of slippery growth. Watch your footing. Ramps are particularly dangerous around the edges because of deep water. Proceed down with caution.

When launching, back the trailer slowly into the water until the boat begins to float. Once the boat is floating, push it away from the trailer while a second person pulls the dolly out. Hold on to the boat at the bow, never allow it to get away from you and use bow and stern lines to move the boat to a dock nearby and secure it. Don't forget to use fenders.

If there is an offshore breeze, you can simply sail away. With an onshore breeze the waves break close to the ramp, so it is important to get away as quickly as possible. Never get between the boat and shore when there are breaking waves. To keep the boat from banging around, aim the bow directly into the waves.

When you are bringing the boat in, back the trailer into the water. Point the front of the trailer directly up the ramp so that it will be aligned with the bow pointing toward shore and the boat can easily be pulled out. Your centerboard should be up, the sails down, and the rudder out before you put the boat on the trailer. If you are lifting a boat out of the water, use three people, if possible, one on each side and one at the bow. If there are only two people, it is best to have one on each side.

If you are beaching the boat without a ramp, have the sails down, the centerboard up, and the rudder out before you get to the beach, and keep the boat outside the breaking waves until you are ready to lift it out. Watch for a smooth set of waves before taking it all the way in. Try to find a sandy part of the beach, one that is away from gravel. Again, never get between the hull of your boat and the shore, because the surf can roll the boat over on top of you. And whatever system you use, never leave your boat unattended.

MARINAS AND YACHT CLUBS

You may decide to keep your boat at a marina. Many marinas have launching ramps or a hoist, as well as dinghy service, docks, and a clubhouse with lockers and showers. Or you might choose to keep your boat at a yacht club. While most yacht clubs offer more limited services, they usually provide docks, a clubhouse, and probably swimming and sailing lessons. And of course yacht clubs provide a much more extensive social program and a chance to make friends with people of similar interests.

BOAT MAINTENANCE

To get the most out of your boat and sails, you must maintain them properly. Wash them down with fresh water every time after sailing. Salt can do a lot of damage to your boat's finish and working parts. Replace broken parts so that your boat is always in optimum working order. Be sure to store your boat properly. If you keep it on land, store it hull up to preserve the shape if you are leaving it for long periods. If you keep it in a berth, tie it properly to avoid damage from rough weather. Use covers to keep out water and leaves, etc.

Your sails also require care. Use sail covers, as synthetic sails are harmed by long exposure to sunlight. Use sail bags if you have them. Fold your sails smoothly to avoid wrinkling. (In light air an uneven surface will cause turbulence in the flow of air across the sail.)

When washing salt from your sails, use fresh water so they will dry properly. Never allow sails to flap in heavy wind; this weakens the fabric. Only hoist the sails to their design limits between the black bands on the mast.

Any boat with electrical devices such as lights and an electric-start motor will have a battery, wires and fuses. Check for loose or corroded connections and frayed wire insulation. Also make sure you have spare fuses and bulbs on board before casting off your dock lines.

A FINAL WORD

Simply finishing this book and its course of instruction does not make someone a proficient sailor. Only through practice will the skills taught in these lessons become a part of the individual. When you can react instinctively to a situation, instead of working through it mechanically, you've taken a major step toward becoming a competent sailor.

Review this book regularly. There will always be something that was not learned or fully understood the first time around. The review will stimulate you to think of all the things that can happen on a sailboat in terms of anticipation, preparation, and execution. Never think that you have learned it all. Nature-the wind and water-has a grand way of teaching humility to the overconfident.

Now that you have completed the Basic Sailing and Basic Coastal Cruising standards, you may wish to acquire actual certification. To do so, you should be tested by an American Sailing Association certified instructor and receive a signed ASA Sailing Log Book. Further information may be obtained directly from the American Sailing Association, P. O. Box 12079, Marina del Rey, California 90295, Phone (310) 822-7171, Fax (310) 822-4741, Email info@american-sailing.com, Website www.american-sailing.com

ANSWERS TO REVIEW QUESTIONS

PART ONE

Question 1.
A. Aloft
headstay 11
backstay shroud 8
mast 9
boom 10
boom vang 14
topping lift 13
mainsheet 15
B. On Deck and Below
tiller 7
lifelines 3
rudder 6
stern 5
hull 1
bow 4
keel 2
C. Sails
jib 17 jib sheet 18
mainsail 16
head 19
clew 21
tack 20
luff 24
foot 25
leech 22
batten 23

Question 2.
b) into the wind

Question 3.
deck cleat B
winch E
block D
fairlead C
cam cleat A

Question 4.
displacement and planing

Question 5.
powerboat

Question 6.
false

Question 7.
true

Question 8.
5 persons

PART TWO

Question 1.
b) smooth air flow

Question 2.
b) close-hauled

Question 3.
c) eased out all the way

Question 4.
c) an accidental jibe

Question 5.
b) head to wind

Question 6.

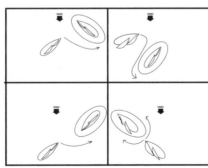

Question 7.
a) boat ahead and being overtaken
Question 8.

a) when overtaking,
c) when the power vessel is limited in its maneuverability by a narrow channel and
d) when the sailboat is also under power.

Question 9. A port tack boat shall give way to boat on starboard tack.

Question 10.
When two sailboats are approaching on the same tack, the windward boat shall stay clear of the leeward boat.

PART THREE

Question 1.
keep a person from falling overboard.

Question 2.
Heat Escape Lessening Position

Question 3.
Do remove wet clothing when in shelter
Do wrap in a sleeping bag or blank with external heat source.
Do call for medical assistance, even medium cases.

Question 4.
Do not administer fluids unless victim is totally conscious.
Do not massage victim.
Do not administer alcohol.

PART FOUR

Question 1.
fathoms, feet, and meters; meters

Question 2
a) port

Question 3.
c) splits into two routes.

Question 4.
1. swim area
2. rock
3. slow

Question 5.
anchor, chain, and rode

Question 6. a) acts as shock absorber
b) prevents rode from chafing on rocks

Question 7.
a) shelter
b) room to swing
c) sufficient water depth
d) good holding ground

Question 8.
a) nylon
b) Dacron
c) nylon
d) Dacron
e) polyethylene or polypropylene

Question 9.
fore and aft; maneuvering a vessel for docking and undocking

part five

Question 1.
self-bailing cockpit 6
through-hull fitting 5
pintle 3
gudgeon 2
rudderpost 4
tiller 1
turnbuckle 7
chainplate 8

Question 2.
a) left to right 4
b) right to left 1
c) toward us 3
d) away from us 2

Question 3.

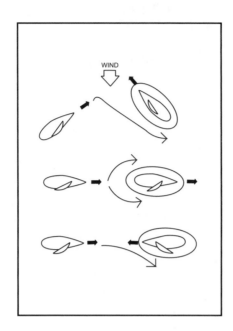

Question 4.
one short; one short; five or more short blasts

Question 5.
one prolonged blast

Question 6.
Type I

Question 7.
2 B-I or 1 B-II

Question 8.
Class B

Question 9.
d) all of the above (Note that other procedures are recommended, such as alerting authorities to your situation by radio and use of fire extinguishers.)

Question 10.
Class A

part six

Question 1.
a) bowline, a loop for attaching temporarily
b) clove hitch, for attaching to a spar temporarily
c) reef knot, for reefing the sails
d) round turn and two half hitches, for attaching to a spar or piling
e) figure eight, a stopper knot

Question 2.
b) 150% genoa

Question 3.
b) low pressure systems

Question 4.
b) cold fronts

Question 5.
a) cumulonimbus clouds: thunderstorms
b) low rolling clouds: line squalls

question 6.

a) Come about or jibe.
b) Determine the source and extent of the problem.
c) Position the boat to put the strain on the strongest part of the rig.
d) Determine another method of control.
e) Stop the engine and clear away the line.

FLOAT PLAN

Complete this plan before you go boating. Leave it with a reliable person either at a marina or elsewhere. Ask that person to notify the Coast Guard or other local authority if you do not return as scheduled.
DO NOT FILE THIS PLAN WITH THE COAST GUARD.
Cancel the plan when you return.

Name of your vessel _____
Your name _____ Telephone _____
Address _____

DESCRIPTION OF VESSEL

Type _____ Color _____
Color of Trim _____ Registration Number _____
Length _____ Sails _____ Make- _____
Engines: NumberType _____ Horsepower _____
Fuel Capacity _____ Canvas Top? _____ Color of Top _____

SURVIVAL EQUIPMENT (Check as appropriate)

PFDs _____ Flares- _____ Mirror _____ Signal Flag- _____
Smoke Signals _____ Signaling Flashlight _____
Food _____
Emergency Water _____
Anchor _____ Amount of Line _____ Paddle _____
Radio: Yes/No _____ Type _____ EPIRB _____ Frequencies _____
Raft or Dinghy _____

OTHER PEOPLE ON BOARD

Name	Age	Address and Telephone Number
_____	_____	_____
_____	_____	_____
_____	_____	_____

TRIP DETAILS

Depart: Date _____ Time _____ Return: Date _____ Time _____
Going to: _____ Via _____
Return via _____ Latest Time of Return _____

IF TRAILERING

Auto License _____ State _____ Type and Make _____
Trailer License _____ State _____ Color of Auto _____
Where Parked _____

NOTIFICATION

If Not Returned by _____ (time) Call the Coast Guard
at _____ or
Local Authority at _____

IMPORTANT–It is mandatory that all items be completed when the information is available.

SAMPLE BOATING ACCIDENT REPORT

COMPLETE ALL BLOCKS (PRINT OR TYPE ALL INFORMATION. INDICATE THOSE NOT APPLICABLE BY "NA." THOSE UNKNOWN BY "UN")

1. OPERATOR'S NAME AND ADDRESS AGE _____	2. RENTED BOAT	3. OPERATOR'S EXPERIENCE

2. RENTED BOAT
- ☐ Yes
- ☐ No

3. OPERATOR'S EXPERIENCE

THIS TYPE OF BOAT	OTHER BOAT OPERATING EXPERIENCE
☐ UNDER 20 HOURS	☐ UNDER 20 HOURS
☐ 20 TO 100 HOURS	☐ 20 TO 100 HOURS
☐ 100 TO 500 HOURS	☐ 100 TO 500 HOURS
☐ OVER 500 HOURS	☐ OVER 500 HOURS

HOME PHONE (   )   WORK PHONE (   )

4. OWNER'S NAME AND ADDRESS

HOME PHONE (   )   WORK PHONE (   )

5. NUMBER OF PERSONS ON BOARD

6. NUMBER OF PERSONS TOWED (I.E. SKIING ETC.)

7. FORMAL INSTRUCTION IN BOATING SAFETY
- ☐ NONE
- ☐ USCG AUXILIARY
- ☐ US POWER SQUADRON
- ☐ AMERICAN RED CROSS
- ☐ STATE
- ☐ OTHER (SPECIFY)

VESSEL NO. 1 (YOUR VESSEL)

8. BOAT NUMBER	9. BOAT NAME	10. BOAT MANUFACTURER	11. BOAT MODEL	12. MFGR. HULL IDENT. NO.

13. TYPE OF BOAT
- ☐ OPEN MOTORBOAT
- ☐ CABIN MOTORBOAT
- ☐ AUXILIARY SAIL
- ☐ SAIL ONLY
- ☐ HOUSEBOAT
- ☐ RAFT
- ☐ CANOE
- ☐ KAYAK
- ☐ JET SKI/WETBIKE
- ☐ ROWBOAT
- ☐ OTHER (SPECIFY)

14. HULL MATERIAL
- ☐ WOOD
- ☐ ALUMINUM
- ☐ STEEL
- ☐ FIBERGLASS
- ☐ RUBBER/VINYL
- ☐ PLASTIC
- ☐ OTHER (SPECIFY) _____

15. PROPULSION
- ☐ OUTBOARD
- ☐ INBOARD
- ☐ INBOARD-OUTBOARD
- ☐ JET
- ☐ SAIL
- ☐ PADDLE/OARS
- ☐ OTHER (SPECIFY)

TYPE OF FUEL _____

16. BOAT DATA
NUMBER OF ENGINES _____   LENGTH _____
MAKE OF ENGINE _____   BEAM (WIDTH) _____
HORSEPOWER (TOTAL) _____   DEPTH (TOP OF INNER
YEAR BUILT _____   TRANSOM TO KEEL) _____
(ENGINE)   YEAR BUILT (BOAT) _____

17. PRIMARY BOAT USE
- ☐ RECREATIONAL
- ☐ COMMERCIAL
- ☐ FOR-HIRE
- ☐ WORK BOAT

18. PREVIOUS ACCIDENTS INVOLVING THIS BOAT

DATES

VESSEL NO. 2 (OTHER VESSEL INVOLVED)

19. BOAT NUMBER	20. BOAT NAME	21. BOAT MANUFACTURER	22. BOAT MODEL	23. MFGR. HULL IDENT. NO.

24. NAME OF OPERATOR   AGE _____

HOME PHONE (   )
WORK PHONE (   )

25. ADDRESS

26. NAME OF OWNER

HOME PHONE (   )
WORK PHONE (   )

27. ADDRESS

28. WITNESSES

NAME	AGE _____	ADDRESS	TELEPHONE NUMBER ( )
NAME	AGE _____	ADDRESS	TELEPHONE NUMBER ( )
NAME	AGE _____	ADDRESS	TELEPHONE NUMBER ( )

ACCIDENT DATE AND LOCATION

29. DATE OF ACCIDENT	30. TIME ___ AM ___ PM	31. NAME OF BODY OF WATER 32. LAST PORT OF CALL	33. LOCATION (AS PRECISELY AS POSSIBLE)

34. STATE	35. NEAREST CITY OR TOWN	36. COUNTY

ENVIRONMENTAL CONDITIONS

37. WEATHER	38. WATER CONDITIONS	39. TEMPERATURE (ESTIMATE)	40. WIND	41. VISIBILITY	42. WHEATHER ENCOUNTERED
☐ CLEAR ☐ RAIN ☐ CLOUDY ☐ SNOW ☐ FOG ☐ HAZY	☐ CALM ☐ CHOPPY ☐ ROUGH ☐ VERY ROUGH ☐ STRONG CURRENT	AIR _____ °F WATER _____ °F	☐ NONE ☐ LIGHT (0 TO 6 MPH) ☐ MODERATE (7 TO 14 MPH) ☐ STRONG (15 TO 25 MPH) ☐ STORM (25 MPH AND OVER)	☐ GOOD ☐ FAIR ☐ POOR	☐ WAS AS FORECAST ☐ NOT AS FORECAST ☐ FORECAST NOT OBTAINED

THIS **CONFIDENTIAL REPORT** IS USED IN RESEARCH FOR THE PREVENTION OF ACCIDENTS, AND A COPY IS FORWARDED TO THE UNITED STATES COAST GUARD.

(COMPLETE BOTH SIDES)

<table>
<tr><td colspan="3" align="center">ACCIDENT DATA</td></tr>
</table>

43. OPERATION AT TIME OF ACCIDENT (CHECK ALL APPLICABLE)	44. TYPE OF ACCIDENT	45. IN YOUR OPINION, CAUSE OF ACCIDENT

43. OPERATION AT TIME OF ACCIDENT (CHECK ALL APPLICABLE)

☐ CRUISING ☐ DRIFTING
☐ MANEUVERING ☐ AT ANCHOR
☐ WATER SKIING ☐ TIED TO DOCK
☐ TOWING ☐ OTHER (USE ITEM 48)
☐ ACCELERATING

44. TYPE OF ACCIDENT

☐ GROUNDING ☐ COLLISION WITH FIXED OBJECT
☐ CAPSIZING ☐ COLLISION WITH FLOATING OBJECT
☐ FLOODING
☐ SINKING ☐ FALL OVERBOARD
☐ FIRE OR EXPLOSION (FUEL) ☐ FALL IN BOAT
☐ FIRE OR EXPLOSION (OTHER THAN FUEL) ☐ PERSON(S) HIT BY BOAT OR PROPELLER
☐ VESSEL(S) COLLISION ☐ OTHER (USE ITEM 48)

45. IN YOUR OPINION, CAUSE OF ACCIDENT

☐ WEATHER CONDITIONS ☐ RESTRICTED VISION
☐ EXCESSIVE SPEED ☐ FAULT OF HULL
☐ NO PROPER LOOKOUT ☐ FAULT OF MACHINERY
☐ OVERLOADING ☐ FAULT OF EQUIPMENT
☐ IMPROPER LOADING ☐ FATIGUE
☐ HAZARDOUS WATERS ☐ OTHER (SPECIFY)
☐ ALCOHOL _____
☐ DRUGS

---

46. PERSONAL FLOTATION DEVICES (PFD)

WAS THE BOAT ADEQUATELY EQUIPPED WITH COAST GUARD APPROVED PERSONAL FLOTATION DEVICES?

☐ YES ☐ NO

WHERE THEY ACCESSIBLE? ☐ YES ☐ NO
WHERE THEY USED? ☐ YES ☐ NO

WAS THE VESSEL CARRYING <u>NONAPPROVED</u>

LIFESAVING DEVICES? ☐ YES ☐ NO
WERE THEY ACCESSIBLE? ☐ YES ☐ NO
WERE THEY USED? ☐ YES ☐ NO

47. FIRE EXTINGUISHERS

WAS APPROVED TYPE FIRE FIGHTING EQUIPMENT ABOARD?

☐ YES ☐ NO

WHERE THEY USED? (IF "YES", LIST TYPES(S) AND NUMBER)

☐ YES ☐ NO

---

48. ACCIDENT DESCRIPTION

DESCRIBE WHAT HAPPENED AND WHAT COULD HAVE PREVENTED THIS ACCIDENT. (INCLUDE FAILURE OF EQUIPMENT. EXPLAIN CAUSE OF DEATH OR INJURY, MEDICAL TREATMENT, ETC. USE SKETCH IF HELPFUL. IF NEEDED, CONTINUE DESCRIPTION ON ADDITIONA PAPER.)

GLOSSARY

abaft Toward the stern.

abeam At right angles to the centerline of a boat.

aboard On or in a boat; close to a boat.

aft, after Toward the stern.

aground With the hull or keel of a boat touching the bottom.

aloft Overhead.

amidships Between fore and aft; the middle of the boat.

anchor A device shaped so as to grip the bottom. It is secured to a line from the boat to hold it in the desired position.

astern Behind the stern of a boat.

athwartships Across the beam of a boat.

awash Immersed in water.

backstay A wire support from the mast to the stern of the boat.

bail To remove water from the boat.

ballast Weight placed in the bottom of the boat to give it stability.

bare poles With all sails down.

battens Thin wooden or plastic strips placed in pockets in the leech of a sail to help hold its form.

beam The width of a boat at its widest point.

beam wind A wind that blows across the boat from side to side.

bearing The compass (magnetic) direction from one object to another.

beat To sail to windward.

belay To make secure.

bend To secure (for example, a sail to a spar or a line to a sail).

bight Loop.

bilge The very lowest part of a boat's interior, where water is most likely to collect.

blanket To take wind from a sail

block A nautical pulley.

boat hook A device for catching hold of a ring bolt or line when coming alongside a pier or picking up a mooring.

bolt rope Rope secured to the edge of a sail to give it strength and to facilitate adjusting foot and luff tension.

boom The spar to which the foot of the sail is attached with lacing, slides, or a groove.

boom vang A line to steady the boom when off the wind.

bow Forward part of the boat.

bowsprit A spar extending forward from the bow.

breast line Docking line leading roughly at right angles from the boat's sides.

bridle Rope span with ends secured for the sheet block to ride on.

broach To spin out of control and capsize or come close to a capsize; loss of steering.

buoy Any floating object anchored in one place to mark a position or provide a mooring.

by the lee On a run, having the wind coming slightly from the side on which the sails are trimmed.

can A buoy, used to mark a channel, colored green or black and given an odd number.

capsize To tip over.

careen To place a boat on her side so that work may be carried out on her underwater parts.

carry away To break or tear loose.

cast off To let go of a line when leaving the dock or mooring; to ease sheets.

catboat A sailboat with a single sail.

centerboard A shaped blade attached to the underside of the hull to give the boat lateral resistance when it is sailing to windward.

chafe To damage a line by rubbing.

chainplates Metal plates bolted to the

side of a boat to which shrouds are attached to support the rigging.

chock A device affixed to the deck and used as a guide for an anchor or mooring line.

claw off To clear a lee shore.

cleat A fitting used to secure a line under strain.

clew The outer corner of a sail.

close-hauled The most windward point of sail, on which the wind is at about 45 degrees.

close-winded Describes a craft capable of sailing very close to the wind.

coaming The raised protection around a cockpit.

cockpit The space at a lower level than the deck in which the tiller or wheel is located; a cockpit may be center or aft.

cringle A metal ring worked into the sail.

crutch Support for the boom when the sails are furled.

displacement The weight of water displaced by a boat.

dock The body of water in which the boat sits while tied up to a float or pier (often used to mean the float or pier itself).

downhaul A line attached to the tack of the sail, used to trim the draft forward.

draft 1) The depth or fullness of a sail. 2) The depth of the keel or centerboard in the water.

drift The leeway or movement sideways of a boat.

dry sailing Keeping a boat out of water when not in use.

ease To let out.

fairlead A fitting used to change the direction of a line, giving it a better angle from a sail or block to a winch or cleat.

fall The part of a tackle to which the power is applied in hoisting.

fathom A nautical measurement for the depth of water. One fathom is equal to six feet.

fetch A windward course by which a craft can make her destination without having to tack.

float A floating platform, usually accessible from shore, to which a boat is tied up when docked.

foot The bottom length of a sail.

fore-and-aft In the direction of the keel, from front to back.

forefoot The forward part of the keel, adjoining the lower part of the stem.

foremast The most forward mast of a sailboat having two or more masts.

foresail A jib.

fouled Entangled or clogged.

frames The skeleton of the ship, which holds the hull together and gives support.

free Sailing on any point of sail except close-hauled.

freeboard The distance from the top of the hull to the water.

full-and-by Sailing as close to the wind as possible with all the sails full.

furl To fold or roll a sail on a boom and then secure it with sail ties.

gaff A pole extending from a mast to support the head of a sail.

gasket A piece of rope or canvas used to secure a furled sail.

gear Any equipment pertaining to a sailboat.

genoa An overlapping foresail.

gimbal A device used for suspending the compass so it remains level.

give-way vessel A boat required to keep out of the way of another vessel.

gooseneck A device that secures the boom to the mast.

grommet A metal ring fastened in a sail.

ground tackle Anchor, rode, etc., used to secure a boat to her mooring.

gudgeon A fitting attached to the hull into which the rudder's pintles are inserted.

gunwale The rail of the boat at deck level.

guy A line or wire used to adjust and position the spinnaker pole.

halyard A line used to haul sails up and down the mast.

hard alee The command used in coming about to inform the crew that the helm is being pushed hard to leeward, turning the boat into the wind.

head The top of a sail.

head to wind With the bow headed into the wind and the sails luffing.

headsail Any sail used forward of the mast, a foresail.

headstay A forward stay supporting the mast.

headway Motion forward.

heave to To stop a boat by turning the bow to the wind and holding it there. A boat stopped this way is hove to.

helm The tiller or wheel mechanism by which the boat is steered.

hike To lean over the side of a boat to help counterbalance heeling.

hoist The vertical edge of a sail; to haul aloft.

hull The main body of the boat.

inboard Toward the centerline of the boat; mounted inside the hull.

in irons In the wind's eye and having lost all headway. A boat in irons will not go off **on either tack** Also called in stays.

jib A triangular sail set forward of the mainmast.

jibe To change tack on a downwind course. A boat begins to jibe at the moment when, with the wind aft, the foot of her mainsail crosses her centerline. The boat completes the jibe when the mainsail fills on the new tack.

jibstay A wire supporting the mast to which the luff of the jib is attached.

jumper A stay on the upper forward part of the mast.

keel A heavy fin filled with lead ballast under the hull. It prevents the boat from sideslipping by resisting the lateral force of the wind, and it gives the boat stability.

ketch A two-masted sailing vessel with a small after mast stepped forward of the rudderpost.

knot A nautical unit of speed: 6,076 feet or one nautical mile per hour.

lanyard A line fastened to an object, such as a pail, whistle, knife, or other small tool for purposes of securing it.

lay The twisting of a rope's strands.

lazarette A small space below deck, usually aft, where spare parts are kept or an outboard motor is mounted.

leech The after edge of a sail.

leeward Away from the wind (also lee).

lifeline A wire that encircles the deck to prevent crew members from falling overboard.

light sails Sails made of a lightweight material for use in light winds.

list A leaning sideways due to excess weight on one side.

locker A storage compartment on a boat.

lubber's line A short post inside a compass used as a reference point when steering or taking bearings.

luff 1) The forward vertical edge of a sail. 2) To alter course toward the wind until the boat is head to wind. 3) The flapping of a sail caused by the boat being head to wind.

mainmast The principal mast of a sailboat.

mainsail The largest regular sail on a modem sailboat.

mainsheet The line for controlling the main boom.

marconi A tall mast used with a jibheaded rig.

mizzen The shorter mast aft on a yawl or ketch.

mooring A heavy anchor or weight permanently in position.

mooring buoy A buoy fitted with a ring and used for mooring a boat.

nun A buoy with a conical top, found on the starboard hand on entering a channel and painted red. Nuns are numbered evenly.

offshore Away from the shore.

off the wind Sailing downwind or before the wind.

on the wind Sailing close-hauled.

outboard Away from the centerline of the boat; mounted on the stern.

outhaul The line that pulls the mainsail

away from the mast and tightens the foot of the sail along the boom.

painter A short piece of rope secured to the bow of a small boat and used for making her fast to a dock.

pay off To turn the bow away from the wind.

peak The upper after comer of a gaff sail.

pennant A three-sided flag.

pinch To sail so close to the wind as to allow the sails to luff.

pintle A bolt of metal secured to the rudder and fitting into the gudgeon. The pintle gives a swinging support to the rudder.

point To head close to the wind.

port The left side of a boat as one faces forward.

port tack A course with the wind coming from the port and the sails trimmed on the starboard side.

quarter That portion of a vessel's side near the stern.

rail The outer edge of the deck.

rake The angle of a boat's mast from the vertical.

reach Sailing with a beam wind.

ready about The command given to prepare for coming about.

reef To reduce the area of a sail.

rhumb line The straight-line compass course between two points; hence the shortest course, except over long distances, where the great circle course is shorter.

rig 1) In general, a boat's upper works. 2) To set up the spars and standing and running rigging of a sailboat.

rigging The wire or lines used to adjust sails.

roach The curve of the edge of the sail.

rode The line and chain that secure the anchor to the boat.

rudder A flat wooden shape fitted on the sternpost by pintles and gudgeons.

run Point of sail with the wind aft.

sail ties Lengths of webbing used to secure a furled sad to a boom.

scull To move the rudder rapidly back and forth to propel the boat forward.

seaway An area with rough or moderate waves.

secure To make safe.

set The direction of the leeway of a vessel or of tide or current.

shackle A U-shaped piece of iron or steel with eyes in the ends, closed by a shackle pin.

shake out To let out a reef and hoist the sail.

sheave The wheel of a block pulley.

sheet The line used to control the forward or athwartships movement of a sail.

shrouds Vertical wires that hold the mast upright.

skeg A continuation of the keel aft that protects the propeller and sometimes connects to the heel of the rudder.

spinnaker A balloonlike sail used on a downwind course.

splice To join rope by tucking the strands together.

spreader An athwartships support that holds the shrouds away from the mast.

spring line A line used when the boat is docked to keep her from moving forward and aft.

squall A brief storm that arrives suddenly.

stand-on vessel A vessel that maintains her course and speed.

standing rigging That part of a ship's rigging that is permanently secured and not movable (stays, shrouds, and spreaders).

starboard The right side of a boat as one faces forward.

starboard tack A course with the wind coming from the starboard and the sails trimmed on the port side.

stay A rope of hemp, wire, or iron used for supporting a mast fore-and-aft.

staysail A small triangular sail used forward of the mast on a reaching course.

stem The timber at the extreme forward part of a boat, secured to the forward end of the keel and supporting the bow planks.

step the frame into which the heel of a

mast fits or stops.

stern The after section of the boat.

stow To put away.

strake A row of planks in the hull.

swamp To fill with water.

tack 1) The forward lower corner of a sail, where the luff and foot meet. 2) Any course on which the wind comes from either side of the boat. 3) To change course by passing into the wind.

tackle An arrangement of ropes and blocks to give a mechanical advantage.

tender 1) A small boat employed to go back and forth to the shore from a larger boat. 2) Heeling easily when close-hauled.

thimble An iron ring grooved on the outside for a rope grommet.

thwart The athwartships seat in a boat.

tiller Steering instrument that controls the rudder.

topping lift 1) A line or wire to hold the boom off the deck when not in use (also called a boom lift). 2) A line from the mast to the spinnaker pole, controlling spinnaker pole height.

topside On deck.

transom The stern facing of the hull.

traveler A sliding fitting to which the mainsheet is attached, keeping the boom in the same place as it is moved in and out.

trim 1) To adjust the sails. 2) The position of the sails relative to the wind.

tuning The delicate adjustment of a boat's rigging, sails, and hull to the proper balance to assure the best sailing performance.

turnbuckle A threaded link that pulls two eyes together, used for setting up standing rigging.

veer A change of direction, as in the wind.

wake The waves from a boat.

waterline An imaginary line around the hull at the surface of the water when the boat is on an even keel.

weather The state of the atmosphere at a certain time and place.

well found Well equipped.

whip To bind the strands of a line's end with yarn or cord.

whisker pole A light spar extending from the mast and used to hold the jib out when sailing off the wind.

winch A mechanical device to aid in trimming a line. It consists basically of a coil, on which the line is wound, and a crank to do the winding.

windward Toward the wind, the opposite of leeward.

wing-and-wing Running before the wind with the sails set on both sides.

working sails The regular sails on a boat.

yacht General term for a boat used solely for the personal pleasure of the owner.

yawl A two-masted boat with a small after mast located abaft the steering gear.

INDEX

ACKNOWLEDGMENTS

My many thanks for help of every kind to

Hunter Yachts
Karina Paape
Marti Betz
Kathy Thompson
Janice Jobson
Lenny Shabes
Peter Isler
Fred Hills
Charles E. Kanter
Mark Robinson
Hank Bernbaum
Daniel Maxim

John Van Osdol
Julia Garver
Clyde Hungerford
Dudley Overton
John Peterson
Erik Macklin
Cindy Wise
Carole Bright
Evelyn DeChantillon
Kathy Christensen
Greg Hillman
Flor Restrepo
Harry Munns

You and the ASA

A continuing relationship

An ASA school doesn't just teach people how to sail. It teaches them how to sail better; to become more competent and confident in their abilities. A broad curriculum of courses allows you to continue seeking new challenges ... reaching for new heights. We'll teach you how to cruise coastal waters; how to skipper your own charter boat; how to navigate with electronics and by the stars; how to set off across oceans. You can learn it all or any single aspect of sailing which interests you. Experienced sailors are welcome too and can receive internationally recognized credentials through successfully completing the appropriate examination. With an ASA school, you are assured of professional training and the best value for your sail education dollar.

The ASA Progression

The ASA curriculum is composed of seven levels, from basic sailing to ocean passagemaking. Certification at any of these levels opens the door to an expanded world of sailing opportunity. Your ASA Log Book outlines in detail the Standards and Certification requirements for all levels of training. Below is a brief description of the various levels.

1. ASA BASIC SAILING-Daysail a boat up to approx. 26 feet in moderate wind and sea without supervision. No previous navigation or sailing skills required.

2. BASIC COASTAL CRUISING-Skipper or crew aboard a 20 to 30-foot auxiliary sailboat in moderate winds and sea. ASA Basic Sailing certification required. Basic Sailing and Basic Coastal Cruising courses can be taken simultaneously.

3. BAREBOAT CHARTERING-Skipper or crew a 30 to 50-foot auxiliary sailboat by day in coastal waters. Boat systems and maintenance included. Basic Coastal Cruising Certification required.

4. COASTAL NAVIGATION-Navigational theory required to safely navigate a sailboat in coastal or inland waters. Meets Advanced Coastal Cruising Standard. No previous certification required.

5. ADVANCED COASTAL CRUISING–Skipper or crew a 30 to 50-foot auxiliary sailboat, day or night, in coastal waters, in any weather. Certification in Basic Coastal Cruising and Coastal Navigation required.

6. CELESTIAL NAVIGATION-Celestial navigation theory required to safely navigate a vessel on an offshore passage. Meets Offshore Standard. No previous certification required.

7. OFFSHORE-Skipper or crew a 30 to 50-foot auxiliary sailboat, day or night, offshore, in any weather. Certification in Advanced Coastal Cruising and Celestial Navigation required.

EXPERIENCED SAILORS TAKE NOTE ... You need not enroll in a course of instruction to receive Certification-credentials will be awarded upon successful completion of the appropriate examination taken at an ASA sailing school. Challenge the Standards and receive the credentials you deserve to back up your experience!

Team Members Receive Special Preference

To our members the ASA means more than certification and Vessel Assist educational excellence. It's smart business! When you join the ASA, you become a member of America's strongest and fastest growing team. Check out these membership benefits!

Each issue is packed with news and information for active sailors who need to know. Articles on navigation, cruising, learning to sail and stories about real people and their adventures make American Sailing one of the premiere journals of its kind. Only ASA members can get American Sailing; don't look for it in stores.

 Marine Insurance Discounts

Boat owners can save a bundle with ASA membership. Save at least 5% over regular, quoted rates. With today's insurance costs that can really add up!

Rental, Charter and Instruction Discounts
Present the ASA membership card at selected charter companies and sailing schools throughout the United States and you sail at a preferred rate. Worldwide charter companies including The Moorings and Stardust Marine honor the ASA card for charter and travel discounts

ASA Travel Service!
Unbelievable 10% rebate on all airline tickets. Hundreds of hotels throughout the United States offer ASA members discounts up to 50%. These aren't second rate hotels and you will certainly recognize Hilton, Radisson and Ramada to name a few.

ASA Gold Mastercard
Put your name under the ASA logo on a gold Mastercard that offers a competitive interest rate, no annual fee the first year and up to $15,000 credit limit. A portion of each purchase also goes to the ASA charitable educational fund.

Vessel Assist

The Boat Owner's Auto Club you cannot afford not to belong to!

FREE ONE YEAR MEMBERSHIP in Vessel Assist is available to all ASA members. An Associate Membership in VA entitles you to:

- Group rate insurance program
- Free towing, free jump starts and free delivery of necessary parts, fuel, etc.
- 24 hour toll free dispatch and claims center
- Coverage worldwide on any boat you own or legally charter
- Immediate and reliable member response
- Fully insured U.S. Coast Guard licensed professional
- Ungrounding when soft aground, on-scene service
- First Alert Cruise Log Float Plan Service
- Special discounted rates for services at a home berth non-emergency service and savings on fuel, parts, etc. from marine vendors

Free One year subscription to SAIL Magazine, America's most popular sailing magazine.

Discounts on Books! Videos! Sailing Gear!

PLUS LOTS MORE!
Join the Team!

- ❑ $39 one-year individual
- ❑ $55 two-year individual
- ❑ $20 additional family member, per year
- ❑ $75 one-year family (list additional members)
- ❑ $99 two-year family (list additional members)
- ❑ $300 individual lifetime membership
- ❑ $500 family lifetime membership (list additional members)

Name _____

Street Address _____

City _____ State _____ Zip _____

❑ Check or M.O. ❑ Mastercar ❑Visa ❑Amex

Card # _____ Expires _____

Signature _____